8th Workshop on Balto-Slavic Natural Language Processing (BSNLP 2021)

Online
20 April 2021

ISBN: 978-1-7138-2958-4

Printed from e-media with permission by:

Curran Associates, Inc.
57 Morehouse Lane
Red Hook, NY 12571

Some format issues inherent in the e-media version may also appear in this print version.

Association for Computational Linguistics
209 N. Eighth Street
Stroudsburg, Pennsylvania 18360

Phone: 1-570-476-8006
Fax: 1-570-476-0860

acl@aclweb.org

Additional copies of this publication are available from:

Curran Associates, Inc.
57 Morehouse Lane
Red Hook, NY 12571 USA
Phone: 845-758-0400
Fax: 845-758-2633
Email: curran@proceedings.com
Web: www.proceedings.com

EACL 2021

Proceedings of the 8th BSNLP Workshop on Balto-Slavic Natural Language Processing,

Co-located with the 16th European Chapter of the Association for Computational Linguistics (EACL)

April 20, 2021

Preface

This volume contains the papers presented at BSNLP-2021: the eighth workshop on Balto-Slavic Natural Language Processing. The workshop is organized by ACL SIGSLAV, the Special Interest Group on NLP in Slavic Languages of the Association for Computational Linguistics.

The BSNLP workshops have been convening for over a decade, with a clear vision and purpose. On one hand, the languages from the Balto-Slavic group play an important role due to their widespread use and diverse cultural heritage. These languages are spoken by about one-third of all speakers of the official languages of the European Union, and by over 400 million speakers worldwide. The political and economic developments in Central and Eastern Europe place societies where Balto-Slavic languages are spoken at the center of rapid technological advancement and growing European consumer markets.

On the other hand, research on theoretical and applied NLP in some of these languages still lag behind the "major" languages, such as English and other Western European languages. In comparison to English, which has dominated the digital world since the advent of the Internet, many of these languages still lack resources, processing tools and applications—especially those with smaller speaker bases.

The Balto-Slavic languages pose a wealth of fascinating scientific challenges. The linguistic phenomena specific to the Balto-Slavic languages—complex morphology and free word order—present non-trivial problems for the construction of NLP tools, and require rich morphological and syntactic resources.

The BSNLP workshop aims to bring together researchers in NLP for Balto-Slavic languages from academia and industry. We aim to stimulate research, foster the creation of tools and dissemination of new results. The workshop serves as a forum for the exchange of ideas and experience and for discussing shared problems. One fascinating aspect of Slavic and Baltic languages is their structural similarity, as well as an easily recognizable lexical and inflectional inventory spanning the groups, which—despite the lack of mutual intelligibility—creates a special environment in which researchers can fully appreciate the shared problems and solutions.

In order to stimulate research and collaboration further, we have organized the third BSNLP Challenge: a shared task on multilingual named entity recognition. Due to rich inflection, free word order, derivation, and other phenomena present in the Slavic languages, work on named entities poses a challenging task. Fostering research and development on the problems of named entities — detecting mentions of names, lemmatization (normalization), classification, and cross-lingual matching — is crucial for cross-lingual information access and wider use of NLP in Slavic languages. This third edition of the shared task covered six languages: Bulgarian, Czech, Polish, Russian, Slovene, and Ukrainian. If further covered five types of named entities: persons, locations, organizations, events, and products.

We received 11 regular paper submissions, and we selected 8 of them for presentation. The papers cover topics ranging from pre-training BERT-style transformers for Slavic languages to paraphrasing, text simplification, sentiment analysis, abusive language recognition, and inappropriate language detection.

Ten teams registered to participate in the NE Challenge, of which eight submitted results, and six also submitted system description papers. These papers are included in this volume, and their work is discussed in the special session dedicated to the Challenge.

This workshop's presentations—the regular Workshop papers and the Shared Task Challenge—cover at least ten Balto-Slavic languages: Bosnian, Bulgarian, Croatian, Czech, Montenegrin, Polish, Russian, Serbian, Slovene, Ukrainian.

This workshop continues the proud tradition established by the earlier BSNLP workshops, which were held in conjunction with the following venues:

1. ACL 2007 Conference in Prague, Czech Republic;
2. IIS 2009: Intelligent Information Systems, in Kraków, Poland;
3. TSD 2011: 14th International Conference on Text, Speech and Dialogue in Plzeň, Czech Republic;
4. ACL 2013 Conference in Sofia, Bulgaria;
5. RANLP 2015 Conference in Hissar, Bulgaria;
6. EACL 2017 Conference in Valencia, Spain.
7. ACL 2019 Conference in Florence, Italy

We sincerely hope that this work will help stimulate further growth of our rich and exciting field.

The BSNLP'2021 Organizers: Bogdan Babych, Olga Kanishcheva, Preslav Nakov, Jakub Piskorski, Lidia Pivovarova, Vasyl Starko, Josef Steinberger, Roman Yangarber, Michał Marcińczuk, Senja Pollak, Pavel Přibáň, Marko Robnik-Šikonja

Organizers:

Bogdan Babych (Heidelberg University, Germany)
Olga Kanishcheva (Kharkiv Polytechnic Institute, Ukraine)
Preslav Nakov (Qatar Computing Research Institute, HBKU, Qatar)
Jakub Piskorski (Joint Research Centre of the European Commission, Ispra, Italy)
Lidia Pivovarova (University of Helsinki, Finland)
Vasyl Starko (Ukrainian Catholic University, Ukraine)
Josef Steinberger (University of West Bohemia, Czech Republic)
Roman Yangarber (University of Helsinki, Finland)
Michał Marcińczuk (Wrocław University of Technology, Poland)
Senja Pollak (Jožef Stefan Institute, Ljubljana, Slovenia)
Pavel Přibáň (University of West Bohemia, Czech Republic)
Marko Robnik-Šikonja (University of Ljubljana, Slovenia)

Program Committee:

Željko Agić (Corti ApS, Copenhagen, Denmark)
Radovan Garabik (Comenius University in Bratislava, Slovakia)
Tomas Krilavičius (Vytautas Magnus University, Kaunas, Lithuania)
Cvetana Krstev (University of Belgrade, Serbia)
Vladislav Kubon (Charles University, Prague, Czech Republic)
Nikola Ljubešić (Jožef Stefan Institute, Ljubljana, Slovenia)
Natalia Loukachevitch (Lomonosov Moscow State University Moscow, Russia)
Preslav Nakov (Qatar Computing Research Institute, HBKU, Qatar)
Maciej Ogrodniczuk (Polish Academy of Sciences, Poland)
Petya Osenova (Bulgarian Academy of Sciences, Bulgaria)
Alexander Panchenko (Skoltech, Moscow, Russia)
Jakub Piskorski (Joint Research Centre, Ispra, Italy/PAS, Warsaw, Poland)
Lidia Pivovarova (University of Helsinki, Finland)
Senja Pollak (Jožef Stefan Institute, Ljubljana, Slovenia)
Marko Robnik-Šikonja (University of Ljubljana, Slovenia)
Alexandr Rosen (Charles University, Prague)
Tanja Samardžić (University of Geneva, Switzerland)
Agata Savary (University of Tours, France)
Serge Sharoff (University of Leeds, UK)
Stan Szpakowicz (University of Ottawa, Canada)
Irina Temnikova (Sofia University, Bulgaria)
Ivan Vulić (University of Cambridge, UK)
Miloš Jakubíček (Lexical Computing, Czech Republic UK)
Roman Yangarber (University of Helsinki, Finland)
Daniel Zeman (Charles University, Czech Republic)

Table of Contents

Workshop Program

No Day Set (continued)

HerBERT: Efficiently Pretrained Transformer-based Language Model for Polish

Robert Mroczkowski[1] **Piotr Rybak**[1] **Alina Wróblewska**[2] **Ireneusz Gawlik**[1,3]

[1]ML Research at Allegro.pl
[2]Institute of Computer Science, Polish Academy of Sciences
[3]Department of Computer Science, AGH University of Science and Technology
`{firstname.lastname}@allegro.pl, alina@ipipan.waw.pl`

Abstract

BERT-based models are currently used for solving nearly all Natural Language Processing (NLP) tasks and most often achieve state-of-the-art results. Therefore, the NLP community conducts extensive research on understanding these models, but above all on designing effective and efficient training procedures. Several ablation studies investigating how to train BERT-like models have been carried out, but the vast majority of them concerned only the English language. A training procedure designed for English does not have to be universal and applicable to other especially typologically different languages. Therefore, this paper presents the first ablation study focused on Polish, which, unlike the isolating English language, is a fusional language. We design and thoroughly evaluate a pretraining procedure of transferring knowledge from multilingual to monolingual BERT-based models. In addition to multilingual model initialization, other factors that possibly influence pretraining are also explored, i.e. training objective, corpus size, BPE-Dropout, and pretraining length. Based on the proposed procedure, a Polish BERT-based language model – HerBERT – is trained. This model achieves state-of-the-art results on multiple downstream tasks.

1 Introduction

Recent advancements in self-supervised pretraining techniques drastically changed the way we design Natural Language Processing (NLP) systems. Even though, pretraining has been present in NLP for many years (Mikolov et al., 2013; Pennington et al., 2014; Bojanowski et al., 2017), only recently we observed a shift from task-specific to general-purpose models. In particular, the BERT model (Devlin et al., 2019) proved to be a dominant architecture and obtained state-of-the-art results for a variety of NLP tasks.

While most of the research related to analyzing and improving BERT-based models focuses on English, there is an increasing body of work aimed at training and evaluation of models for other languages, including Polish. Thus far, a handful of models specific for Polish has been released, e.g. Polbert[1], first version of HerBERT (Rybak et al., 2020), and Polish RoBERTa (Dadas et al., 2020).

Aforementioned works lack ablation studies, making it difficult to attribute hyperparameters choices to models performance. In this work, we fill this gap by conducting an extensive set of experiments and developing an efficient BERT training procedure. As a result, we were able to train and release a new BERT-based model for Polish language understanding. Our model establishes a new state-of-the-art on the variety of downstream tasks including semantic relatedness, question answering, sentiment analysis and part-of-speech tagging.

To summarize, our contributions are:

1. development and evaluation of an efficient pretraining procedure for transferring knowledge from multilingual to monolingual language models based on work by Arkhipov et al. (2019),

2. detailed analysis and an ablation study challenging the effectiveness of Sentence Structural Objective (SSO, Wang et al., 2020), and Byte Pair Encoding Dropout (BPE-Dropout, Provilkov et al., 2020),

3. release of HerBERT[2] – a BERT-based model for Polish language understanding, which achieves state-of-the-art results on KLEJ Benchmark (Rybak et al., 2020) and POS tagging task (Wróblewska, 2020).

[1]`https://github.com/kldarek/polbert`
[2]`https://huggingface.co/allegro/herbert-large-cased`

Proceedings of the 8th BSNLP Workshop on Balto-Slavic Natural Language Processing, pages 1–10
April 20, 2021.

The rest of the paper is organized as follows. In Section 2, we provide an overview of related work. After that, Section 3 introduces the BERT-based language model and experimental setup used in this work. In Section 4, we conduct a thorough ablation study to investigate the impact of several design choices on the performance of downstream tasks. Next, in Section 5 we apply drawn conclusions and describe the training of HerBERT model. In Section 6, we evaluate HerBERT on a set of eleven tasks and compare its performance to other state-of-the-art models. Finally, we conclude our work in Section 7.

2 Related Work

The first significant ablation study of BERT-based language pretraining was described by Liu et al. (2019). Authors demonstrated the ineffectiveness of Next Sentence Prediction (NSP) objective, the importance of dynamic token masking, and gains from using both large batch size and large training dataset. Further large-scale studies analyzed the relation between the model and the training dataset sizes (Kaplan et al., 2020), the amount of compute used for training (Brown et al., 2020) and training strategies and objectives (Raffel et al., 2019).

Other work focused on studying and improving BERT training objectives. As mentioned before, the NSP objective was either removed (Liu et al., 2019) or enhanced either by predicting the correct order of sentences (Sentence Order Prediction (SOP), Lan et al., 2020) or discriminating between previous, next and random sentence (Sentence Structural Objective (SSO), Wang et al., 2020). Similarly, the Masked Language Modelling (MLM) objective was extended to either predict spans of tokens (Joshi et al., 2019), re-order shuffled tokens (Word Structural Objective (WSO), Wang et al., 2020) or replaced altogether with a binary classification problem using mask generation (Clark et al., 2020).

For tokenization, the Byte Pair Encoding algorithm (BPE, Sennrich et al., 2016) is commonly used. The original BERT model used WordPiece implementation (Schuster and Nakajima, 2012), which was later replaced by SentencePiece (Kudo and Richardson, 2018). Gong et al. (2018) discovered that rare words lack semantic meaning. Provilkov et al. (2020) proposed a BPE-Dropout technique to solve this issue.

All of the above work was conducted for English language understanding. There was little research into understanding how different pretraining techniques affect BERT-based models for other languages. The main research focus was to train BERT-based models and report their performance on downstream tasks. The first such models were released for German[3] and Chinese (Devlin et al., 2019), recently followed by Finnish (Virtanen et al., 2019), French (Martin et al., 2020; Le et al., 2020), Polish (Rybak et al., 2020; Dadas et al., 2020), Russian (Kuratov and Arkhipov, 2019), and many other languages[4]. Research on developing and investigating an efficient procedure of pretraining BERT-based models was rather neglected in these languages.

Language understanding for low-resource languages has also been addressed by training jointly for several languages at the same time. That approach improves performance for moderate and low-resource languages as showed by Conneau and Lample (2019). The first model of this kind was the multilingual BERT trained for 104 languages (Devlin et al., 2019) followed by Conneau and Lample (2019) and Conneau et al. (2020).

3 Experimental Setup

In this section, we describe the experimental setup used in the ablation study. First, we introduce the corpora we used to train models. Then, we give an overview of the language model architecture and training procedure. In particular, we describe the method of transferring knowledge from multilingual to monolingual BERT-based models. Finally, we present the evaluation tasks.

3.1 Training Data

We gathered six corpora to create two datasets on which we trained HerBERT. The first dataset (henceforth called *Small*) consists of corpora of the highest quality, i.e. NKJP, Wikipedia, and Wolne Lektury. The second dataset (*Large*) is over five times larger as it additionally contains texts of lower quality (CCNet and Open Subtitles). Below, we present a short description of each corpus. Additionally, we include the basic corpora statistics in Table 1.

NKJP (Narodowy Korpus Języka Polskiego, eng. *National Corpus of Polish*) (Przepiórkowski, 2012) is a well balanced collection of Polish texts. It

[3] `https://deepset.ai/german-bert`

[4] `https://huggingface.co/models`

Corpus	Tokens	Documents	Avg len
Source Corpora			
NKJP	1357M	3.9M	347
Wikipedia	260M	1.4M	190
Wolne Lektury	41M	5.5k	7447
CCNet Head	2641M	7.0M	379
CCNet Middle	3243M	7.9M	409
Open Subtitles	1056M	1.1M	961
Final Corpora			
Small	1658M	5.3M	313
Large	8599M	21.3M	404

Table 1: Overview of all data sources used to train HerBERT. We combine them into two corpora. The *Small* corpus consists of the highest quality text resources: NKJP, Wikipedia, and Wolne Lektury. The *Large* corpus consists of all sources. *Avg len* is the average number of tokens per document in each corpus.

consists of texts from many different sources, such as classic literature, books, newspapers, journals, transcripts of conversations, and texts crawled from the internet.

Wikipedia is an online encyclopedia created by the community of Internet users. Even though it is crowd-sourced, it is recognized as a high-quality collection of articles.

Wolne Lektury (eng. *Free Readings*)[5] is a collection of over five thousand books and poems, mostly from 19th and 20th century, which have already fallen in the public domain.

CCNet (Wenzek et al., 2020) is a clean monolingual corpus extracted from Common Crawl[6] dataset of crawled websites.

Open Subtitles is a popular website offering movie and TV subtitles, which was used by Lison and Tiedemann (2016) to curate and release a multilingual parallel corpus from which we extracted its monolingual Polish part.

3.2 Language Model

Tokenizer We used Byte-Pair Encoding (BPE) tokenizer (Sennrich et al., 2016) with the vocabulary size of 50k tokens and trained it on the most representative parts of our corpus, i.e annotated subset of the NKJP, and the Wikipedia.

Subword regularization is supposed to emphasize the semantic meaning of tokens (Gong et al., 2018; Provilkov et al., 2020). To verify its impact on training language model we used a BPE-Dropout (Provilkov et al., 2020) with a probability of dropping a merge equal to 10%.

Architecture We followed the original BERT (Devlin et al., 2019) architectures for both BASE (12 layers, 12 attention heads and hidden dimension of 768) and LARGE (24 layers, 16 attention heads and hidden dimension of 1024) variants.

Initialization We initialized models either randomly or by using weights from XLM-RoBERTa (Conneau et al., 2020). In the latter case, the parameters for all layers except word embeddings and token type embeddings were copied directly from the source model. Since XLM-RoBERTa does not use the NSP objective and does not have the token type embeddings, we took them from the original BERT model.

To overcome the difference in tokenizers vocabularies we used a method similar to (Arkhipov et al., 2019). If a token from the target model vocabulary was present in the source model vocabulary then we directly copied its weights. Otherwise, it was split into smaller units and the embedding was obtained by averaging sub-tokens embeddings.

Training Objectives We trained all models with an updated version of the MLM objective (Joshi et al., 2019; Martin et al., 2020), masking ranges of subsequent tokens belonging to single words instead of individual (possibly subword) tokens. We replaced the NSP objective with SSO. The other parameters were kept the same as in the original BERT paper. Training objective is defined in Equation 1.

$$\mathcal{L} = \mathcal{L}_{\text{MLM}}(\theta) + \alpha \cdot \mathcal{L}_{\text{SSO}}(\theta) \tag{1}$$

where α is the SSO weight.

3.3 Tasks

KLEJ Benchmark The standard method for evaluating pretrained language models is to use a diverse collection of tasks grouped into a single benchmark. Such benchmarks exist in many languages, e.g. English (GLUE, Wang et al., 2019), Chinese (CLUE, Xu et al., 2020), and Polish (KLEJ, Rybak et al., 2020).

[5] `https://wolnelektury.pl`
[6] `http://commoncrawl.org/`

Following this paradigm we first verified the quality of assessed models with KLEJ. It consists of nine tasks: name entity classification (**NKJP-NER**, Przepiórkowski, 2012), semantic relatedness (**CDSC-R**, Wróblewska and Krasnowska-Kieraś, 2017), natural language inference (**CDSC-E**, Wróblewska and Krasnowska-Kieraś, 2017), cyberbullying detection (**CBD**, Ptaszynski et al., 2019), sentiment analysis (**PolEmo2.0-IN**, **PolEmo2.0-OUT**, Kocoń et al., 2019, **AR**, Rybak et al., 2020), question answering (**Czy wiesz?**, Marcinczuk et al., 2013), and text similarity (**PSC**, Ogrodniczuk and Kopeć, 2014).

POS Tagging and Dependency Parsing All of the KLEJ Benchmark tasks belong to the classification or regression type. It is therefore difficult to assess the quality of individual token embeddings. To address this issue, we further evaluated HerBERT on part-of-speech tagging and dependency parsing tasks.

For tagging, we used the manually annotated subset of NKJP (Degórski and Przepiórkowski, 2012), converted to the CoNLL-U format by Wróblewska (2020). We evaluated models performance on a test set using accuracy and F1-Score.

For dependency parsing, we applied Polish Dependency Bank (Wróblewska, 2018) from the Universal Dependencies repository (release 2.5, Zeman et al., 2019).

In addition to three Transformer-based models, we also included models trained with static embeddings. The first one did not use pretrained embeddings while the latter utilized fastText (Bojanowski et al., 2017) embeddings trained on Common Crawl.

The models are evaluated with the standard metrics: UAS (unlabeled attachment score) and LAS (labelled attachment score). The gold-standard segmentation was preserved. We report the results on the test set.

4 Ablation Study

In this section, we analyze the impact of several design choices on downstream task performance of Polish BERT-based models. In particular, we focus on initialization, corpus size, training objective, BPE-Dropout, and the length of pretraining.

4.1 Experimental Design

Hyperparameters Unless stated otherwise, in all experiments we trained $\text{BERT}_{\text{BASE}}$ model initialized with XLM-RoBERTa weights for 10k iterations using a linear decay schedule of the learning rate with a peak value of $7 \cdot 10^{-4}$ and a warm-up of 500 iterations. We used a batch size of 2560.

Evaluation Different experimental setups were compared using the average score on the KLEJ Benchmark. The validation sets are used for evaluation and we report the results corresponding to the median values of the five runs. Since only six tasks in KLEJ Benchmark have validation sets the scores are not directly comparable to those reported in Section 6. We used Welch's t-test (Welch, 1947) with a p-value of 0.01 to test for statistical differences between experimental variants.

4.2 Results

Initialization One of the main goals of this work is to propose an efficient strategy to train a monolingual language model. We began with investigating the impact of pretraining the language model itself. For this purpose, the following experiments were designed.

Init	Pretraining	BPE	Score
	Ablation Models		
Random	No	-	58.15 ± 0.33
XLM-R	No	-	<u>83.15 ± 1.22</u>
Random	Yes	No	85.65 ± 0.43
XLM-R	Yes	No	<u>88.80 ± 0.15</u>
Random	Yes	Yes	85.78 ± 0.23
XLM-R	Yes	Yes	<u>**89.10 ± 0.19**</u>
	Original Models		
XLM-R	-	-	88.82 ± 0.15

Table 2: Average scores on KLEJ Benchmark depending on the initialization scheme: Random – initialization with random weights, XLM-R – initialization with XLM-RoBERTa weights. We used $\text{BERT}_{\text{BASE}}$ model trained for 10k iterations with the SSO weight equal to 1.0 on the *Large* corpus. The best score within each group is underlined, the best overall is bold.

First, we fine-tuned randomly initialized BERT model on KLEJ Benchmark tasks. Note that this model is not pretrained in any way. As expected, the results on the KLEJ Benchmark are really poor with the average score equal to 58.15.

Next, we evaluated the BERT model initialized

with XLM-RoBERTa weights (see Table 2). It achieved much better average score than the randomly initialized model (83.15 vs 58.15), but it was still not as good as the original XLM-RoBERTa model (88.82%). The difference in the performance can be explained by the transfer efficiency. The method of transferring token embeddings between different tokenizers proves to retain most information, but not all of it.

To measure the impact of initialization on pretraining optimization, we trained the aforementioned models for 10k iterations. Beside MLM objective, we used SSO loss with $\alpha = 1.0$ and conducted experiments with both enabled and disabled BPE-Dropout. Models initialized with XLM-RoBERTa achieve significantly higher results than models initialized randomly, 89.10 vs 85.78 and 88.80 vs 85.65 for pretraining with and without BPE-Dropout respectively.

Models initialized with XLM-RoBERTa achieved similar results to the original XLM-RoBERTa (the differences are not statistically significant). It proves that it is possible to quickly recover from the performance drop caused by a tokenizer conversion procedure and obtain a much better model than the one initialized randomly.

Corpus Size As mentioned in Section 2, previous research show that pretraining on a larger corpus is beneficial for downstream task performance (Kaplan et al., 2020; Brown et al., 2020). We investigated this by pretraining $\text{BERT}_{\text{BASE}}$ model on both *Small* and *Large* corpora (see Section 3.1). To mitigate a possible impact of confounding variable, we also vary the weight of SSO loss and usage of BPE-Dropout (see Table 3).

As expected, the model pretrained on a *Large* corpus performs better on downstream tasks. However, the difference is statistically significant only for the experiment with SSO weight equal to 1.0 and BPE-Dropout enabled. Therefore it's not obvious whether a larger corpus is actually beneficial.

Corpus	SSO	BPE	Score
Small	1.0	Yes	88.73 ± 0.08
Large	1.0	Yes	89.10 ± 0.19
Small	0.1	Yes	88.90 ± 0.24
Large	0.1	Yes	**89.37 ± 0.25**
Small	0.0	Yes	89.18 ± 0.15
Large	0.0	Yes	89.25 ± 0.21
Small	0.0	No	89.12 ± 0.29
Large	0.0	No	89.28 ± 0.26

Table 3: Average scores on KLEJ Benchmark depending on a corpus size. We used $\text{BERT}_{\text{BASE}}$ model trained for 10k iterations with or without BPE-Dropout and with various SSO weights. The best score within each group is underlined, the best overall is bold.

Sentence Structural Objective Subsequently, we tested SSO, i.e. the recently introduced replacement for the NSP objective, which proved to be ineffective. We compared models trained with three values of SSO weight α (see Section 3.2): 0.0 (no SSO), 0.1 (small impact of SSO), and 1.0 (SSO equally important as MLM objective) (see Table 4).

The experiment showed, that SSO actually hurts downstream task performance. The differences between enabled and disabled SSO are statistically significant for two out of three experimental setups. The only scenario for which the negative effect of SSO is not statistically significant is using the Large corpus and BPE-dropout. Overall, the best results are achieved using a small SSO weight but the differences are not significantly different from disabling SSO.

SSO	Corpus	BPE	Score
0.0	Small	Yes	89.18 ± 0.15
0.1	Small	Yes	88.90 ± 0.24
1.0	Small	Yes	88.73 ± 0.08
0.0	Large	Yes	89.25 ± 0.21
0.1	Large	Yes	89.37 ± 0.25
1.0	Large	Yes	89.10 ± 0.19
0.0	Large	No	89.28 ± 0.26
0.1	Large	No	**89.45 ± 0.18**
1.0	Large	No	88.80 ± 0.15

Table 4: Average scores on KLEJ Benchmark depending on a SSO weight. We used $\text{BERT}_{\text{BASE}}$ model trained for 10k iterations with BPE-Dropout. The best score within each group is underlined, the best overall is bold.

BPE-Dropout The BPE-Dropout could be beneficial for downstream task performance, but its impact is difficult to assess due to many confounding variables.

The model initialization with XLM-RoBERTa weights means that token embedding is already semantically meaningful even without additional pretraining. However, for both random and XLM-RoBERTa initialization the BPE-Dropout is beneficial.

BPE	Init	SSO	Corpus	Score
No	Random	1.0	Large	85.65 ± 0.43
Yes	Random	1.0	Large	$\underline{85.78 \pm 0.23}$
No	XLM-R	1.0	Large	88.80 ± 0.15
Yes	XLM-R	1.0	Large	$\underline{89.10 \pm 0.19}$
No	XLM-R	0.0	Large	$\underline{\mathbf{89.28 \pm 0.26}}$
Yes	XLM-R	0.0	Large	89.25 ± 0.21
No	XLM-R	0.0	Small	89.12 ± 0.29
Yes	XLM-R	0.0	Small	$\underline{89.18 \pm 0.15}$

Table 5: Average scores on KLEJ Benchmark depending on usage of BPE-Dropout. We used $\text{BERT}_{\text{BASE}}$ model trained for 10k iterations on a large corpus. The best score within each group is underlined, the best overall is bold.

According to the results (see Table 5), none of the reported differences is statistically significant and we can only conclude that BPE-Dropout does not influence the model performance.

Length of Pretraining The length of pretraining in terms of the number of iterations is commonly considered an important factor of the final quality of the model (Kaplan et al., 2020). Even though it seems straightforward to validate this hypothesis in practice it is not so trivial.

When pretraining Transformer-based models linear decaying learning rate is typically used. Therefore, increasing the number of training iterations changes the learning rate schedule and impacts the training. In our initial experiments usage of the same learning rate caused the longer training to collapse. Instead, we chose the learning rate for which the value of loss function after 10k steps was similar. We found that the learning rate equal to $3 \cdot 10^{-4}$ worked best for training in 50k steps.

Using the presented experiment setup, we tested the impact of pretraining length for two values of SSO weight: 1.0 and 0.1. In both cases, the model pretrained with more iterations achieves only slightly better but statistically significant results (see Table 6).

# Iter	LR	SSO	Score
10k	$7 \cdot 10^{-4}$	1.0	89.10 ± 0.19
50k	$3 \cdot 10^{-4}$	1.0	$\underline{89.43 \pm 0.10}$
10k	$7 \cdot 10^{-4}$	0.1	89.37 ± 0.25
50k	$3 \cdot 10^{-4}$	0.1	$\underline{\mathbf{89.87 \pm 0.22}}$

Table 6: Average scores on KLEJ Benchmark depending training length. We used $\text{BERT}_{\text{BASE}}$ model trained on a large corpus with BPE-Dropout. The best score within each group is underlined, the best overall is bold.

5 HerBERT

In this section, we apply conclusions drawn from the ablation study (see Section 4) and describe the final pretraining procedure used to train HerBERT model.

Pretraining Procedure HerBERT was trained on the *Large* corpus. We used Dropout-BPE in tokenizer with a probability of a drop equals to 10%. Finally, HerBERT models were initialized with weights from XLM-RoBERTa and were trained with the objective defined in Equation 1 with SSO weight equal to 0.1.

Optimization We trained $\text{HerBERT}_{\text{BASE}}$ using Adam optimizer (Kingma and Ba, 2014) with parameters: $\beta_1 = 0.9$, $\beta_2 = 0.999$, $\epsilon = 10^{-8}$ and a linear decay learning rate schedule with a peak value of $3 \cdot 10^{-4}$. Due to the initial transfer of weights from the already trained model, the warm-up stage was set to a relatively small number of 500 iterations. The whole training took 50k iterations.

Training of $\text{HerBERT}_{\text{LARGE}}$ was longer (60k iterations) and had a more complex learning rate schedule. For the first 15k we linearly decayed the learning rate from $3 \cdot 10^{-4}$ to $2.5 \cdot 10^{-4}$. We observed the saturation of evaluation metrics and decided to drop the learning rate to $1 \cdot 10^{-4}$. After training for another 25k steps and reaching the learning rate of $7 \cdot 10^{-5}$ we again reached the plateau of evaluation metrics. In the last phase of training, we dropped the learning rate to $3 \cdot 10^{-5}$ and trained for 20k steps until it reached zero. Additionally, during the last phase of training, we disabled both BPE-Dropout and dropout within the Transformer itself as suggested by Lan et al. (2020).

Model	AVG	NKJP-NER	CDSC-E	CDSC-R	CBD	PolEmo2.0-IN	PolEmo2.0-OUT	Czy wiesz?	PSC	AR
Base Models										
XLM-RoBERTa	84.7 ± 0.29	91.7	93.3	93.4	66.4	90.9	77.1	64.3	97.6	87.3
Polish RoBERTa	85.6 ± 0.29	94.0	94.2	94.2	63.6	90.3	76.9	71.6	98.6	87.4
HerBERT	86.3 ± 0.36	94.5	94.5	94.0	67.4	90.9	80.4	68.1	98.9	87.7
Large Models										
XLM-RoBERTa	86.8 ± 0.30	94.2	**94.7**	93.9	67.6	92.1	81.6	70.0	98.3	88.5
Polish RoBERTa	87.5 ± 0.29	94.9	93.4	94.7	69.3	**92.2**	81.4	74.1	**99.1**	88.6
HerBERT	**88.4 ± 0.19**	**96.4**	94.1	**94.9**	**72.0**	**92.2**	**81.8**	**75.8**	98.9	**89.1**

Table 7: Evaluation results on KLEJ Benchmark. *AVG* is the average score across all tasks. Scores are reported for test set and correspond to median values across five runs. The best scores within each group are underlined, the best overall are in bold.

Both $\text{HerBERT}_{\text{BASE}}$ and $\text{HerBERT}_{\text{LARGE}}$ models were trained with a batch size of 2560.

6 Evaluation

In this section, we introduce other top-performing models for Polish language understanding and compare their performance on evaluation tasks (see Section 3.3) to HerBERT.

6.1 Models

According to the KLEJ Benchmark leaderboard[7] the three top-performing models of Polish language understanding are XLM-RoBERTa-NKJP[8], Polish RoBERTa, and XLM-RoBERTa. These are also the only three models available in LARGE architecture variant.

Unfortunately, the XLM-RoBERTa-NKJP model is not publicly available, so we cannot use it for our evaluation. However, it has the same average score as the runner-up (Polish RoBERTa) which we compare HerBERT with.

6.2 Results

KLEJ Benchmark Both variants of HerBERT achieved the best average performance, significantly outperforming Polish RoBERTa and XLM-RoBERTa (see Table 7). Regarding BASE models, $\text{HerBERT}_{\text{BASE}}$ improves the state-of-the-art result by 0.7pp and for $\text{HerBERT}_{\text{LARGE}}$ the improvement is even bigger (0.9pp). In particular, $\text{HerBERT}_{\text{BASE}}$ scores best on eight out of nine tasks (tying on PolEmo2.0-OUT, performing slightly worse on CDSC-R) and $\text{HerBERT}_{\text{LARGE}}$ in seven out of nine tasks (tying in PolEmo2.0-IN, performing worse in CDSC-E and PSC). Surprisingly, $\text{HerBERT}_{\text{BASE}}$ is better than $\text{HerBERT}_{\text{LARGE}}$ in CDSC-E. The same behaviour is noticeable for Polish RoBERTa, but not for XLM-RoBERTa. For other tasks, the LARGE models are always better. Summing up, $\text{HerBERT}_{\text{LARGE}}$ is the new state-of-the-art Polish language model based on the results of the KLEJ Benchmark.

It is worth emphasizing that the proposed procedure for efficient pretraining by transferring knowledge from multilingual to monolingual language allowed HerBERT to achieve better results than Polish RoBERTa even though it was optimized with around ten times shorter training.

POS Tagging HerBERT achieves overall better results in terms of both accuracy and F1-Score. $\text{HerBERT}_{\text{BASE}}$ beats the second-best model (i.e. Polish RoBERTa) by a margin of 0.33pp (F1-Score by 0.35pp) and $\text{HerBERT}_{\text{LARGE}}$ by a margin of 0.09pp (F1-Score by 0.12pp). It should be em-

[7] `https://klejbenchmark.com/leaderboard/`

[8] XLM-RoBERTa-NKJP is XLM-RoBERTa model additionally fine-tuned on NKJP corpus.

Model	Accuracy	F1-Score
Base Models		
XLM-RoBERTa	95.97 ± 0.04	95.79 ± 0.05
Polish RoBERTa	96.13 ± 0.03	95.92 ± 0.03
HerBERT	96.46 ± 0.04	96.27 ± 0.04
Large Models		
XLM-RoBERTa	97.07 ± 0.05	96.93 ± 0.05
Polish RoBERTa	97.21 ± 0.02	97.05 ± 0.03
HerBERT	**97.30 ± 0.02**	**97.17 ± 0.02**

Table 8: Part-of-speech tagging results on NKJP dataset. Scores are reported for the test set and are median values across five runs. Best scores within each group are underlined, best overall are bold.

Model	UAS	LAS
Static Embeddings		
Plain	90.58 ± 0.07	87.35 ± 0.12
FastText	92.20 ± 0.14	89.57 ± 0.13
Base Models		
XLM-RoBERTa	95.14 ± 0.07	93.25 ± 0.12
Polish RoBERTa	95.41 ± 0.24	93.65 ± 0.34
HerBERT	95.18 ± 0.22	93.24 ± 0.23
Large Models		
XLM-RoBERTa	95.38 ± 0.02	93.66 ± 0.07
Polish RoBERTa	**95.60 ± 0.18**	**93.90 ± 0.21**
HerBERT	95.11 ± 0.04	93.32 ± 0.02

Table 9: Dependency parsing results on Polish Dependency Bank dataset. Scores are reported for the test set and are median values across three runs. Best scores within each group are underlined, best overall are bold.

phasized that while the improvements may appear to be minor, they are statistically significant. All results are presented in Table 8.

Dependency Parsing The dependency parsing results are much more ambiguous than in other tasks. As expected, the models with static fastText embeddings performed much worse than Transformer-based models (around 3pp difference for UAS, and 4pp for LAS). In the case of Transformer-based models, the differences are less noticeable. As expected, the LARGE models outperform the BASE models. The best performing model is Polish RoBERTa. HerBERT models performance is the worst across Transformer-based models except for the UAS score which is slightly better than XLM-RoBERTa for BASE models. All results are presented in Table 9.

7 Conclusion

In this work, we conducted a thorough ablation study regarding training BERT-based models for Polish language. We evaluated several design choices for pretraining BERT outside of English language. Contrary to Wang et al. (2020), our experiments demonstrated that SSO is not beneficial for the downstream task performance. It also turned out that BPE-Dropout does not increase the quality of a pretrained language model.

As a result of our studies we developed and evaluated an efficient pretraining procedure for transferring knowledge from multilingual to monolingual BERT-based models. We used it to train and release HerBERT – a Transformer-based language model for Polish. It was trained on a diverse multi-source corpus. The conducted experiments confirmed its high performance on a set of eleven diverse linguistic tasks, as HerBERT turned out to be the best on eight of them. In particular, it is the best model for Polish language understanding according to the KLEJ Benchmark.

It is worth emphasizing that the quality of the obtained language model was even more impressive considering its short training time. Due to multilingual initialization, $\text{HerBERT}_{\text{BASE}}$ outperformed Polish $\text{RoBERTa}_{\text{BASE}}$ even though it was trained with a smaller batch size (2560 vs 8000) for a fewer number of steps (50k vs 125k). The same behaviour is also visible for $\text{HerBERT}_{\text{LARGE}}$. Additionally, we conducted a separate ablation study to confirm that the success of HerBERT is caused by the described initialization scheme. It showed that in fact, it was the most important factor to improved the quality of HerBERT.

We believe that the proposed training procedure and detailed experiments will encourage NLP researchers to cost-effectively train language models for other languages.

References

Mikhail Arkhipov, Maria Trofimova, Yuri Kuratov, and Alexey Sorokin. 2019. Tuning multilingual transformers for language-specific named entity recognition. In *Proceedings of the 7th Workshop on Balto-Slavic Natural Language Processing*, pages 89–93, Florence, Italy. Association for Computational Linguistics.

Piotr Bojanowski, Edouard Grave, Armand Joulin, and Tomas Mikolov. 2017. Enriching word vectors with subword information. *Transactions of the Association for Computational Linguistics*, 5:135–146.

Tom B. Brown, Benjamin Mann, Nick Ryder, Melanie Subbiah, Jared Kaplan, Prafulla Dhariwal et al. 2020. Language models are few-shot learners. *CoRR*, abs/2005.14165.

Kevin Clark, Minh-Thang Luong, Quoc V. Le, and Christopher D. Manning. 2020. ELECTRA: pre-training text encoders as discriminators rather than generators. In *8th International Conference on Learning Representations, ICLR 2020, Addis Ababa, Ethiopia, April 26-30, 2020*. OpenReview.net.

Alexis Conneau, Kartikay Khandelwal, Naman Goyal, Vishrav Chaudhary, Guillaume Wenzek, Francisco Guzmán et al. 2020. Unsupervised cross-lingual representation learning at scale. In *Proceedings of the 58th Annual Meeting of the Association for Computational Linguistics*, pages 8440–8451, Online. Association for Computational Linguistics.

Alexis Conneau and Guillaume Lample. 2019. Cross-lingual language model pretraining. In H. Wallach, H. Larochelle, A. Beygelzimer, F. d'Alché-Buc, E. Fox, and R. Garnett, editors, *Advances in Neural Information Processing Systems 32*, pages 7059–7069. Curran Associates, Inc.

Sławomir Dadas, Michał Perełkiewicz, and Rafał Poświata. 2020. Pre-training polish transformer-based language models at scale.

Łukasz Degórski and Adam Przepiórkowski. 2012. *Recznie znakowany milionowy podkorpus NKJP*, pages 51–58.

Jacob Devlin, Ming-Wei Chang, Kenton Lee, and Kristina Toutanova. 2019. Bert: Pre-training of deep bidirectional transformers for language understanding. In *Proceedings of the 2019 Conference of the North American Chapter of the Association for Computational Linguistics: Human Language Technologies, Volume 1 (Long and Short Papers)*, pages 4171–4186.

Chengyue Gong, Di He, Xu Tan, Tao Qin, Liwei Wang, and Tie-Yan Liu. 2018. Frage: Frequency-agnostic word representation. In S. Bengio, H. Wallach, H. Larochelle, K. Grauman, N. Cesa-Bianchi, and R. Garnett, editors, *Advances in Neural Information Processing Systems 31*, pages 1334–1345. Curran Associates, Inc.

Mandar Joshi, Danqi Chen, Yinhan Liu, Daniel S. Weld, Luke Zettlemoyer, and Omer Levy. 2019. Spanbert: Improving pre-training by representing and predicting spans. *arXiv preprint arXiv:1907.10529*.

Jared Kaplan, Sam McCandlish, Tom Henighan, Tom B Brown, Benjamin Chess, Rewon Child et al. 2020. Scaling laws for neural language models. *arXiv preprint arXiv:2001.08361*.

Diederik P. Kingma and Jimmy Ba. 2014. Adam: A method for stochastic optimization. Cite arxiv:1412.6980Comment: Published as a conference paper at the 3rd International Conference for Learning Representations, San Diego, 2015.

Jan Kocoń, Piotr Miłkowski, and Monika Zaśko-Zielińska. 2019. Multi-level sentiment analysis of PolEmo 2.0: Extended corpus of multi-domain consumer reviews. In *Proceedings of the 23rd Conference on Computational Natural Language Learning (CoNLL)*, pages 980–991, Hong Kong, China. Association for Computational Linguistics.

Taku Kudo and John Richardson. 2018. SentencePiece: A simple and language independent subword tokenizer and detokenizer for neural text processing. In *Proceedings of the 2018 Conference on Empirical Methods in Natural Language Processing: System Demonstrations*, pages 66–71, Brussels, Belgium. Association for Computational Linguistics.

Yuri Kuratov and Mikhail Arkhipov. 2019. Adaptation of deep bidirectional multilingual transformers for russian language.

Zhenzhong Lan, Mingda Chen, Sebastian Goodman, Kevin Gimpel, Piyush Sharma, and Radu Soricut. 2020. ALBERT: A lite BERT for self-supervised learning of language representations. In *8th International Conference on Learning Representations, ICLR 2020, Addis Ababa, Ethiopia, April 26-30, 2020*. OpenReview.net.

Hang Le, Loïc Vial, Jibril Frej, Vincent Segonne, Maximin Coavoux, Benjamin Lecouteux et al. 2020. FlauBERT: Unsupervised language model pre-training for French. In *Proceedings of the 12th Language Resources and Evaluation Conference*, pages 2479–2490, Marseille, France. European Language Resources Association.

Pierre Lison and Jörg Tiedemann. 2016. Opensubtitles2016: Extracting large parallel corpora from movie and tv subtitles. In *Proceedings of the Tenth International Conference on Language Resources and Evaluation (LREC 2016)*, Paris, France. European Language Resources Association (ELRA).

Yinhan Liu, Myle Ott, Naman Goyal, Jingfei Du, Mandar Joshi, Danqi Chen et al. 2019. Roberta: A robustly optimized bert pretraining approach. *arXiv preprint arXiv:1907.11692*.

Michał Marcinczuk, Marcin Ptak, Adam Radziszewski, and Maciej Piasecki. 2013. Open dataset for development of polish question answering systems. In *Proceedings of the 6th Language & Technology Conference: Human Language Technologies as a Challenge for Computer Science and Linguistics, Wydawnictwo Poznanskie, Fundacja Uniwersytetu im. Adama Mickiewicza.*

Louis Martin, Benjamin Muller, Pedro Javier Ortiz Suárez, Yoann Dupont, Laurent Romary, Éric de la Clergerie et al. 2020. CamemBERT: a tasty French language model. In *Proceedings of the 58th Annual Meeting of the Association for Computational Linguistics*, pages 7203–7219, Online. Association for Computational Linguistics.

Tomas Mikolov, Ilya Sutskever, Kai Chen, Greg S Corrado, and Jeff Dean. 2013. Distributed representations of words and phrases and their compositionality. In *Advances in neural information processing systems*, pages 3111–3119.

Maciej Ogrodniczuk and Mateusz Kopeć. 2014. The Polish Summaries Corpus. In *Proceedings of the Ninth International Conference on Language Resources and Evaluation, LREC 2014.*

Jeffrey Pennington, Richard Socher, and Christopher Manning. 2014. Glove: Global vectors for word representation. In *Proceedings of the 2014 Conference on Empirical Methods in Natural Language Processing (EMNLP)*, pages 1532–1543, Doha, Qatar. Association for Computational Linguistics.

Ivan Provilkov, Dmitrii Emelianenko, and Elena Voita. 2020. BPE-dropout: Simple and effective subword regularization. pages 1882–1892.

Adam Przepiórkowski. 2012. *Narodowy korpus języka polskiego*. Naukowe PWN.

Michal Ptaszynski, Agata Pieciukiewicz, and Paweł Dybała. 2019. Results of the poleval 2019 shared task 6: First dataset and open shared task for automatic cyberbullying detection in polish twitter. *Proceedings of the PolEval 2019 Workshop*, page 89.

Colin Raffel, Noam Shazeer, Adam Roberts, Katherine Lee, Sharan Narang, Michael Matena et al. 2019. Exploring the limits of transfer learning with a unified text-to-text transformer. *CoRR*, abs/1910.10683.

Piotr Rybak, Robert Mroczkowski, Janusz Tracz, and Ireneusz Gawlik. 2020. KLEJ: Comprehensive benchmark for polish language understanding. In *Proceedings of the 58th Annual Meeting of the Association for Computational Linguistics*, pages 1191–1201, Online. Association for Computational Linguistics.

Mike Schuster and Kaisuke Nakajima. 2012. Japanese and korean voice search. In *2012 IEEE International Conference on Acoustics, Speech and Signal Processing (ICASSP)*, pages 5149–5152. IEEE.

Rico Sennrich, Barry Haddow, and Alexandra Birch. 2016. Neural machine translation of rare words with subword units. *In Association for Computational Linguistics (ACL)*, pages 1715–1725.

Antti Virtanen, Jenna Kanerva, Rami Ilo, Jouni Luoma, Juhani Luotolahti, Tapio Salakoski et al. 2019. Multilingual is not enough: Bert for finnish.

Alex Wang, Amanpreet Singh, Julian Michael, Felix Hill, Omer Levy, and Samuel R. Bowman. 2019. GLUE: A multi-task benchmark and analysis platform for natural language understanding. In the Proceedings of ICLR.

Wei Wang, Bin Bi, Ming Yan, Chen Wu, Jiangnan Xia, Zuyi Bao et al. 2020. Structbert: Incorporating language structures into pre-training for deep language understanding. In *8th International Conference on Learning Representations, ICLR 2020, Addis Ababa, Ethiopia, April 26-30, 2020*. OpenReview.net.

B. L. Welch. 1947. THE GENERALIZATION OF 'STUDENT'S' PROBLEM WHEN SEVERAL DIFFERENT POPULATION VARLANCES ARE INVOLVED. *Biometrika*, 34(1-2):28–35.

Guillaume Wenzek, Marie-Anne Lachaux, Alexis Conneau, Vishrav Chaudhary, Francisco Guzmán, Armand Joulin et al. 2020. CCNet: Extracting high quality monolingual datasets from web crawl data. In *Proceedings of the 12th Language Resources and Evaluation Conference*, pages 4003–4012, Marseille, France. European Language Resources Association.

Alina Wróblewska. 2018. Extended and enhanced polish dependency bank in universal dependencies format. In *Proceedings of the Second Workshop on Universal Dependencies (UDW 2018)*, pages 173–182. Association for Computational Linguistics.

Alina Wróblewska. 2020. Towards the conversion of National Corpus of Polish to Universal Dependencies. In *Proceedings of the 12th Language Resources and Evaluation Conference*, pages 5308–5315, Marseille, France. European Language Resources Association.

Alina Wróblewska and Katarzyna Krasnowska-Kieraś. 2017. Polish evaluation dataset for compositional distributional semantics models. In *Proceedings of the 55th Annual Meeting of the Association for Computational Linguistics (Volume 1: Long Papers)*, pages 784–792.

Liang Xu, Xuanwei Zhang, Lu Li, Hai Hu, Chenjie Cao, Weitang Liu et al. 2020. Clue: A chinese language understanding evaluation benchmark.

Daniel Zeman, Joakim Nivre, Mitchell Abrams, Noëmi Aepli, Željko Agić, Lars Ahrenberg et al. 2019. Universal dependencies 2.5. LINDAT/CLARIAH-CZ digital library at the Institute of Formal and Applied Linguistics (ÚFAL), Faculty of Mathematics and Physics, Charles University.

Russian Paraphrasers: Paraphrase with Transformers

Alena Fenogenova
SberDevices, Sberbank, Russia
alenush93@gmail.com

Abstract

This paper focuses on generation methods for paraphrasing in the Russian language. There are several transformer-based models (Russian and multilingual) trained on a collected corpus of paraphrases. We compare different models, contrast the quality of paraphrases using different ranking methods and apply paraphrasing methods in the context of augmentation procedure for different tasks. The contributions of the work are the combined paraphrasing dataset, fine-tuned generated models for Russian paraphrasing task and additionally the open source tool for simple usage of the paraphrasers.

1 Introduction

One of the prominent features of any natural language is its diversity. Variability and ambiguity of natural languages lead to infinity of sequence combinations and one can always form a new sentence that has never been said before. However, there are approaches to automatic construction of texts with roughly the same meaning: paraphrases. Paraphrasing is expressing the meaning of an input sequence in alternative ways while maintaining grammatical and syntactical correctness. Paraphrases are of a great use in diverse applications on downstream NLP tasks and are presented in two main task forms: 1) Paraphrase identification - detecting if a pair of text inputs has the same meaning; classification task. 2) Paraphrase generation - producing paraphrases allows for the creation of more varied and fluent text; generation task.

The identification of paraphrases is very useful in many tasks, such as multi-document summarization (identifying paraphrases allows to condense information repeated across documents), question answering (checking the sequences of the tests, keyword matching to find answers), semantic parsing and search (to find the same queries or documents) and many others (Lewis et al., 2020).

In this work we will discuss paraphrase generation applicability. Paraphrase generation is used in different NLP applications (for example, in chatbots to diversify responses (Lippe et al., 2020)) and sub-tasks. Paraphrasers can be used to augment datasets with new data. For question answering systems, paraphrasing questions can not just increase the number of data examples for training ML-models (Xu et al., 2020), but are also used to match them with key words in the knowledge base. Paraphrasers can help generate adversarial examples to evaluate model robustness - increasing the stability of ML-models: training models on a wide variety of examples in different styles, with different sentiment, but the same meaning or intent of the user. The demand for targeting paraphrasers for generating specific writing styles is also trending now (Xu et al., 2012; Bolshakov and Gelbukh, 2004). This type of paraphrasing performs different types of style transfer, such as changing style from rude to polite, or from professional to simple language.

There are some general approaches for paraphrase generation. Rule-based approaches (Meteer and Shaked, 1988) and data-driven methods (Madnani and Dorr, 2010) are the oldest ones. Currently, the most common approach is to consider the task as supervised learning using sequence-to-sequence models (Gupta et al., 2018). The unsupervised approaches (Niu et al., 2020) are also very common. Other methods proposed include use of Deep Reinforcement Learning (Qian et al., 2019; Siddique et al., 2020). Fine-tuning with large language models such as GPT2 is also a valuable approach that can be considered supervised (Witteveen and Andrews, 2019) or unsupervised (Hegde and Patil, 2020).

The majority of the resources and methods for

Proceedings of the 8th BSNLP Workshop on Balto-Slavic Natural Language Processing, pages 11–19

paraphrasing are proposed for the English language. For the Russian language there were several attempts of paraphrase corpora creation (Pronoza et al., 2015; Gudkov et al., 2020). In 2016 the collection of the Russian paraphrase corpus and the Paraphrase Detection Shared Task (Pivovarova et al., 2017) were organized, which attracted attention to the topic and led to a number of further works on the identification of paraphrases (Kuratov and Arkhipov, 2019) and sentence similarity experiments (Kravchenko, 2017; Boyarsky and Kanevsky, 2017).

In this paper, we compare different language models for paraphrase generation in Russian, namely rugpt2-large, rugpt3-large, and multilingual models - mT5. We prove that all these models can generate good Russian paraphrases and test different ranking methods on generated examples. We provide the combined paraphrasing dataset, fine-tuned generated models for Russian paraphrasing task, augmentation experiments on data for common NLP tasks, and additionally present the open source tool for user-friendly usage of the Russian paraphrasers.

This paper is structured as follows: in section 2 we present the methodology - the dataset we use 2.1, models we fine-tune 2.2, and range strategies for paraphrasers output 2.3; section 3 is devoted to evaluation and analysis of the paraphraser performance and results - the models scores 3.1, the augmentation procedure with paraphrasers 3.2, and 3.3 the discussion about the results in the context of paraphrase application; and section 4 concludes the paper.

2 Methodology

Language models achieve impressive results when trained in a semi-supervised manner to predict the next word or words in a sequence. They can be fine-tuned and used for a variety of downstream NLP tasks (text classification, sentiment analysis, NER etc.). Good examples of such large language models that can be used for text generation are GPT-2, GPT-3, and mT5. In this section, we present our experiments with these models for Russian trained on the prepared dataset.

2.1 Dataset

Historically there are several approaches that have been used to construct paraphrasing datasets.

1. *translation-based paraphrasing* is based on the parallel data from different languages - if two Russian texts are translated to the same text in another language, then they are likely paraphrases of each other;

2. *argument-distribution paraphrasing* - if two predicates have the same meaning and they normally appear with the same arguments, they could be changed with their vector pairs;

3. *event-based paraphrasing* - the source for paraphrases is multiple descriptions of the same news event, as various news reporters are likely to choose different words to describe the same event.

Dataset	Total	news	speech
Train	410k	210k	200k
Validation	200k	100k	100k
Test	4017	2056	1961

Table 1: The dataset statistics and distribution.

The event-based approach was chosen for the creation of the Russian paraphrase corpus (Pivovarova et al., 2017). For experiments in this paper the dataset we use consists of two main parts: 1) news data from ParaPhraserPlus[1] for train and validation set and Shared task golden test for test set 2) conversational data from subtitles[2] (that were generated in an argument-distribution approach) and dialogues of users with chatbots (further in the text called *speech*). The distribution of the parts and data sizes are presented in Table 1. The test set was checked manually and further in the evaluation we assume that golden set contains high quality paraphrases to compare with.

Thus, the dataset presents two domains: informal style (speech subset, also presented in question form) and formal (news headlines). The speech subset of the data was checked for grammatical errors and typos with Yandex.Speller[3]. It was also filtered by metrics ROUGE-L (Lin, 2004) with threshold between 0.95 and 0.5. The example of the data is presented in Figure 1.

The news subset of the corpus was converted into the format of sentence pairs: $sentence_i == sentenceparaphrase_i$. Additionally, we automatically checked the cases when the information in

[1] http://paraphraser.ru/download/

[2] https://github.com/rysshe/paraphrase/tree/master/data

[3] https://yandex.ru/dev/speller/

the paraphrase sentence was excessive, for instance, $sentence_1$ *Jose Mourinho on the verge of being fired at Manchester United.* and $sentence_2$ *Mourinho could be fired if Manchester United lose to Burnley on Saturday*. The second sentence contains more information about the game, it is timing and the opposing team; in data it is permissible to have extra information in the reference sentence, but not in the paraphrase. Our experiments show that the generative models (fine-tuned on such structured data) generated more diverse sentences with absolutely out of control new information and names that could not be defined as paraphrases. It was the reason for the filtration of the pairs, where paraphrase sentence has length much longer than reference sentence or contains significantly more NER, date, and address information (the tool natasha[4] was used to detect entities). We set thresholds empirically and not strictly in order to exclude extremely inappropriate cases and kept the sentences where the entities or their number are the same, such as, *Poroshenko asked **the head of Turkey** not to recognize the presidential elections in the Crimea* and *Poroshenko urged **Erdogan** not to recognize the presidential elections in Crimea*.

2.2 Models

The idea of paraphrase generation is to build a model that reads a sequence of words and then generates a different sequence of words with the same meaning. Paraphrase generation task can be defined as generating a target sentence T for a reference sentence P where the newly generated target sentence T is semantically similar to reference sentence P.

We chose three pre-trained language models that are available for Russian:

1. ruGPT2-large[5] is a model by SberDevices team trained as a Russian analogue of OpenAI GPT-2 model (Radford et al., 2019). GPT-2 is an auto-regressive model, has up-to 1.5 Billion parameters, was trained on 40GB of Internet text to predict the next word. ruGPT2 was trained on 1024 context length with transformers on 170GB data on 64 GPUs 3 weeks.

2. ruGPT3-large is almost analogous to famous GPT-3 (Brown et al., 2020). ruGPT3 was trained on Internet text on 1024 context length with transformers on 80 billion tokens around 3 epochs, and then was fine-tuned on 2048 context.

3. mT5 (Xue et al., 2020) - Multilingual T5 (mT5) by Google is a massively multilingual pre-trained text-to-text transformer model, trained on the mC4 corpus, covering 101 languages including Russian. We trained three mT5 models on the same data: mT5-small, mT5-base and mT5-large.

We used Huggingface Transformers Library[6] to fine-tune the models on a sentence reconstruction task to generate paraphrases. Input data for GPT-based models were in the format:

$$<s> P_i === T_i </s>$$

. Input data for mT5 models contained the sequence "rephrase: " and looked like the following:

$$perephrasiruj : P_i </s>$$

and target format:

$$<s> T_i </s>$$

.

All the models were trained on a single GPU Tesla V100-SXM3 32 Gb for 3-5 epochs takes 28 minutes per epoch; validation set's perplexity was used to do early stopping.

Once the model was fine-tuned, it was able to produce paraphrases in a way it was trained. If one fed in any reference phrase with the same sequence token "===" or "rephrase:", the model generated paraphrases on demand.

2.3 Candidate range

After the model was trained, we sampled from the model from test sentences as conditional input. It allowed to generate different multiple candidate sentences for the single reference sentence. We have tested different parameters (we use the interface of Hugging face, so the parameters are basic for generation: top_p, top_k sampling parameters, $temperature$, etc.), but finally used $temperature = 1.0$, $top_k = 10$, $top_p = 0.9$, $maxlength = length(P) + 10$, $repetitionpenalty = 1.5$ for GPT-based models

[4]https://github.com/natasha/natasha

[5]https://github.com/sberbank-ai/ru-gpts

[6]https://huggingface.co/

```
0.749 Куда отправиться на каникулах? => Куда поехать на каникулах?

0.799 Куда бы тебе хотелось поехать? => Куда бы тебе хотелось отправиться?

0.714 В какую страну тебе хотелось бы направиться? => В какое государство тебе хотелось бы направиться?

0.727 Куда тебе хотелось бы отправиться сейчас? => Куда тебе хотелось бы съездить?

0.545 Можешь назвать любимое мобильное приложение? => Какое твоё самое любимое мобильное приложение?

0.666 Твоё самое любимое моб приложение? => Есть любимое моб приложение?

0.545 Какое у тебя самое любимое приложение?  => У тебя какое любимое приложение?
```

Figure 1: Dialogues data example

and $temperature = 1.0$, $top_k = 50$, $top_p = 0.95$, $maxlength = 150$, $repetitionpenalty = 1.5$ - for mT5 models.

Still the quality of generating multiple outputs varies, and we can select from n examples (where $n = 10$) the best quality paraphrases based on a number of criteria or one of the range strategies to filter output down to a set of satisfactory results.

We suggest 5 types of the candidate range: 1) cosine sentence similarity between reference sentence and generated one; 2) pairwise cosine sentence similarity between n generated sentences and the reference; 3) syntax based approach; 4) BLEU best; 5) ROUGE-L best.

The first two strategies are based on sentence similarity scores received with SentenceTransformers[7]. It is a Python framework for state-of-the-art sentence and text embeddings, created based on the initial paper Sentence-BERT: Sentence Embeddings using Siamese BERT-Networks (Reimers and Gurevych, 2019). One can use this framework to compute sentence / text embeddings for more than 100 languages. These embeddings can then be compared with cosine-similarity e.g. to find sentences with a similar meaning. We used *paraphrase-xlm-r-multilingual-v1* (Reimers and Gurevych, 2020; Thakur et al., 2020) model for paraphrase identification task (paraphrase mining). It is a multilingual version (including Russian) of *distilroberta-base-paraphrase-v1* (multilingual knowledge distilled version of multilingual Universal Sentence Encoder), trained on parallel data for 50+ languages. In the first strategy we ranged pairwise n candidates comparing cosine sentence similarities between a reference sentence and the generated one and chose the best ones (or set a distance threshold from which we are confident it is a good paraphrase).

In the second strategy we used paraphrase mining[8], the task of finding paraphrases in a corpus of sentences. The framework allows to find paraphrases in a list of sentences. Thus, we input all generated sentences and the reference one and model outputs the paraphrases.

The syntax based approach is based on the idea that arguments in the reference sentences and in the target sentence will be the same. Thus we can count the number of syntactic subjects and repeated tokens in both sentences and range the most coincidental ones. For syntax parsing we used Deeppavlov Bert Syntargus model[9]. The final two range strategies were using ROUGE-L scores and BLEU pairwise scores to choose the best from n candidates. We eliminated candidates with scores more than 0.9 and less than 0.3.

The most stable range strategy in our experiments was the first one - cosine sentence similarity between a reference sentence and the generated candidate.

3 Evaluation

We propose a two-step evaluation procedure: 1) universal metrics between gold testset examples and generated models outputs and 2) application of paraphrasers on downstream tasks where we augment data. Additionally, we will discuss the quality of the paraphrases evaluated by humans on subset of examples.

3.1 Results

To measure the quality of paraphrase generation we used average ROUGE-L, BLEU-n metrics and average cosine distance between reference and generated (calculated with model for paraphrase

[7]https://github.com/UKPLab/sentence-transformers

[8]https://www.sbert.net/examples/applications/paraphrase-mining/README.html

[9]http://docs.deeppavlov.ai/en/master/features/models/syntaxparser.html

identification task) sentences. BLEU-n calculates n gram overlap (unigrams, bigrams and trigrams), ROUGE-L measures the longest matching sequence.

Thus, we first ranged candidates as described in section 2.3, counted average scores between them for each example in the testset and got average scores for all testset examples. The results of the models are presented in Table 3. It is worth mentioning that in the process of ranging candidates we eliminated examples that were very similar by Levenshtein distance with the reference sentence (the cases when paraphraser changes case or adds punctuation symbols are not what we want).

We can observe that the golden set results have the highest scores, still the average results of the filtered models are high. The best results by ROUGE and BLEU scores are demonstrated by the mT5-small model, however it is interesting that the mt5-base and large models scores are lower, while the average candidates cosine similarity in these models is higher. It is due to the fact that if we explore generated sequences we find out that the mT5 model generates sequences that do not have great variability. For example, it is likely to generate sentences that differ only in punctuation symbols or prepositions from the reference sentence. In other words, the metrics of average cosine similarity is more reliable when paraphrases are expected to be more diverse. Thus, in order to choose the best model one need to pay attention to the metrics which are more appropriate for one's task.

The range step of the candidates is of a great importance. We took the results of mT5-small and gpt3 models. In Table 2 we present the scores depending on the different range strategies. One can see that the results vary a lot. Without filtration GPT-based model performed much worse by all the metrics. The mT5 model after filtration had even higher scores by BLEU and ROUGE metrics, but they decreased with average cosine similarity. Therefore, depending on the model and the result one expects, the range strategy should be different.

3.2 Data augmentation

In addition to general metrics, we tested if augmenting the training data with the use of paraphrasers could help to improve the performance of the model on the down-stream tasks. For this purpose we applied fine-tuned models to paraphrase examples in the training samples and, thus, augmenting the training data.

To demonstrate how paraphrases perform with default parameters on a down-stream task, we chose the following datasets:

1. RuSentiment[10] (Rogers et al., 2018) - dataset for sentiment analysis of social media posts in Russian.

2. TERRa (Shavrina et al., 2020) - Textual Entailment Recognition for Russian, a part of Russian SuperGLUE benchmark[11]. This task requires to recognize, given two text fragments, whether the meaning of one text is entailed (can be inferred) from the other text. To augment data we paraphrased the premise in each sample, kept the hypothesis and the labels, but shuffled the extended training set.

3. DaNetQA (Glushkova et al., 2020) - Russian yes/no Question Answering Dataset, a part of Russian SuperGLUE benchmark (Shavrina et al., 2020). In this dataset we paraphrased only questions and kept the paragraphs in the original format.

We took mT5-base model with range strategy of pairwise cosine similarity and default parameters. For each task we created a baseline solution as an example of paraphrasers applicability on simple setups for common tasks. For DaNetQA we made simple sequence classification with *DeepPavlov/rubert-base-cased* embeddings trained 10 epochs. For ruSentiment we used a Logistic regression classifier as a baseline. The tf-idf baseline provided by the organizers was used for TERRa.

We can see in Table 4 that the results are slightly different for all the tasks. On the TERRa task there was an increase in the performance. However, in ruSentiment we observed decrease of performance on the test set, as well as in DaNetQA, where the quality was almost the same. During the evaluation procedure the performance on training set for all the tasks was increasing. It is worth to mention that we use paraphrasers from the library with the default, same parameters for all three tasks, and even with them the results do not decrease significantly.

The results of the experiment are quite controversial. On the one hand, we did not observe a significant decrease in the performance on the set,

[10] http://text-machine.cs.uml.edu/projects/rusentiment/
[11] https://russiansuperglue.com/tasks

Model	Strategy	CS	BLEU-1	BLEU-2	BLEU-3	ROUGE-L
mT5-small	cosine similarity	0.781	0.49	0.35	0.21	0.49
mT5-small	paraphrase mining	0.776	0.58	0.45	0.30	0.58
mT5-small	syntax	0.775	0.55	0.41	0.26	0.56
mT5-small	best rouge	0.770	0.44	0.29	0.15	0.43
mT5-small	best bleu	0.772	0.53	0.40	0.26	0.53
mT5-small	all candidates	0.761	0.54	0.40	0.27	0.54
rugpt3	cosine similarity	0.754	0.41	0.27	0.15	0.42
rugpt3	paraphrase mining	0.740	0.42	0.28	0.17	0.43
rugpt3	syntax	0.737	0.42	0.27	0.16	0.42
rugpt3	best rouge	0.733	0.35	0.22	0.12	0.37
rugpt3	best bleu	0.735	0.37	0.24	0.13	0.38
rugpt3	all candidates	0.727	0.36	0.24	0.13	0.38

Table 2: Scores of the mT5-small model and rugpt3 with different range strategies.

Paraphraser	Cosine similarity	BLEU-1	BLEU-2	BLEU-3	ROUGE-L
golden set	0.848	0.57	0.43	0.28	0.58
mT5-small	0.781	0.49	0.35	0.21	0.49
mT5-base	0.798	0.35	0.23	0.12	0.37
mT5-large	0.802	0.40	0.25	0.12	0.41
rugpt2	0.717	0.43	0.29	0.17	0.44
rugpt3	0.754	0.41	0.27	0.15	0.42

Table 3: Scores of the models average

Dataset	Orig	Aug	+examples
DaNetQA	0.621	0.62	1750
ruSent	0.674	0.666	5550
TERRa	0.471	0.475	5600

Table 4: Augmentation results on test sets of the mT5-base model and number of generated examples that were added.

on the other hand, we suppose to see increase of performance with larger sizes of the dataset. One of possible explanations for this is that there was no new information in the added training set, the labels and the meaning were the same, which caused better performance during the training stage and possible overfitting. Examples of sentiment data are very short, with specific lexicon, emojis etc., which also could influence the results. DaNetQA dataset assumes YES/NO questions format, while the paraphraser could change the form of the question heavily and decrease the performance. Additionally, we believe that for every downstream task it is essential to choose a model and parameters more appropriate for the data on each step: generation, ranking, and evaluation. However, these hypotheses need further augmentation testing.

3.3 Discussion

The generated sentences are of different quality; all of the fine-tuned models are able to produce appropriate paraphrases, as well as some of them contain extra information, some typos, agreement errors or different meaning. In Figure 2 one can see the best candidates examples for three of the models. Table 5 represents the distribution of three classes: 1) good, 2) bad and 3) paraphrasers with extra information or some grammatical errors. We took 50 examples from testset, generated the paraphrases with each model, took best candidates and manually checked the number of examples for each class. The GPT2 is more stable; GPT3 is tend to produce more diverse paraphrases and add extra information that changes sense or makes it controversial; mT5 model makes more mistakes or instead changes the reference sentence not much.

The number of inappropriate candidates is significant and the procedure of candidates range and model parameters setup is crucial and should be specific for every task where we want to use paraphrasers generated on large language models. Each model has its own generating traits. For instance, GPT-based models are likely to generate more off-top sentences and the diversity of their answers is high. We also noticed the tendency of GPT-based models to change the quality of generation examples depending on the max length. mT5 models prefer to change sentences in small pieces: change argument in the sentence on its synonym or add/cut more punctuation and symbols. Therefore, mT5-base results are rated higher with BLEU and ROUGE scores, but the examples do not differ much from reference sentences. The suitability of multilingual models to Russian has no doubts, the results are comparable. Additionally mT5-models are much faster in generation than GPT-based.

We believe the paraphrasers will be useful in many applications, thus we provide the dataset and fine-tuned models in hugging-face format in open source. The library with paraphrasers and some of range strategies for them is also available[12]. We hope everyone can find the perfect Russian paraphraser for oneself.

Model	Good	Extra info/Typos	Bad
GPT2	70%	17%	13%
GPT3	56%	34%	10%
mT5-base	63%	21%	16%

Table 5: Human evaluation of paraphrasers performance. All results were scored manually by people. The distribution is presented in percentage.

4 Conclusion

Paraphrase generation with large language models achieves impressive results. Our experiments show that both multilingual and Russian-oriented models are able to quickly learn the task of paraphrasing through fine-tuning training on a prepared Russian set of paraphrase examples. This paper contributions are the corpus of paraphrases, 5 fine-tuned models for the Russian language, comparison of them, range strategies for finding the best candidates, and the open source library in Python for convenient use of the pre-trained paraphrasers.

In future work, we would like to further explore the effectiveness of generated paraphrasers for different augmentation experiments and evaluate the models robustness in terms of reconstruction and generated paraphrases.

[12]https://github.com/RussianNLP/russian$_paraphrasers$

References

Igor A Bolshakov and Alexander Gelbukh. 2004. Synonymous paraphrasing using wordnet and internet. In *International Conference on Application of Natural Language to Information Systems*, pages 312–323. Springer.

Kirill Boyarsky and Eugeni Kanevsky. 2017. Effect of semantic parsing depth on the identification of paraphrases in russian texts. In *Conference on Artificial Intelligence and Natural Language*, pages 226–241. Springer.

Tom B Brown, Benjamin Mann, Nick Ryder, Melanie Subbiah, Jared Kaplan, Prafulla Dhariwal, Arvind Neelakantan, Pranav Shyam, Girish Sastry, Amanda Askell, et al. 2020. Language models are few-shot learners. *arXiv preprint arXiv:2005.14165*.

Taisia Glushkova, Alexey Machnev, Alena Fenogenova, Tatiana Shavrina, Ekaterina Artemova, and Dmitry I Ignatov. 2020. Danetqa: a yes/no question answering dataset for the russian language. *arXiv preprint arXiv:2010.02605*.

Vadim Gudkov, Olga Mitrofanova, and Elizaveta Filippskikh. 2020. Automatically ranked russian paraphrase corpus for text generation. *arXiv preprint arXiv:2006.09719*.

Ankush Gupta, Arvind Agarwal, Prawaan Singh, and Piyush Rai. 2018. A deep generative framework for paraphrase generation. In *Proceedings of the AAAI Conference on Artificial Intelligence*, volume 32.

Chaitra Hegde and Shrikumar Patil. 2020. Unsupervised paraphrase generation using pre-trained language models. *arXiv preprint arXiv:2006.05477*.

Dmitry Kravchenko. 2017. Paraphrase detection using machine translation and textual similarity algorithms. In *Conference on artificial intelligence and natural language*, pages 277–292. Springer.

Yuri Kuratov and Mikhail Arkhipov. 2019. Adaptation of deep bidirectional multilingual transformers for russian language. *arXiv preprint arXiv:1905.07213*.

Mike Lewis, Marjan Ghazvininejad, Gargi Ghosh, Armen Aghajanyan, Sida Wang, and Luke Zettlemoyer. 2020. Pre-training via paraphrasing. *arXiv preprint arXiv:2006.15020*.

Chin-Yew Lin. 2004. Rouge: A package for automatic evaluation of summaries. In *Text summarization branches out*, pages 74–81.

Phillip Lippe, Pengjie Ren, Hinda Haned, Bart Voorn, and Maarten de Rijke. 2020. Diversifying task-oriented dialogue response generation with prototype guided paraphrasing. *arXiv preprint arXiv:2008.03391*.

Nitin Madnani and Bonnie J Dorr. 2010. Generating phrasal and sentential paraphrases: A survey of data-driven methods. *Computational Linguistics*, 36(3):341–387.

Models	Examples
	Скрипач Большого театра погиб после падения в оркестровую яму.
rugpt2	- Скрипач Большого театра скончался после падения в оркестровую яму. (+) - Скрипач Большого театра упал в оркестровую яму и скончался. (+) - Скрипач Большого театра упал в оркестровую яму и умер. (+) - Скрипач Большого театра упал в оркестровую яму и умер от падения. (+-)
rugpt3	- В Большом театре после падения в оркестровую яму погиб скрипач. (+) - В Большом театре подтвердили смерть скрипача от падения в оркестровую яму. (extra info) - При падении в оркестровую яму в Большом театре погиб скрипач. (+) - Упавший в оркестровую яму Скрипач Большого театра умер в больнице. (extra info)
mt5-base	- Более 200 человек погибли при падении в оркестрову яму. (-) - В Большом театре погиб скрыпач после падения в оркестровую яму. (typo) - Скрипач "Большого театра" погиб при падении в оркестровую яму. (+) - Скрипач Большого театра погиб при падении в оркестровую яму. (+)

Figure 2: Generated examples for sentence *Bolshoi Theater violinist dies after falling into orchestra pit.* + is a good generated paraphrase, - is not appropriate paraphrase, *extra info* means the generally good paraphrase but it contains more information than the reference ones.

Marie Meteer and Varda Shaked. 1988. Strategies for effective paraphrasing. In *Coling Budapest 1988 Volume 2: International Conference on Computational Linguistics*.

Tong Niu, Semih Yavuz, Yingbo Zhou, Huan Wang, Nitish Shirish Keskar, and Caiming Xiong. 2020. Unsupervised paraphrase generation via dynamic blocking. *arXiv preprint arXiv:2010.12885*.

Lidia Pivovarova, Ekaterina Pronoza, Elena Yagunova, and Anton Pronoza. 2017. Paraphraser: Russian paraphrase corpus and shared task. In *Conference on Artificial Intelligence and Natural Language*, pages 211–225. Springer.

Ekaterina Pronoza, Elena Yagunova, and Anton Pronoza. 2015. Construction of a russian paraphrase corpus: unsupervised paraphrase extraction. In *Russian Summer School in Information Retrieval*, pages 146–157. Springer.

Lihua Qian, Lin Qiu, Weinan Zhang, Xin Jiang, and Yong Yu. 2019. Exploring diverse expressions for paraphrase generation. In *Proceedings of the 2019 Conference on Empirical Methods in Natural Language Processing and the 9th International Joint Conference on Natural Language Processing (EMNLP-IJCNLP)*, pages 3164–3173.

Alec Radford, Jeffrey Wu, Rewon Child, David Luan, Dario Amodei, and Ilya Sutskever. 2019. Language models are unsupervised multitask learners. *OpenAI blog*, 1(8):9.

Nils Reimers and Iryna Gurevych. 2019. Sentence-bert: Sentence embeddings using siamese bert-networks. In *Proceedings of the 2019 Conference on Empirical Methods in Natural Language Processing*. Association for Computational Linguistics.

Nils Reimers and Iryna Gurevych. 2020. Making monolingual sentence embeddings multilingual using knowledge distillation. In *Proceedings of the 2020 Conference on Empirical Methods in Natural Language Processing*. Association for Computational Linguistics.

Anna Rogers, Alexey Romanov, Anna Rumshisky, Svitlana Volkova, Mikhail Gronas, and Alex Gribov. 2018. Rusentiment: An enriched sentiment analysis dataset for social media in russian. In *Proceedings of the 27th international conference on computational linguistics*, pages 755–763.

Tatiana Shavrina, Alena Fenogenova, Anton Emelyanov, Denis Shevelev, Ekaterina Artemova, Valentin Malykh, Vladislav Mikhailov, Maria Tikhonova, Andrey Chertok, and Andrey Evlampiev. 2020. Russiansuperglue: A russian language understanding evaluation benchmark. *arXiv preprint arXiv:2010.15925*.

AB Siddique, Samet Oymak, and Vagelis Hristidis. 2020. Unsupervised paraphrasing via deep reinforcement learning. In *Proceedings of the 26th ACM SIGKDD International Conference on Knowledge Discovery & Data Mining*, pages 1800–1809.

Nandan Thakur, Nils Reimers, Johannes Daxenberger, and Iryna Gurevych. 2020. Augmented sbert: Data augmentation method for improving bi-encoders for pairwise sentence scoring tasks. *arXiv preprint arXiv:2010.08240*.

Sam Witteveen and Martin Andrews. 2019. Paraphrasing with large language models. *arXiv preprint arXiv:1911.09661*.

Silei Xu, Sina J Semnani, Giovanni Campagna, and Monica S Lam. 2020. Autoqa: From databases to qa semantic parsers with only synthetic training data. *arXiv preprint arXiv:2010.04806*.

Wei Xu, Alan Ritter, Bill Dolan, Ralph Grishman, and Colin Cherry. 2012. Paraphrasing for style. In *Proceedings of COLING 2012*, pages 2899–2914.

Linting Xue, Noah Constant, Adam Roberts, Mihir Kale, Rami Al-Rfou, Aditya Siddhant, Aditya Barua, and Colin Raffel. 2020. mt5: A massively multilingual pre-trained text-to-text transformer. *arXiv preprint arXiv:2010.11934*.

Abusive Language Recognition in Russian

Kamil Saitov
Innopolis University
Russian Federation
saitov66@gmail.com

Leon Derczynski
IT University of Copenhagen
Denmark
ld@itu.dk

Abstract

Abusive phenomena are commonplace in language on the web. The scope of recognizing abusive language is broad, covering many behaviours and forms of expression. This work addresses automatic detection of abusive language in Russian. The lexical, grammatical and morphological diversity of Russian language present potential difficulties for this task, which is addressed using a variety of machine learning approaches. We present a dataset and baselines for this task.

1 Introduction

Unfortunately, hate speech and abusive language are prevalent on the internet (Waseem and Hovy, 2016), often creating an aggressive environment for users. This can include cyber-bullying or threats towards individuals and groups. Reducing this content is difficult: it is harmful for humans to moderate.[1] Thus, there is a critical need for abusive language recognition systems, which would help social networks and forums filter abusive language. Moreover, with platforms taking increased control over which content to surface, automatic abuse recognition is more important than ever.

One problem arises when the subjectivity of the matter is considered. Abusive language is hard for humans to recognize universally (Waseem, 2016). This indicates that the collection and labeling of data should be thorough and objective, which could be reached through e.g. large-scale crowd-sourced data annotation (Sabou et al., 2014).

NLP research in the area is nascent, with existing solutions oriented mostly towards English language (Vidgen and Derczynski, 2020), which, despite sometimes being mistakenly considered as "universal" (Bender, 2019), is very different grammatically and lexically from many languages, especially those using non-Latin characters (e.g. Russian, Japanese etc). This paper addresses abusive language detection in Russian. One issue with recognition of abusive language in Russian is the limited number of sources of labeled data relative to English (Andrusyak et al., 2018; Zueva et al., 2020; Smetanin, 2020; Potapova and Gordeev, 2016). Thus, the collection and labeling of data presents an additional challenge, and we present both dataset and models.

2 Abusive Language Definition

In this case, we use the OLID annotation definition of abusive language (Zampieri et al., 2019). This covers profanity, and targeted and untargeted insults and threats, against both groups and individuals. Specifically, in accordance this scheme, we consider the use of racial and other group-targeted slurs abusive.

3 Dataset

3.1 Data collection

We searched for publicly available datasets containing considerable amounts of abusive language.

Russian Troll Tweets is a repository consisting of 3 million tweets.[2] This was filtered to only Cyrillic texts. This data is not labeled, thus a subset of the data was labeled manually for use in this research. During labeling, the data turned out to contain significantly less abusive language than expected. An additional resource, the RuTweetCorp (Rubtsova, 2013), was also annotated for abusive language.

In search for sources rich in abusive language, the "South Park" TV show was found. The Russian subtitles for it embodied a high density of profanity, hate-speech, racism, sexism, various examples of

[1] https://www.theverge.com/2020/5/12/21255870/facebook-content-moderator-settlement-scola-ptsd-mental-health

[2] https://github.com/fivethirtyeight/russian-troll-tweets

Proceedings of the 8th BSNLP Workshop on Balto-Slavic Natural Language Processing, pages 20–25
April 20, 2021.

ethnicity and nationality abuse. The subtitles from more than four seasons of the series yielded many instances of abusive language. This data, Russian South Park (RSP), was annotated manually. Inter-annotator agreement (IAA; computed with Cohen's Kappa) over the whole dataset is 0.68 among three L1[3] Russian annotators.

To complement this, the Kaggle "Russian Language Toxic Comments" dataset (RTC) was also annotated. The dataset contains more than 14 000 labeled samples of hate speech. In Section 4, the performance of models trained on RSP data will be compared to that including RTC. More than 1500 samples are in the RSP dataset, and more than 15 000 samples are in total, adding the RTC data.

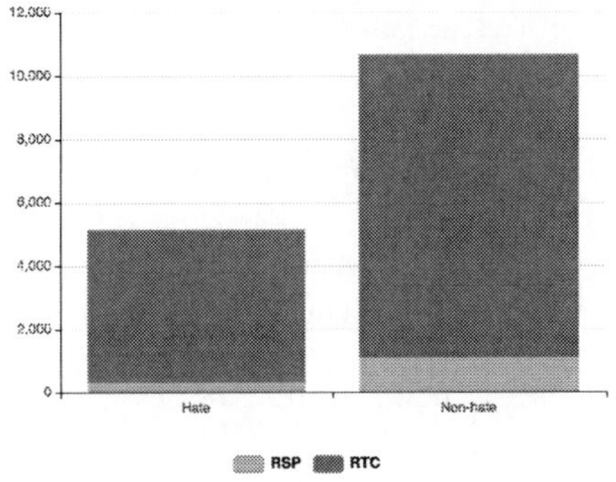

Figure 1: Dataset parts size and balance

		Instances	Tokens
Total	Abusive	5 904	133 180
	Non-abusive	9 893	192 307
RSP	Abusive	307	4 356
	Non-abusive	1 078	18 189
RTC	Abusive	5 597	128 824
	Non-abusive	8 815	174 118

Table 1: Word & token distribution across RSP

As well as in many *in situ* abusive language research, an abusive language lexicon was also constructed. The text data that was collected previously contained a fair amount of such vocabulary, however, the dictionary should not be limited by the dataset. HateBase (Tuckwood, 2017) contains only 17 abusive Russian words. VK, the largest social network in Russia and CIS, has an abusive speech filter dictionary published unofficially, containing a large lexicon of abusive words.[4] Another source is *russki-mat*,[5] an open dictionary of Russian curse words with proper explanations and examples of usage. Overall, the multiple-source lexicon built contains more than 700 unique terms. As can be seen from Table 2, abuse-bearing sentences contain four times more uppercased words and 25 times more abusive words than non-abusive sentences.

[3]I.e. as first language

[4]Common Knowledge Russian Tweets, http://study.mokoron.com/

[5]http://www.russki-mat.net/home.php

Words	mean	deviation
Uppercase (abusive)	0.02	0.007
Profane (absuive)	0.05	0.003
Uppercase (non-abusive)	0.005	0.00019
Profane (non-abusive)	0.002	0.00005

(a) At sentence level

Words	mean	deviation
Uppercase (abusive)	0.02	0.0003
Profane (absuive)	0.03	0.0004
Uppercase (non-abusive)	0.006	1.84E-05
Profane (non-abusive)	0.003	3.80E-06

(b) Across the whole dataset

Table 2: Uppercase and profane word distribution across the dataset

4 Experiments

4.1 Data Preprocessing

The stages of pre-processing are the following:

1. Balance the dataset. The initial dataset no-hate/hate distribution is $1078/307$ for the RSP dataset and $8815/5597$ for the RSP+RTC dataset. The no-hate portion of the dataset is under-sampled so that this proportion is consistent.

2. Strip URLs. Remove the links from texts.

3. Adjust platform-specific text. All Twitter mentions, hashtags and retweet are shown by a set of distinct symbols (# for hasthtag, @ for retweet). These tags might hold information on whether the tweet is targeted at a particular person or not.

4. Orthographic normalisation. Replace Russian ë and Ë to the corresponding e and E. These letters are mostly interchangeable in Russan language, thus it is the standard preprocessing routine when working with Russian text data.

5. Tokenization. Splitting the sentences into separate words and punctuation. The tokenization is done with NLTK library's word_tokenize() method.

6. Lemmatize terms. Lemmatization is reducing the word into its normal form. In case of Russian language, most researchers prefer stemming over lemmatization, however, if stemming is used, the search for offensive words in sentences would become intractable. The lemmatization is done with pymorphy2 (Korobov, 2015) - a morphological analyzer library specifically for Russian language.

7. Remove stop words from the text. Such words are common interjections, conjugations, prepositions, that do not need to be seen as features in the future modelling of the data.

8. TF-IDF vectorization. Turn the words into frequency vectors for each sample.

9. Train-test split Randomly split the ready data into train and test sets with 80/20 proportion.

4.2 Feature Extraction

Additional features beyond the text itself are included. Since abusive or hateful comments are anticipated to be also negative in sentiment, sentiment analysis is included. The sentiment was automatically predicted for the RTC dataset, for which a FastText (Bojanowski et al., 2017) embedding induced over RuSentiment (Rogers et al., 2018) was used, achieving F1 of 0.71, high for sentiment classifiers for Russian.

Upper-casing full words is a popular tone-indicating technique (Derczynski et al., 2015). Since one cannot "shout" in the internet, the intent of a higher-tone is expressed with upper-casing. Therefore, the number of fully-uppercased words is counted for each sample.

We also count the number of offensive words (from our lexicon) contained in a sentence. This feature is expected to be important, since abusive language is often combined with profanity, though this kind of sampling is not without bias (Vidgen and Derczynski, 2020).

4.3 Baseline Results [no RTC data]

The baseline model is a binary Linear Support Vector Classifier with default L2 loss and squared-hinge loss. The model was chosen to be an SVC because similar work for other languages suggest that it can be effective for this type of task (Frisiani et al., 2019).

The overall F1-score is up to 0.75, depending on the seed and parameters. The F1-score on the RSP+RTC Comments dataset is higher, up to 0.87, again, depending on the seed and parameters (Figure 2). Analysing the incorrectly classified samples, it turns out that the main difficulty the model has is

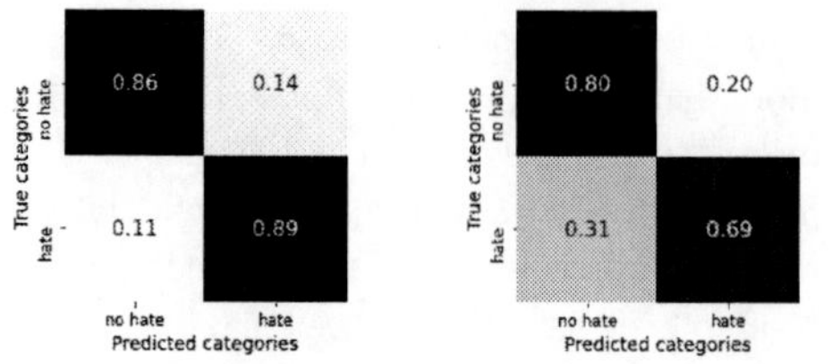

(a) with RTC data (b) no RTC data

Figure 2: Confusion matrixes of the baseline model

longer texts as well as texts containing swear words that cannot be converted to initial form due to distortion through slang/word formation. An example of this is the following:

> В чем проблема? Деградируй до неандертальца и х*ярь (heavily distorted slang) п*дарасов (misspelling)
>
> *What is the problem? Degrade to a Neanderthal level and kick those f*ggots*

The following example is a stereotypical hate speech sentence - it is all upper-cased, it uses abusive words and contains numerous insults. The baseline model recognizes it well:

> КРЫМОТРЕД НАРУШАЕТ ПРАВИЛА РАЗДЕЛА Т.К В НЕМ НЕТ ОБСУЖДЕНИЯ ПОЛИТИКИ. СВОБОДНОЕ ОБЩЕНИЕ ЭТО В Ь. ЭТО ТОЖЕ САМОЕ ЕСЛИ Я НА ДОСКЕ О ПОЛИТИКЕ СОЗДАМ ТРЕД О ШЛ*ХАХ. ТАК ЧТО У*БЫВАЙТЕ В Б ИЛИ НВР СО СВОИМ ЧАТИКОМ ПРЕСТАРЕЛЫХ Г*МОСЕКОВ!
>
> *CRIMEA THREAD VIOLATES THE RULES OF THE FORUM BECAUSE THE RULES DOES NOT ALLOW POLITICS DISCUSSION. THIS IS THE SAME IF I START DISCUSSING SL*TS ON A POLITICS FORUM. SO GET THE F*CK OUT OF HERE AND GO TO ¡another forum¿ AND TAKE YOUR WHOLE OLD F*GGOTS PARTY WITH YOU!*

4.4 Skip stopword exclusion

Although removing stop words from tokenized text is common practice, leaving them in might yield different results. This is the case here. The results are better on both datasets. F1-score over the RTC+RSP dataset is 0.88 (Figure 3).

4.5 Without balancing the dataset

In this experiment, the datasets are not balanced, thus the proportion of hate/no-hate is 1/2 in the combined RTC+RSP dataset and 1/10 in the RSP. As can be seen in Figure 4, true positives decrease by a small amount and the false negatives have risen up by a large margin, causing a decrease in overall model performance.

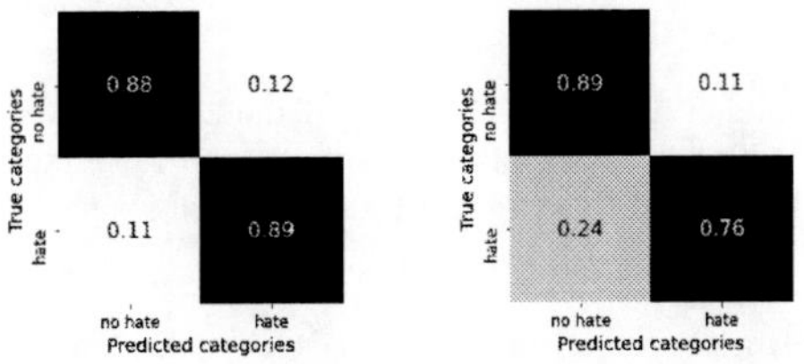

(a) with RTC data (b) no RTC data

Figure 3: Improved recall and precision on both datasets without stopword filtering

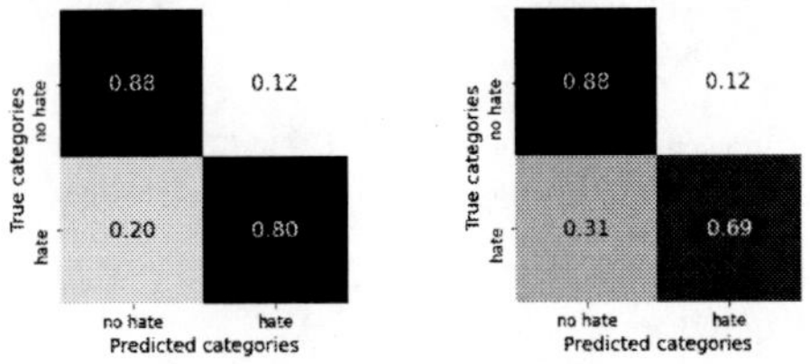

(a) with RTC data (b) no RTC data

Figure 4: Performance without giving balancing instance weights

4.6 Deep Learning

Neural network-based approaches often show promising results on various NLP tasks. In fact, some of the best methods for hate-speech detection in English are BERT, CNN, GRU/LSTM-based techniques (Zampieri et al., 2020). We investigated these methods over RSP.

Model	F1	Recall	Precision
RuBERT	0.85	0.86	0.84
mBERT	0.76	0.73	0.79

(a) BERT variant performance

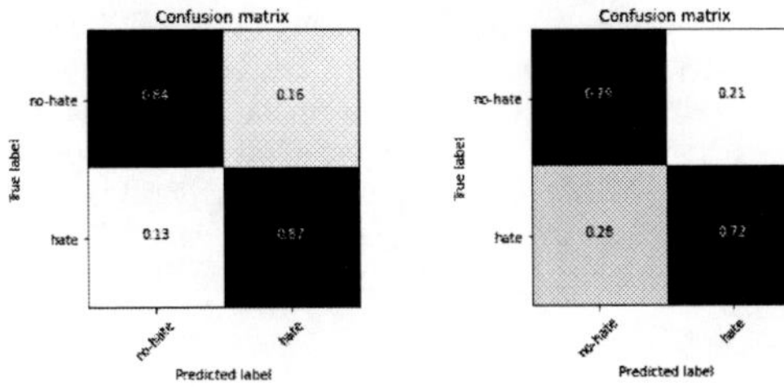

(b) RuBERT (c) mBERT

Figure 5: Performance of BERT variations over the combined dataset

4.6.1 RuBERT

RuBERT (Burtsev et al., 2018) is the original Bidirectional Encoder Representations from Transformers (Devlin et al., 2019) model but trained on Russian Wikipedia pages. The fine-tuning needed to be made includes training the last, classifier layer of the network. The results are promising, reaching F1-score of 0.85 on the whole training dataset (confusion matrix in Figure 5).

The model is able to correctly recognize the following sample as hate-speech:

> Посмотрел Утомленных солнцем 2. И оказалось, что это хороший фильм, такая высокобюджетная артхаусятина, к которой могут быть претензии только потому, что сп*здили-распилили и вообще ТАК НЕ БЫВАЕТ. Ну н*хуй этих критиков. Обзоры длиннее фильмов, петросянство хуже рашкокомедий, еб*нутая ненависть и до*бки по мелочам.
>
> *Watched Burnt by the Sun 2. Turns out it's a pretty good movie, a high-budget arthouse-ish film, the only downside possible is that most of the budget has been corruptly-stolen and THE PLOT IS NOT REALISTIC. F*ck those critics. The review texts are longer than the movie itself, jokes are worse than <humor in Russian-produced comedies>, f*cked up hate and f*cking nagging about small errors.*

4.6.2 mBERT

mBERT is multilingual BERT (Devlin et al., 2019), again trained on Wikipedia pages of over a hundred languages, mainly of non-Latin alphabets. Russian is Cyrillic, thus the model has the potential in Russian hate-speech recognition domain. The fine-tuning is the same as for RuBERT.

The results (Figure 5) showed worse performance than RuBERT, up to 0.76 F1-score. The reason for the lower performance is probably in the concept of generalisation of BERT to multiple languages, as opposed to RuBERT, which is trained exclusively on Russian language.

The following is an example of a sample which has been incorrectly classified as no-hate with both BERT-based models, as well as the baseline model:

> Вонючий совковый скот прибежал и ноет. А вот и сторонник демократии и свободы слова закукарекал.
>
> *The stinking soviet cattle came running and whining. And here is the supporter of democracy and freedom of speech starting to croak.*

The sentence does not contain any especially abusive vocabulary, but rather the words "stinking", "cattle", "croak" in this context (in relation to people) are abusive.

4.7 Analysis

For the largest dataset of Russian abusive language samples (RSP+RTC) and the LinearSVC model, the best-case is 0.88. This is a good result for such a simple model compared to typical results in other languages (Zampieri et al., 2020). Our suggestion is that the reason for such a good score is the correct data preprocessing and, even more importantly, feature selection.

Processing	RTC+RSP	RSP only
Base	0.86	0.75
No stopword removal	**0.88**	**0.83**
No dataset balancing	0.85	0.80

Table 3: Ablations over data processing steps, with SVM classifier (F-scores)

RuBERT still struggles mainly with recognizing longer texts and texts with misspellings. Another barrier for this model in particular is when a text contains many named entities, because word representations might not contain entity surface forms (Augenstein et al., 2017) or individual entities may not be representative of the typical context of a given abusive language phenomena.

An example of the above-mentioned criteria is the following long sentence with many named entities (NEs) and misspellings:

> Сторонники бандеровцев (NE) (леваков (NE), выступавших за бесклассовое (misspelling) общество и борьбу с капитализмом) и карлика-душителя котов Степана Бандеры (NE), который, как известно, боролся с расизмом, поддерживал Идель-Урал (NE) и называл побратимами исламских борцов за свободу из Азербайджана (NE), не пользуются симпатиями у правых европейцев.

The mistakes made by mBERT are roughly a superset of those made by RuBERT. This suggests that information mBERT can gain from other languages is not particularly helpful for this task.

5 Conclusion

This paper presented data, models and experiments for abusive language detection in Russian. By choosing the right preprocessing techniques and language-specific feature selection it is possible to achieve state-of-the-art performance on par with best-performing English language models, even using a simple SVM model. This indicates that, given sufficient diversity of data, abusive language detection solutions can be rapidly developed for new languages.

The code and data for this research are publicly available at: `https://github.com/Sariellee/Russan-Hate-speech-Recognition`

References

Bohdan Andrusyak, Mykhailo Rimel, and Roman Kern. 2018. Detection of abusive speech for mixed sociolects of Russian and Ukrainian Languages. In *Proceedings of RASLAN*, pages 77–84.

Isabelle Augenstein, Leon Derczynski, and Kalina Bontcheva. 2017. Generalisation in named entity recognition: A quantitative analysis. *Computer Speech & Language*, 44:61–83.

Emily Bender. 2019. The #BenderRule: On Naming the Languages We Study and Why It Matters. *The Gradient*.

Emily M Bender and Batya Friedman. 2018. Data statements for natural language processing: Toward mitigating system bias and enabling better science. *Transactions of the Association for Computational Linguistics*, 6:587–604.

Piotr Bojanowski, Edouard Grave, Armand Joulin, and Tomas Mikolov. 2017. Enriching word vectors with subword information. *Transactions of the Association for Computational Linguistics*, 5:135–146.

Mikhail Burtsev, Alexander Seliverstov, Rafael Airapetyan, Mikhail Arkhipov, Dilyara Baymurzina, Nickolay Bushkov, Olga Gureenkova, Taras Khakhulin, Yurii Kuratov, Denis Kuznetsov, et al. 2018. DeepPavlov: Open-source library for dialogue systems. In *Proceedings of ACL 2018, System Demonstrations*, pages 122–127.

Leon Derczynski, Diana Maynard, Giuseppe Rizzo, Marieke Van Erp, Genevieve Gorrell, Raphaël Troncy, Johann Petrak, and Kalina Bontcheva. 2015. Analysis of named entity recognition and linking for tweets. *Information Processing & Management*, 51(2):32–49.

Jacob Devlin, Ming-Wei Chang, Kenton Lee, and Kristina Toutanova. 2019. BERT: Pre-training of Deep Bidirectional Transformers for Language Understanding. In *Proceedings of the 2019 Conference of the North American Chapter of the Association for Computational Linguistics: Human Language Technologies, Volume 1 (Long and Short Papers)*, pages 4171–4186.

Nicolò Frisiani, Alexis Laignelet, and Batuhan Güler. 2019. Combination of multiple deep learning architectures for offensive language detection in tweets. *arXiv preprint arXiv:1903.08734*.

Mikhail Korobov. 2015. Morphological analyzer and generator for russian and ukrainian languages. In Mikhail Yu. Khachay, Natalia Konstantinova, Alexander Panchenko, Dmitry I. Ignatov, and Valeri G. Labunets, editors, *Analysis of Images, Social Networks and Texts*, volume 542 of *Communications in Computer and Information Science*, pages 320–332. Springer International Publishing.

Rodmonga Potapova and Denis Gordeev. 2016. Detecting state of aggression in sentences using CNN. In *International Conference on Speech and Computer*, pages 240–245.

Anna Rogers, Alexey Romanov, Anna Rumshisky, Svitlana Volkova, Mikhail Gronas, and Alex Gribov. 2018. RuSentiment: An enriched sentiment analysis dataset for social media in Russian. In *Proceedings of the 27th international conference on computational linguistics*, pages 755–763.

YV Rubtsova. 2013. A method for development and analysis of short text corpus for the review classification task. In *Proceedings of Conferences Digital Libraries: Advanced Methods and Technologies, Digital Collections, RCDL*, pages 269–275.

Marta Sabou, Kalina Bontcheva, Leon Derczynski, and Arno Scharl. 2014. Corpus annotation through crowdsourcing: Towards best practice guidelines. In *Proceedings of LREC*, pages 859–866.

Sergey Smetanin. 2020. Toxic Comments Detection in Russian. In *Computational Linguistics and Intellectual Technologies: Proceedings of the International Conference "Dialogue 2020"*.

Christopher Tuckwood. 2017. Hatebase: Online database of hate speech. *The Sentinal Project. Available at: https://www. hatebase. org*.

Bertie Vidgen and Leon Derczynski. 2020. Directions in abusive language training data, a systematic review: Garbage in, garbage out. *PLoS one*, 15(12):e0243300.

Zeerak Waseem. 2016. Are you a racist or am i seeing things? Annotator influence on hate speech detection on twitter. In *Proceedings of the first workshop on NLP and computational social science*, pages 138–142.

Zeerak Waseem and Dirk Hovy. 2016. Hateful symbols or hateful people? Predictive features for hate speech detection on twitter. In *Proceedings of the NAACL Student Research Workshop*, pages 88–93.

Marcos Zampieri, Preslav Nakov, Sara Rosenthal, Pepa Atanasova, Georgi Karadzhov, Hamdy Mubarak, Leon Derczynski, Zeses Pitenis, and Çağrı Çöltekin. 2020. SemEval-2020 Task 12: Multilingual Offensive Language Identification in Social Media (OffensEval 2020).

Nadezhda Zueva, Madina Kabirova, and Pavel Kalaidin. 2020. Reducing unintended identity bias in Russian hate speech detection. In *Proceedings of the Fourth Workshop on Online Abuse and Harms*, pages 65–69.

A Data Statement

This appendix describes metadata for RSP, following Bender and Friedman (2018).

A. Curation rationale The texts were taken from the South Park TV series in order to gather a corpus relatively rich in various forms of abusive language.

B. Language variety Scripted Russian translated at high standard from US English. BCP47 `ru-RU`

C. Speaker demographic The text is transcribed from words of Russian actors, mostly male, portraying characters who are both adults and children. The child characters (age eight) make up most of the speech content. The scripts were originally written by two US males from Colorado, over a period where they were aged 20-something to 40-something.

D. Annotator demographic Native Russian speakers, male, twenties, university students.

E. Speech situation This is scripted TV speech; it's not know how much latitude the voice actors were afforded over wording.

F. Text characteristics The content is deliberately somewhat foul-mouthed and very informal; political satire and social commentary are common themes.

Detecting Inappropriate Messages on Sensitive Topics that Could Harm a Company's Reputation*

Nikolay Babakov[‡], Varvara Logacheva[‡], Olga Kozlova[†], Nikita Semenov[†], and Alexander Panchenko[‡]
[‡]Skolkovo Institute of Science and Technology, Moscow, Russia
[†]Mobile TeleSystems (MTS), Moscow, Russia
{n.babakov,v.logacheva,a.panchenko}@skoltech.ru
{oskozlo9,nikita.semenov}@mts.ru

Abstract

Not all topics are equally "flammable" in terms of toxicity: a calm discussion of turtles or fishing less often fuels inappropriate toxic dialogues than a discussion of politics or sexual minorities. We define a set of *sensitive* topics that can yield inappropriate and toxic messages and describe the methodology of collecting and labeling a dataset for appropriateness. While toxicity in user-generated data is well-studied, we aim at defining a more fine-grained notion of *inappropriateness*. The core of inappropriateness is that it can harm the reputation of a speaker. This is different from toxicity in two respects: (i) inappropriateness is topic-related, and (ii) inappropriate message is not toxic but still unacceptable. We collect and release two datasets for Russian: a topic-labeled dataset and an appropriateness-labeled dataset. We also release pre-trained classification models trained on this data.

1 Introduction

The classification and prevention of toxicity (malicious behaviour) among users is an important problem for many Internet platforms. Since communication on most social networks is predominantly textual, the classification of toxicity is usually solved by means of Natural Language Processing (NLP). This problem is even more important for developers of chatbots trained on a large number of user-generated (and potentially toxic) texts. There is a well-known case of Microsoft Tay chatbot[1] which was shut down because it started producing racist, sexist, and other offensive tweets after having been fine-tuned on user data for a day.

However, there exists a similar and equally important problem, which is nevertheless overlooked by the research community. This is a problem of texts which are not offensive as such but can express inappropriate views. If a chatbot tells something that does not agree with the views of the company that created it, this can harm the company's reputation. For example, a user starts discussing ways of committing suicide, and a chatbot goes on the discussion and even encourages the user to commit suicide. The same also applies to a wide range of *sensitive* topics, such as politics, religion, nationality, drugs, gambling, etc. Ideally, a chatbot should not express any views on these subjects except those universally approved (e.g. that drugs are not good for your health). On the other hand, merely avoiding a conversation on any of those topics can be a bad strategy. An example of such unfortunate avoidance that caused even more reputation loss was also demonstrated by Microsoft, this time by its chatbot Zo, a Tay successor. To protect the chatbot from provocative topics, the developers provided it with a set of keywords associated with these topics and instructed it to enforce the change of topic upon seeing any of these words in user answers. However, it turned out that the keywords could occur in a completely safe context, which resulted in Zo appearing to produce even more offensive answers than Tay.[2] Therefore, simple methods cannot eliminate such errors.

Thus, our goal is to make a system that can predict if an answer of a chatbot is *inappropriate* in any way. This includes toxicity, but also any answers which can express undesirable views and approve or prompt user towards harmful or illegal actions. To the best of our knowledge, this problem has not been considered before. We formalize it and present a dataset labeled for the presence of such inappropriate content.

Even though we aim at a quite specific task – detection of inappropriate statements in the output

*Warning: the paper contains textual data samples which can be considered offensive or inappropriate.

[1]https://www.theverge.com/2016/3/24/11297050/tay-microsoft-chatbot-racist

[2]https://www.engadget.com/2017-07-04-microsofts-zo-chatbot-picked-up-some-offensive-habits.html

Proceedings of the 8th BSNLP Workshop on Balto-Slavic Natural Language Processing, pages 26–36
April 20, 2021.

of a chatbot to prevent the reputational harm of a company, in principle, the datasets could be used in other use-cases e.g. for flagging inappropriate frustrating discussion in social media.

It is also important to discuss the ethical aspect of this work. While it can be considered as another step towards censorship on the Internet, we suggest that it has many use-cases which serve the common good and do not limit free speech. Such applications are parental control or sustaining of respectful tone in conversations online, *inter alia*. We would like to emphasize that our definition of sensitive topics does not imply that any conversation concerning them need to be banned. Sensitive topics are just topics that should be considered with extra care and tend to often flame/catalyze toxicity.

The contributions of our work are three-fold:

- We define the notions of sensitive topics and inappropriate utterances and formulate the task of their classification.
- We collect and release two datasets for Russian: a dataset of user texts labeled for sensitive topics and a dataset labeled for inappropriateness.
- We train and release models which define a topic of a text and define its appropriateness.

We open the access to the produced datasets, code, and pre-trained models for the research use.[3]

2 Related Work

There exist a large number of English textual corpora labeled for the presence or absence of toxicity; some resources indicate the degree of toxicity and its topic. However, the definition of the term "toxicity" itself is not agreed among the research community, so each research deals with different texts. Some works refer to any unwanted behaviour as toxicity and do not make any further separation (Pavlopoulos et al., 2017). However, the majority of researchers use more fine-grained labeling. The Wikipedia Toxic comment datasets by Jigsaw (Jigsaw, 2018, 2019, 2020) are the largest English toxicity datasets available to date operate with multiple types of toxicity (*toxic*, *obscene*, *threat*, *insult*, *identity hate*, etc). Toxicity differs across multiple axes. Some works concentrate solely on major offence (*hate speech*) (Davidson et al., 2017), others research more subtle assaults (Breitfeller et al., 2019). Offenses can be directed towards an individual, a group, or undirected (Zampieri et al., 2019), explicit or implicit (Waseem et al., 2017).

Insults do not necessarily have a topic, but there certainly exist toxic topics, such as sexism, racism, xenophobia. Waseem and Hovy (2016) tackle sexism and racism, Basile et al. (2019) collect texts which contain sexism and aggression towards immigrants. Besides directly classifying toxic messages for a topic, the notion of the topic in toxicity is also indirectly used to collect the data: Zampieri et al. (2019) pre-select messages for toxicity labeling based on their topic. Similarly, Hessel and Lee (2019) use topics to find controversial (potentially toxic) discussions.

Such a topic-based view of toxicity causes unintended bias in toxicity detection – a false association of toxicity with a particular topic (LGBT, Islam, feminism, etc.) (Dixon et al., 2018; Vaidya et al., 2020). This is in line with our work since we also acknowledge that there exist acceptable and unacceptable messages within toxicity-provoking topics. The existing work suggests algorithmic ways for debiasing the trained models: Xia et al. (2020) train their model to detect two objectives: toxicity and presence of the toxicity-provoking topic, Zhang et al. (2020) perform re-weighing of instances, Park et al. (2018) create pseudo-data to level off the balance of examples. Unlike our research, these works often deal with one topic and use topic-specific methods.

The main drawback of topic-based toxicity detection in the existing research is the ad-hoc choice of topics: the authors select a small number of popular topics manually or based on the topics which emerge in the data often, as Ousidhoum et al. (2019). Banko et al. (2020) suggest a taxonomy of harmful online behaviour. It contains toxic topics, but they are mixed with other parameters of toxicity (e.g. direction or severity). The work by Salminen et al. (2020) is the only example of an extensive list of toxicity-provoking topics. This is similar to *sensitive topics* we deal with. However, our definition is broader — sensitive topics are not only topics that attract toxicity, but they can also create unwanted dialogues of multiple types (e.g. incitement to law violation or to cause harm to oneself or others).

3 Inappropriateness and Sensitive Topics

Consider the following conversation with an unmoderated chatbot:

[3]https://github.com/skoltech-nlp/inappropriate-sensitive-topics

- User: When did the Armenian Genocide happen?
- Chatbot: In 1915
- User: Do you want to repeat it?
- Chatbot: Sure

This discussion is related to the topics "politics" and "racism" and can indeed cause reputation damage to a developer. In some countries, such as France, it is a criminal offense to deny the Armenian Genocide during World War I.[4] Note, however, that no offensive or toxic words were employed. Detection of such content is thus desirable.

The notion of *inappropriateness* of a text in our setting is tightly related to this text's topic. This is different from the notion of *toxicity* which does not have to be topic-dependent. Toxic texts are undoubtedly inappropriate in the sense that they should not appear in a respectful conversation. Still, they have been actively researched, so we do not consider them in our work.

3.1 Definitions

We define **sensitive topic** as a topic which *has a high chance of yielding a discussion which can harm the speaker's reputation*. This suggests that there are no universally sensitive topics; their safety depends on the context and the goals of a conversation. The context may include the level of formality, the rules of a company that created the chatbot, the laws of the country where it operates. It is also important to emphasize that a message should not necessarily be banned for touching a sensitive topic. Instead, we introduce the notion of *appropriateness* acceptable statements on a sensitive topic.

We define **inappropriate message** as a message *on a sensitive topic which can frustrate the reader and/or harm the reputation of the speaker*. This definition is hard to formalize, so we rely on the intuitive understanding of appropriateness which is characteristic of human beings and is shared by people belonging to the same culture. Namely, we ask people if a given statement of a chatbot can harm the reputation of the company which developed it. We thus use human judgments as a main measure of appropriateness.

3.2 List of Sensitive Topics

We manually select the set of sensitive topics which often fuel inappropriate statements. This set is heterogeneous: it includes topics related to dangerous or harmful practices (such as drugs or suicide), some of which are legally banned in most countries (e.g. terrorism, slavery) or topics that tend to provoke aggressive argument (e.g. politics) and may be associated with inequality and controversy (e.g. minorities) and thus require special system policies aimed at reducing conversational bias, such as response postprocessing.

This set of topics is based on the suggestions and requirements provided by legal and PR departments of a large Russian telecommunication company. It could, for instance, be used to moderate a corporate dialogue system or flag inappropriate content for children, therefore mitigating possible operational damages. While this list is by no mean comprehensive, we nevertheless believe it could be useful in practical applications and as a starting point for work in this direction.

The list of the sensitive topics is as follows:

- **gambling**;
- **pornography**, description of sexual intercourse;
- **prostitution**;
- **slavery**, human trafficking;
- **suicide**: incitement to suicide, discussion of ways to commit suicide,
- **social injustice** and inequality, social problems, class society;
- **religion**;
- **terrorism**;
- **weapons**;
- **offline crime** (murder, physical assault, kidnapping and other), prison, legal actions;
- **online crime**: breaking of passwords and accounts, viruses, pirated content, stealing of personal information;
- **politics**, military service, past and current military conflicts;
- **body shaming**, people's appearances and clothes;
- **health shaming**, physical and mental disorders, disabilities;
- **drugs**, alcohol, tobacco;
- **racism** and ethnicism;
- **sexual minorities**;
- **sexism**, stereotypes about a particular gender.

4 Topic Labeling

Our final goal is to label the data with *inappropriateness*, and the sensitive topics are not a goal *per se*, but mainly a way to define inappropriateness. Therefore, we use sensitive topics as a way of data

[4]https://www.bbc.com/news/world-europe-16677986

Text	Appropriate	Reason	Sensitive topic
Killing is not a big deal. They have killed no-name ni**a not a politician	✘	Justifying murder	offline crime, racism
This is a violation of the Criminal Law	✔	Shaming the fact of breaking law	offline crime
Religion is the highest level of violence. The believer is forced to believe in infancy.	✘	Insulting the feeling of religious people	religion
Christians, how do you feel about the Gentiles?	✔	Common question about religion	religion
I will earn some money and grab some prostitutes for weekend	✘	Popularisation of prostitution	prostitution
It's good that prostitution is prohibited here	✔	Shaming the prostitution	prostitution

Table 1: Examples of appropriate and inappropriate samples related to sensitive topics (translated from Russian).

pre-selection. Analogously to toxicity, inappropriateness does not often occur in randomly picked texts, so if we label all the messages we retrieve, the percentage of inappropriate utterances among them will be low. Thus, our labeling process includes three stages: (i) we collect the dataset of sentences on sensitive topics, (ii) we build a classifier of sensitive topics on this dataset, (iii) we collect the texts on sensitive topics using the classifier and then label them as appropriate or inappropriate.

4.1 Data Selection

We retrieve the initial pool of texts from general sources with diverse topics, then filter them and hire crowd workers to label them for the presence of sensitive topics manually. We use the data from the following sources:

- 2ch.hk – a platform for communication in Russian similar to Reddit. The site is not moderated, suggesting a large amount of toxicity and controversy; this makes it a practical resource for our purposes. We retrieve 4.7 million sentences from it.
- Otvet.Mail.ru – a question-answering platform that contains questions and answers of various categories and is also not moderated. We take 12 million sentences from it.

To pre-select the data for topic labeling, we manually create large sets of keywords for each sensitive topic. We first select a small set of words associated with a topic and then extract semantically close words using pre-trained word embeddings from RusVectōrēs[5] and further extend the keyword list (this can be done multiple times). In addition to that, for some topics we use existing lists of associated slang on topical websites, e.g. drugs[6] and weapons.[7]

User-generated content which we collect for labeling is noisy and can contain personal information (e.g. usernames, email addresses, or even phone numbers), so it needs cleaning. At the same time, some non-textual information such as emojis is valuable and should be kept intact, so the cleaning should not be too rigorous. Thus, we remove links to any websites, usernames, long numbers, and other special characters such as HTML tags.

4.2 Crowdsourced Labeling

The labeling is performed in a crowdsourcing platform Yandex.Toloka.[8] It was preferred to other analogous platforms like Amazon Mechanical Turk because the majority of its workers are Russian native speakers.

The task of topic labeling is naturally repre-

[5]https://rusvectores.org/ru/associates/

[6]http://www.kantuev.ru/slovar

[7]https://guns.allzip.org/topic/15/626011.html

[8]https://toloka.yandex.ru

sented as a multiple-choice task with the possibility to select more than one answer: the worker is shown the text and possible topics and is asked to choose one or more of them. However, as far as we define 18 sensitive topics, choosing from such a long list of options is difficult. Therefore, we divide the topics into three clusters:

- **Cluster 1**: gambling, pornography, prostitution, slavery, suicide, social injustice,
- **Cluster 2**: religion, terrorism, weapons, offline crime, online crime, politics,
- **Cluster 3**: body shaming, health shaming, drugs, racism, sex minorities, sexism.

Cluster 1 is associated with undesirable behavior; cluster 2 deals with crimes, military actions, and their causes; cluster 3 is about the offense. However, this division is not strict and was performed to ease the labeling process. Checking a text for one of six topics is a realistic task while selecting from 18 topics is too high a cognitive load.

Each cluster has a separate project in Yandex.Toloka. Every candidate text is passed to all three projects: we label each of them for all 18 topics. An example of a task interface is shown in Figure 1.

Before labeling the examples, we ask users to perform **training**. It consists of 20 questions with pre-defined answers. To be admitted to labeling, a worker has to complete the training with at least 65% correct answers. In addition to that, we perform extra training during labeling. One of each ten questions given to a worker has a pre-defined correct answer. If a worker makes a mistake in this question, she is shown the correct answer with an explanation.

Likewise, we perform **quality control** using questions with pre-defined answers: one of ten questions given to the worker is used to control her performance. If the worker gives incorrect answers to more than 25% of control questions, she is banned from further labeling, and her latest answers are discarded.

For the topic labeling task, the average performance of workers on control and training tasks was between 65 and 70%.

In addition to that, we control the speed of task accomplishment. If a user answers ten questions (one page of questions) in less than 20 seconds, this almost certainly indicates that she has not read the examples and selected random answers. Such workers are banned. To ensure the diversity of answers we allow one user to do at most 50 pages of tasks (500 tasks) per 12 hours.

Each sample is labeled in each project by 3 to 5 workers. We use **dynamic overlap** technique implemented in Toloka. An example is first labeled by the minimum number of workers. If they agree, their answer is considered truth. Otherwise, the example is given for extra labeling to more workers to clarify the true label. This allows separating the occasional user mistakes from inherently ambiguous examples.

We aggregate multiple answers into one score using the aggregation method by Dawid and Skene (1979). This is an iterative method that maximizes the probability of labeling taking into account the worker agreement, i.e. it trusts more the workers who agree with other workers often. The result of this algorithm is the score from 0 to 1 for each labeled example which is interpreted as the label confidence.

Besides the aggregation purposes, we use the confidence score as a measure of worker agreement.[9] Since the low score of an example is the sign of either the ambiguity of this example or the low reliability of annotators who labeled it, we assume that the high confidence indicates that the task is interpreted by all workers in a similar way and does not contain inherent contradictions. The average confidence of labeling in our topic dataset is 0.995.

4.3 Crowdsourcing Issues

While collecting manual topic labels, we faced some problems. First, some topics require special knowledge to be labeled correctly. For example, users tend to label any samples about programming or computer hardware as "online crime", even if there is no discussion of any crime. Likewise, some swear words, e.g. "whore", can be used as a general offense and not refer to a prostitute. However, this is not always clear to crowd workers or even to the authors of this research. This can make some sensitive topics unreasonably dependent on such kinds of keywords.

[9] We cannot use Cohen's or Fleiss kappa which are usually employed to measure the inter-annotator agreement because these scores are inapplicable in the crowdsourcing scenario. While Fleiss kappa implies that we have a relatively small number of annotators (usually up to 5) each of whom labels a large percentage of examples, in the crowdsourcing setting we have a much larger number of workers, each labeling only a small number of sentences.

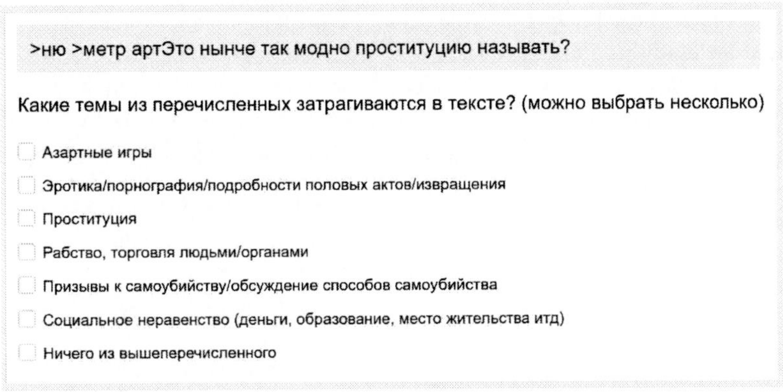

Figure 1: Example of topic labeling task. Translation: upper line – text for labeling: "*Nude* – is it a new name for prostitution?", middle line – task: "Which topics does the text touch? (You can select more than one)", possible answers: "Gambling, pornography, prostitution, slavery, suicide, social inequality, nothing of the above".

Secondly, it is necessary to keep the balance of samples on different topics. If there are no samples related to the topics presented to the worker within numerous tasks she can overthink and try to find the topic in unreasonably fine details of texts. For example, if we provide three or four consecutive sets of texts about weapons and topic "weapons" is not among the proposed topics, the worker will tend to attribute these samples to other remotely similar topics, e.g. "crime", even though the samples do not refer to crime.

We should also point out that a different set of topics or labeling setup could yield other problems. It is difficult to foresee them and to find the best solutions for them. Therefore, we also test two alternative approaches to topic labeling which do not use crowd workers.

4.4 Automated Labeling

After having collected almost 10,000 texts on sensitive topics, we were able to train a classifier that predicts the occurrence of a sensitive topic in the text. Although this classifier is not good enough to be used for real-world tasks, we suggest that samples classified as belonging to a sensitive topic with high confidence (more than 0.75 in our experiments) can be considered belonging to this topic. We perform an extra manual check by an expert (one of the authors) to eliminate mistakes. This method is also laborious, but it is an easier labeling scenario than the crowdsourcing task described in Section 4.2. Approving or rejecting a text as an entity of a single class is easier than classify it into one of six topics.

An alternative way of automated topic labeling is to take the data from specialized sources and select topic-attributed messages using a list of keywords *inherent* for a topic, i.e. words which definitely indicate the presence of a topic. This approach can give many false positives when applied to general texts because many keywords can have an idiomatic meaning not related to a sensitive topic. One such example can be the word "addiction" which can be used in entirely safe contexts, e.g. a phrase "I'm addicted to chocolate" should not be classified as belonging to the topic "drugs". However, when occurring in a specialized forum on addictions,[10] this word almost certainly indicates this topic. We define a list of inherent keywords and select messages containing them from special resources related to a particular topic. We then manually check the collected samples.

The disadvantage of this approach is that we cannot handle multilabel samples. However, according to dataset statistics, only 15% of samples had more than one label. Given the limited time and budget, we decided to use this approach to further extend the dataset. The resulting sensitive topics dataset in the form we opensource it is the combination of all three approaches. Specific, nearly 11,000 samples were labeled in a fully manual manner either via crowdsourcing or by members of our team, the rest samples (nearly 14,500) were labeled via the described semi-automatic approaches

5 Appropriateness Labeling

We should again emphasize that not every utterance concerning a sensitive topic should be banned.

[10] `https://nenormaforum.info`

While the topic of a text can be sensitive, the text itself can nevertheless be appropriate. Thus, we collect the texts on sensitive topics and then label them as appropriate or inappropriate.

Our initial plan was to define the appropriate and inappropriate subtopics for each topic. However, determining the appropriateness criteria explicitly turned out to be infeasible. Therefore, we rely on the inherent human intuition of appropriateness. We provide annotators with the following context: a chatbot created by a company produces a given phrase. We ask to indicate if this phrase can harm the reputation of the company. We also reinforce the annotators' understanding of appropriateness with the training examples. As in the topic labeling setup, here we ask the workers to complete the training before labeling the data. We also fine-tune their understanding of appropriateness with extra training during labeling.

Analogously to topic labeling, the appropriateness labeling is performed via Yandex.Toloka crowdsourcing platform. An example of the task interface is given in Figure 2. Our crowdsourcing setup repeats the one we used in the topic labeling project. We perform training and quality control analogously to topic labeling. Although the appropriateness is not explicitly defined, the workers demonstrate a good understanding of it. Their average performance on the training and control tasks is around 75-80%, which indicates high agreement. The average labeling confidence computed via the Dawid-Skene method is 0.956.

The primary sources of the samples passed to appropriateness labeling are the same as in the topic labeling setup (2ch.hk and Otvet.Mail.ru websites). Before handing texts to workers, we filter them as described in Section 4.1 and also perform extra filtering. We filter out all messages containing obscene language and explicit toxicity. We identify toxicity with a BERT-based classifier for toxicity detection. We fine-tune ruBERT model (Kuratov and Arkhipov, 2019) on a concatenation of two Russian Language Toxic Comments datasets released on Kaggle (Kaggle, 2019, 2020).We filter out sentences which were classified as toxic with the confidence greater than 0.75. As mentioned above, toxicity is beyond the scope of our work, because it has been researched before. Therefore, we make sure that messages which can be automatically recognized as toxic are not included in this dataset.

Inappropriate messages in our formulation concern one of the sensitive topics. Therefore, we pre-select data for labeling by automatically classifying them with sensitive topics. We select the data for labeling in the following proportion:

- 1/3 of samples which belong to one or more sensitive topic with high confidence (> 0.75),
- 1/3 of samples classified as sensitive with medium confidence ($0.3 > c < 0.75$). This is necessary in case if multilabel classifier or crowd workers captured uncertain details of sensitive topics,
- 1/3 random samples – these are used to make the selection robust to classifier errors.

The further labeling process is performed analogously to topic labeling. We use the same training and quality control procedures and define the number of workers per example dynamically.

To get the final answer, we use the same Dawid-Skene aggregation method. It aggregates the labels given by workers (0 and 1, which state for "appropriate" and "inappropriate") into a single score from 0 to 1. We interpret this score as the appropriateness level, where the score in the interval [0, 0.2] indicates appropriate sentences, the score in [0.8, 1] means that the sentence is inappropriate, and other scores indicate ambiguous examples.

6 Datasets Statistics

We collected two datasets: (i) the dataset of sensitive topics and (ii) the appropriateness dataset.

The dataset of sensitive topics consists of 25,679 unique samples. 9,946 samples were labeled with a crowdsourcing platform, nearly 1,500 samples were labeled by our team and the rest samples were collected by using keywords from specialized sources. The average confidence of the crowdsourcing annotation is 0.995; the average number of annotations per example is 4.3; the average time to label one example is 10.8 seconds.

The appropriateness dataset consists of 82,063 unique samples. 8,687 of these samples also belong to the sensitive topics dataset and thus have manually assigned topic labels. The other 73,376 samples have topic labels defined automatically using a BERT-based topic classification model (described in Section 7). The average confidence of the annotation is 0.956; the average number of annotations per example is 3.5; the average time to label one example is 7 seconds.

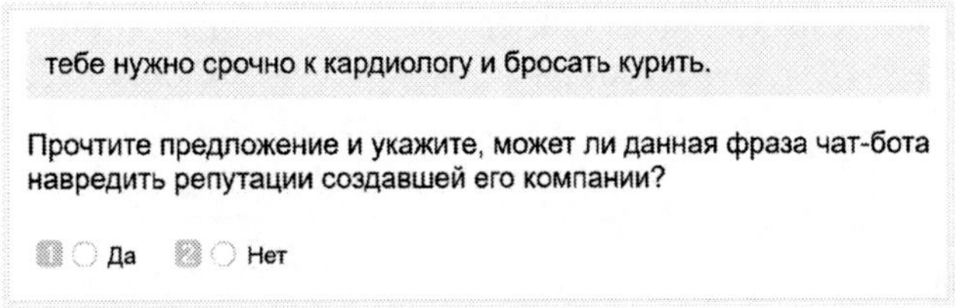

Figure 2: Interface of appropriateness labeling task. Translation: upper line – text: "You should give up smoking and urgently consult cardiologist", middle line – task: "Read the sentence and indicate whether this phrase generated with chatbot can harm the reputation of the company which created this chatbot?", possible answers – "Yes/No"

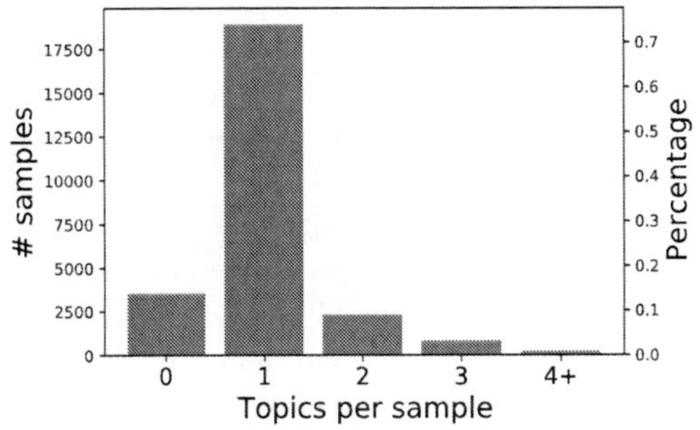

Figure 3: Distribution of samples by number of topics.

Sensitive topic	Topic dataset	Appropriateness dataset
total samples	25,679	82,063
religion	4,110	2,869
drugs	3,870	8,618
sex minorities	1,970	754
health shaming	1,744	7,270
politics	1,593	7,650
weapons	1,530	726
suicide	1,420	1,931
gambling	1,393	2,693
pornography	1,289	2,824
social injustice	1,230	5,294
racism	1,156	3,760
online crime	1,058	3,181
offline crime	1,037	2,206
sexism	1,022	3,644
body shaming	715	3,537
prostitution	634	240
terrorism	577	310
slavery	288	442

Table 2: Number of samples per topic in sensitive topics and appropriateness datasets.

Table 2 shows the number of samples on each sensitive topic in both datasets. While we tried to keep the topic distribution in the topic dataset balanced, some topics (drugs, politics, health shaming) get considerably more samples in the appropriateness dataset. This might be related to the fact that the classifier performance for these topics was good, so utterances classified with these topics with high confidence emerged often.

One sample can relate to more than one topic. Our analysis showed 15% of such examples in the data (see Figure 3). The co-occurrence of topics is not random. It indicates the intersection of multiple topics. The most common co-occurrences are "politics, racism, social injustice", "prostitution, pornography", "sex minorities, pornography". In contrast, 13% of samples in the topic dataset do not touch any sensitive topic. These are examples that were pre-selected for manual topic labeling using keywords and then were labeled as not related to the topics of interest. They were added to the dataset so that the classifier trained on this data does not rely solely on keywords.

The samples in the datasets are mostly single sentences; their average length is 15 words for the appropriateness dataset and 18 words for the topic dataset. The sample length for different topics ranges from 14 to 21 words. We noticed a strong correlation (Spearman's r of 0.72) between the number of samples of a particular topic in the data and the average number of words per sample for this topic. We cannot define if this is a spurious correlation or topics that feature longer sentences tend to be better represented in the data. Longer sentences might be easier to annotate.

7 Evaluation

We confirm the usefulness of the collected data by training classification models on both datasets.

We fine-tune pre-trained ruBERT model (BERT trained on Russian texts (Kuratov and Arkhipov, 2019)) on our data. We use the implementation of BERT-classifier from `deeppavlov`[11] library with pre-trained Conversational RuBERT weights.[12]

7.1 Topic Classifier

We build the topic classifier on 85% of the sensitive topics dataset and use the rest as a test. The proportions of instances of different topics in the training and test subsets are the same.

We measure the classifier performance with F_1-score. The macro-average F_1-score is 0.78. We trained five classifiers with different train-test splits. It turned out that the classifier is unstable, which has already been reported for BERT-based models (Mosbach et al., 2020).

The F_1-scores for individual topics are shown in Figure 4. The score is above 0.8 for 8 out of 18 classes. We noticed that the classifier performance for individual classes is correlated with the number of samples of these classes in the data (Spearman's r of 0.73 – strong correlation). This suggests that the performance could be improved by retrieving more samples of underrepresented classes. However, for some topics (e.g. politics) the score is low despite the fact that they have enough representation in the data. This can indicate the complexity and heterogeneity of a topic.

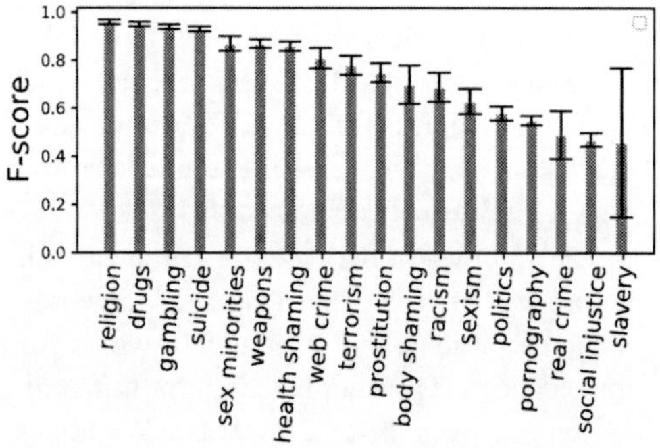

Figure 4: F_1-scores of the BERT-based topic classifier.

7.2 Appropriateness Classifier

Analogously to the topic classifier, we train the appropriateness classifier on 85% of the appropriateness-labeled messages and use the rest for testing. We use the same ruBERT-based model.

ROC-AUC	$0,87 \pm 0,01$
Precision	$0,83 \pm 0,01$
Recall	$0,84 \pm 0,01$
F_1-score	$0,83 \pm 0,01$

Table 3: Performance of the best BERT-based appropriateness classifier (binary classification).

In our data, appropriateness is represented as a number between 0 and 1 where 0 means inappropriate and 1 appropriate. Our initial experiments showed that using samples with low (in)appropriateness confidence for training results in poor results. Therefore, we drop all samples with confidence between 0.2 and 0.8. This results in a decrease of the dataset size to 74,376. Thus, our appropriateness classifier is trained on 63,000 samples. Its performance is outlined in Table 3. The scores are quite high, and the results of training with ten splits are quite stable.

8 Conclusions and Future Work

We introduce the task of detecting inappropriate utterances – utterances that can cause frustration or harm the reputation of a speaker in any way. We define the notion of a sensitive topic tightly related to the notion of appropriateness. We collect two datasets for the Russian language using a large-scale crowdsourcing study. One is labeled with sensitive topics and another with binary appropriateness labeling. We show that while being fine-grained notions, both inappropriateness and sensitivity of the topic can be detected automatically using neural models. Baseline models trained on the new datasets are presented and released.

A promising direction of future work is improving the performance of the presented baselines, e.g. by using the topic and appropriateness labeling jointly, switching to other model architectures, or ensembling multiple models. Another prominent direction of future work is to transfer the notion of appropriateness to other languages by fine-tuning cross-lingual models on the collected datasets.

Acknowledgments

We are grateful to four anonymous reviewers for their helpful suggestions. This work was conducted under the framework of the joint Skoltech-MTS laboratory.

[11] `http://docs.deeppavlov.ai/en/master/_modules/deeppavlov/models/bert/bert_classifier.html#BertClassifierModel`

[12] `http://files.deeppavlov.ai/deeppavlov_data/bert/ru_conversational_cased_L-12_H-768_A-12.tar.gz`

References

Michele Banko, Brendon MacKeen, and Laurie Ray. 2020. A unified taxonomy of harmful content. In *Proceedings of the Fourth Workshop on Online Abuse and Harms*, pages 125–137, Online. Association for Computational Linguistics.

Valerio Basile, Cristina Bosco, Elisabetta Fersini, Debora Nozza, Viviana Patti, Francisco Manuel Rangel Pardo, Paolo Rosso, and Manuela Sanguinetti. 2019. SemEval-2019 task 5: Multilingual detection of hate speech against immigrants and women in twitter. In *Proceedings of the 13th International Workshop on Semantic Evaluation*, pages 54–63, Minneapolis, Minnesota, USA. Association for Computational Linguistics.

Luke Breitfeller, Emily Ahn, David Jurgens, and Yulia Tsvetkov. 2019. Finding microaggressions in the wild: A case for locating elusive phenomena in social media posts. In *Proceedings of the 2019 Conference on Empirical Methods in Natural Language Processing and the 9th International Joint Conference on Natural Language Processing (EMNLP-IJCNLP)*, pages 1664–1674, Hong Kong, China. Association for Computational Linguistics.

Thomas Davidson, Dana Warmsley, Michael Macy, and Ingmar Weber. 2017. Automated hate speech detection and the problem of offensive language.

A. P. Dawid and A. Skene. 1979. Maximum likelihood estimation of observer error-rates using the em algorithm. *Journal of The Royal Statistical Society Series C-applied Statistics*, 28:20–28.

Lucas Dixon, John Li, Jeffrey Sorensen, Nithum Thain, and Lucy Vasserman. 2018. Measuring and mitigating unintended bias in text classification. In *Proceedings of the 2018 AAAI/ACM Conference on AI, Ethics, and Society*, AIES '18, page 67–73, New York, NY, USA. Association for Computing Machinery.

Jack Hessel and Lillian Lee. 2019. Something's brewing! early prediction of controversy-causing posts from discussion features. In *Proceedings of the 2019 Conference of the North American Chapter of the Association for Computational Linguistics: Human Language Technologies, Volume 1 (Long and Short Papers)*, pages 1648–1659, Minneapolis, Minnesota. Association for Computational Linguistics.

Jigsaw. 2018. Toxic comment classification challenge. `https://www.kaggle.com/c/jigsaw-toxic-comment-classification-challenge`. Accessed: 2021-03-01.

Jigsaw. 2019. Jigsaw unintended bias in toxicity classification. `https://www.kaggle.com/c/jigsaw-unintended-bias-in-toxicity-classification`. Accessed: 2021-03-01.

Jigsaw. 2020. Jigsaw multilingual toxic comment classification. `https://www.kaggle.com/c/jigsaw-multilingual-toxic-comment-classification`. Accessed: 2021-03-01.

Kaggle. 2019. Russian language toxic comments. `https://www.kaggle.com/blackmoon/russian-language-toxic-comments`. Accessed: 2021-03-01.

Kaggle. 2020. Toxic russian comments. `https://www.kaggle.com/alexandersemiletov/toxic-russian-comments`. Accessed: 2021-03-01.

Yuri Kuratov and Mikhail Arkhipov. 2019. Adaptation of deep bidirectional multilingual transformers for russian language.

Marius Mosbach, Maksym Andriushchenko, and Dietrich Klakow. 2020. On the stability of fine-tuning bert: Misconceptions, explanations, and strong baselines.

Nedjma Ousidhoum, Zizheng Lin, Hongming Zhang, Yangqiu Song, and Dit-Yan Yeung. 2019. Multilingual and multi-aspect hate speech analysis. In *Proceedings of the 2019 Conference on Empirical Methods in Natural Language Processing and the 9th International Joint Conference on Natural Language Processing (EMNLP-IJCNLP)*, pages 4675–4684, Hong Kong, China. Association for Computational Linguistics.

Ji Ho Park, Jamin Shin, and Pascale Fung. 2018. Reducing gender bias in abusive language detection. In *Proceedings of the 2018 Conference on Empirical Methods in Natural Language Processing*, pages 2799–2804, Brussels, Belgium. Association for Computational Linguistics.

John Pavlopoulos, Prodromos Malakasiotis, and Ion Androutsopoulos. 2017. Deeper attention to abusive user content moderation. In *Proceedings of the 2017 Conference on Empirical Methods in Natural Language Processing*, pages 1125–1135, Copenhagen, Denmark. Association for Computational Linguistics.

Joni Salminen, Sercan Sengün, Juan Corporan, Soon gyo Jung, and Bernard J. Jansen. 2020. Topic-driven toxicity: Exploring the relationship between online toxicity and news topics. *PLoS One*, 15(2).

Ameya Vaidya, Feng Mai, and Yue Ning. 2020. Empirical analysis of multi-task learning for reducing identity bias in toxic comment detection. *Proceedings of the International AAAI Conference on Web and Social Media*, 14(1):683–693.

Zeerak Waseem, Thomas Davidson, Dana Warmsley, and Ingmar Weber. 2017. Understanding abuse: A typology of abusive language detection subtasks. In *Proceedings of the First Workshop on Abusive Language Online*, pages 78–84, Vancouver, BC, Canada. Association for Computational Linguistics.

Zeerak Waseem and Dirk Hovy. 2016. Hateful symbols or hateful people? predictive features for hate speech detection on twitter. In *Proceedings of the NAACL Student Research Workshop*, pages 88–93, San Diego, California. Association for Computational Linguistics.

Mengzhou Xia, Anjalie Field, and Yulia Tsvetkov. 2020. Demoting racial bias in hate speech detection. In *Proceedings of the Eighth International Workshop on Natural Language Processing for Social Media*, pages 7–14, Online. Association for Computational Linguistics.

Marcos Zampieri, Shervin Malmasi, Preslav Nakov, Sara Rosenthal, Noura Farra, and Ritesh Kumar. 2019. Predicting the type and target of offensive posts in social media. In *Proceedings of the 2019 Conference of the North American Chapter of the Association for Computational Linguistics: Human Language Technologies, Volume 1 (Long and Short Papers)*, pages 1415–1420, Minneapolis, Minnesota. Association for Computational Linguistics.

Guanhua Zhang, Bing Bai, Junqi Zhang, Kun Bai, Conghui Zhu, and Tiejun Zhao. 2020. Demographics should not be the reason of toxicity: Mitigating discrimination in text classifications with instance weighting. In *Proceedings of the 58th Annual Meeting of the Association for Computational Linguistics*, pages 4134–4145, Online. Association for Computational Linguistics.

BERTić - The Transformer Language Model for Bosnian, Croatian, Montenegrin and Serbian

Nikola Ljubešić
Jožef Stefan Institute
Jamova cesta 39
Ljubljana, Slovenia
nikola.ljubesic@ijs.si

Davor Lauc
Faculty of Humanities and Social Sciences
Ivana Lučića 3
Zagreb, Croatia
davor.lauc@ffzg.hr

Abstract

In this paper we describe a transformer model pre-trained on 8 billion tokens of crawled text from the Croatian, Bosnian, Serbian and Montenegrin web domains. We evaluate the transformer model on the tasks of part-of-speech tagging, named-entity-recognition, geo-location prediction and commonsense causal reasoning, showing improvements on all tasks over state-of-the-art models. For commonsense reasoning evaluation we introduce COPA-HR - a translation of the Choice of Plausible Alternatives (COPA) dataset into Croatian. The BERTić model is made available for free usage and further task-specific fine-tuning through HuggingFace.

1 Introduction

In recent years, pre-trained transformer models have taken the NLP world by storm (Devlin et al., 2018; Liu et al., 2019; Brown et al., 2020), yielding new state-of-the-art results in various tasks and settings. While such models, requiring significant computing power and data quantity, started to emerge for non-English languages (Martin et al., 2019; de Vries et al., 2019), as well as in multilingual flavours (Devlin et al., 2018; Conneau et al., 2019), there is a significant number of languages for which better models can be obtained with the available pre-training techniques.

This paper describes such an effort - training a transformer language model on more than 8 billion tokens of text written in the Bosnian, Croatian, Montenegrin or Serbian language, all these languages being very closely related, mutually intelligible, and classified under the same HBS (Serbo-Croatian) macro-language by the ISO-693-3 standard.[1]

The name of the model – BERTić – points at two facts: (1) the language model was trained in Zagreb, Croatia, in whose vernacular diminutives ending in *ić* are frequently used (*fotić* eng. photo camera, *smajlić* eng. smiley, *hengić* eng. hanging together), and (2) in all the countries / languages of this model the patronymic surnames end to a great part with the suffix *ić*, with likely diminutive etymology.

The paper is structured as follows: in the following section we describe the data the model is based on, in the third section we give a short description of the modelling performed, and in the fourth section we present a detailed evaluation of the model.

2 Data

As our data basis we use already existing datasets, namely (1) the hrWaC corpus of the Croatian top-level domain, crawled in 2011 (Ljubešić and Erjavec, 2011) and again in 2014 (Ljubešić and Klubička, 2014), (2) the srWaC corpus of the Serbian top-level domain, crawled in 2014 (Ljubešić and Klubička, 2014), (3) the bsWaC corpus of the Bosnian top-level domain, crawled in 2014 (Ljubešić and Klubička, 2014), (4) the cnrWaC corpus of the Montenegrin top-level domain, crawled in 2019, and (5) the Riznica corpus consisting of Croatian literary works and newspapers (Ćavar and Rončević, 2012).

Given that most of the crawls contain data only up to year 2014, we performed new crawls of the Bosnian, Croatian and Serbian top-level domains. We brand these corpora as CLASSLA web corpora given that CLASSLA is the CLARIN knowledge centre for South Slavic languages[2] under which we perform most of the described activities. We deduplicate the CLASSLA corpora by removing

[1] https://iso639-3.sil.org/code_tables/macrolanguage_mappings/data

[2] https://www.clarin.si/info/k-centre/

Proceedings of the 8th BSNLP Workshop on Balto-Slavic Natural Language Processing, pages 37–42
April 20, 2021.

dataset	language	# of words
hrWaC	Croatian	1,250,923,836
CLASSLA-hr	Croatian	1,341,494,461
cc100-hr	Croatian	2,880,490,449
Riznica	Croatian	87,724,737
srWaC	Serbian	493,202,149
CLASSLA-sr	Serbian	752,916,260
cc100-sr	Serbian	711,014,370
bsWaC	Bosnian	256,388,597
CLASSLA-bs	Bosnian	534,074,921
cnrWaC	Montenegrin	79,451,738

Table 1: Datasets used for training the `BERTić` model with their size (in number of words) after deduplication.

identical sentences that were already present in the WaC corpora. The amount of data removed through this deduplication is minor, in all cases in single digit percentages.

We further exploit the recently published cc100 corpora (Conneau et al., 2019) that are based on the CommonCrawl data collection. We perform the same level of deduplication as with the CLASSLA corpora, with every sentence already present in the WaC or CLASSLA corpus being removed from the cc100 corpus. This round of deduplication removed around 15% of the CommonCrawl data.

The resulting sizes of the datasets used for training the `BERTić` model are presented in Table 1. The overall text collection consists of 8,387,681,518 words.

3 Model training

For training this model we selected the Electra approach to training transformer models (Clark et al., 2020). These models are based on training a smaller generator model and the main, larger, discriminator model whose task is to discriminate whether a specific word is the original word from the text, or a word generated by the generator model. The authors claim that the Electra approach is computationally more efficient than the BERT models (Devlin et al., 2018) based on masked language modelling.

As in BERT and similar transformers models, we constructed a WordPiece vocabulary with a vocabulary size of 32 thousand tokens. A WordPiece model was trained using the HuggingFace tokenizers library[3] on the random sample of 10 million paragraphs from the whole dataset. Text pre-processing and cleaning differ from the original BERT only in preserving all Unicode characters, while in the original pre-processing diacritics are removed.

Training of the model was performed to the most part with the hyperparameters set for base-sized models (110 million parameters in 12 transformer layers) as defined in the Electra paper (Clark et al., 2020). Training batch size was kept at 1024, the maximum size for the 8 TPUv3 units on which the training was performed. The training was run for 2 million steps (roughly 50 epochs).

4 Evaluation

In this section we present an exhaustive evaluation of the newly trained `BERTić` model on two token classification tasks – morphosyntactic tagging and named entity recognition, and two sequence classification tasks – geolocation prediction and commonsense causative reasoning.

The reference points in each task are the state-of-the art transformer models covering the macro-language - multilingual BERT (Devlin et al., 2018) and CroSloEngual BERT (Ulčar and Robnik-Šikonja, 2020). While multilingual BERT (`mBERT` onwards) was trained on Wikipedia corpora, CroSloEngual BERT (`cseBERT` onwards) was trained on a similar amount of Croatian data used to train `BERTić`, but without the data from the remaining languages.

4.1 Morphosyntactic tagging

On the task of morphosyntactic tagging (assigning each word one among multiple hundreds of detailed morphosyntactic classes, e.g. `Ncmsay` referring to a common masculine noun, in accusative case, singular number, animate) we compare the three transformer models, `mBERT`, `cseBERT` and `BERTić`. We additionally report results, when available, for the current production tagger for the two languages - the `CLASSLA` tool (Ljubešić and Dobrovoljc, 2019), based on Stanford's Stanza, exploiting static embedding and BiLSTM technology (Qi et al., 2020).

We perform evaluation of the models on this task on four datasets: the Croatian standard language dataset hr500k (Ljubešić et al., 2018), the Croatian non-standard language dataset ReLDI-hr (Ljubešić et al., 2019a), the Serbian standard language dataset

[3] `https://huggingface.co/transformers/main_classes/tokenizer.html`

dataset	language	variety	CLASSLA	mBERT	cseBERT	BERTić
hr500k	Croatian	standard	93.87	94.60	95.74	***__95.81__
reldi-hr	Croatian	non-standard	-	88.87	91.63	***__92.28__
SETimes.SR	Serbian	standard	95.00	95.50	**96.41**	96.31
reldi-sr	Serbian	non-standard	-	91.26	93.54	***__93.90__

Table 2: Average microF1 results on the morphosyntactic annotation task over five training iterations. The highest score per dataset is marked with bold. The statistical significance is tested with the two-sided t-test over the five runs between the two strongest results. Level of significance is labeled with asteriks signs (*** p<=0.001).

dataset	language	variety	CLASSLA	mBERT	cseBERT	BERTić
hr500k	Croatian	standard	80.13	85.67	88.98	****__89.21__
ReLDI-hr	Croatian	non-standard	-	76.06	81.38	****__83.05__
SETimes.SR	Serbian	standard	84.64	**92.41**	92.28	92.02
ReLDI-sr	Serbian	non-standard	-	81.29	82.76	***__87.92__

Table 3: Average F1 results on the named entity recognition task over five training iterations. The highest score per dataset is marked with bold. The statistical significance is tested with the two-sided t-test over the five runs between the two strongest results. Level of significance is labeled with asteriks signs (*** p<=0.001, **** p<=0.0001).

SETimes.SR (Batanović et al., 2018) and the Serbian non-standard Twitter language dataset ReLDI-sr (Ljubešić et al., 2019b).

For each dataset and model we perform hyperparameter optimization via Bayesian search on the wandb.ai platform (Biewald, 2020), allowing for 30 iterations. We optimize the initial learning rate (we search between the values of 9e-6 and 1e-4) and the epoch number (we search between the values of 3 and 15).

We report average microF1 results of five runs per dataset and model in Table 2. The highest score per dataset is marked with bold. The statistical significance is tested with the two-sided t-test over the five runs between the two highest average results. We can observe that the `BERTić` model outperforms all the remaining models, `cseBERT` coming second, on three out of four datasets. Only on the Serbian standard dataset the difference between these two models is insignificant. We argue that this is due to the simplicity of the dataset - it consists of texts from one newspaper only, therefore containing text with little variation even between the training and the testing data.

4.2 Named entity recognition

On the task of named entity recognition we compare the same models on the same datasets as was the case in the previous Section 4.1. We also perform an identical hyperparameter optimisation and experimentation and report the results in Table 3. The results show again that the two best performing models are `cseBERT` and `BERTić` with the latter performing better on three out of four datasets, again, with no significant difference on the standard Serbian task for the same reasons as with the previous task.

4.3 Social media geolocation

In this subsection we compare the three transformer models on the Social Media Geolocation (SMG2020) shared task, which part of the VarDial 2020 Evaluation Campaign (Gaman et al., 2020). The task consists of predicting the exact latitude and longitude of a geo-encoded tweet published in Croatia, Bosnia, Montenegro or Serbia. The shared task winner in 2020 was using the `cseBERT` model (Scherrer and Ljubešić, 2020) in its approach.

We evaluate the model on the two evaluation metrics of the shared task - median and mean of the distance between gold and predicted geolocations. Given the large size of the training dataset (320,042 instances), we do not perform any additional hyperparameter tuning beyond the one performed during the participation in the shared task and apply the same methodology: we fine-tune the transformer model with batch size of 64 for 40 epochs and retain the model with minimum median distance on development data. The results in Table 4 show that the `BERTić` model improved the results of the shared task winner – the `cseBERT` model.

	median	mean
centroid	107.10	145.72
mBERT	42.25	82.05
cseBERT	40.76	81.88
BERTić	**37.96**	**79.30**

Table 4: Median distance and mean distance between gold and predicted geolocation (lower is better) on the task of social media geolocation prediction. The best results are marked in bold. No statistical testing was performed due to a large size of the test dataset (39,723 instances).

	accuracy
random	50.00
mBERT	54.12
cseBERT	61.80
BERTić	****65.76**

Table 5: Average accuracy results on the commonsense causal reasoning task over five training iterations. The highest score per dataset is marked with bold. The statistical significance is tested with the two-sided t-test over the five runs between the two strongest results (** p<=0.01).

4.4 Commonsense causal reasoning

The final evaluation round of the new BERTić model is performed on the task of commonsense causal reasoning on a translation of the COPA dataset (Roemmele et al., 2011) into Croatian, the COPA-HR dataset. The translation is performed by following the methodology laid out while preparing the XCOPA dataset (Ponti et al., 2020), a translation of the COPA dataset into 11 typologically balanced languages.

The dataset consists of 400 training, 100 development and 500 examples. Each instance in the dataset consists of a premise (*The man broke his toe*), a question (*What was the cause?*),[4] and two alternatives, one of them to be chosen by the system as being more plausible (*He got a hole in his sock*, or *He dropped a hammer on his foot*).

While translating the dataset, the translator was also given the task of selecting the more plausible alternative given their translation. The observed agreement between the annotations in the English dataset and the annotations of the Croatian translator was perfect on the training set and the development set, while on the test set one out of 500 choices differed. The problematic example proved to be a rather unclear case – the premise being *I paused to stop talking.*, with the question *What was the cause?*, and the alternatives *I lost my voice.* and *I ran out of breath.*.[5] The dataset is available from the CLARIN.SI repository (Ljubešić, 2021).[6]

The approach taken to benchmarking the three transformer models is that of sentence pair classification, each original instance becoming two sentence pair instances (each sentence pair containing the premise and one alternative), with different models being trained for *cause* and *effect* questions. During evaluation, separate predictions are made on each of the alternatives, the per-class predictions being fed to a softmax function, and the higher positive-class alternative being chosen as the correct one.

The standard evaluation metric for this dataset is accuracy. Given the balanced nature of the test set, the random baseline is 50%. For hyperparameter optimization the same approach was taken as with the token classification tasks.

The results presented in Table 5 show that both language-specific transformer models outperform mBERT significantly, with BERTić obtaining a significant lead over cseBERT.

5 Conclusion

In this paper we have presented a newly published Electra transformer language model, BERTić, trained on more than 8 billion tokens of previously and newly collected web text written in Bosnian, Croatian, Montenegrin or Serbian. We have applied a very thorough evaluation of the model, comparing it primarily to other state-of-the-art transformer models that support the languages in question. We have obtained significant improvements on all four tasks, with no difference obtained only on one single-source-dataset with little text variation and high training and testing data similarity.

The main conclusions we can draw from our results are the following. (1) Although cseBERT and BERTić use a different approach to building transformer language models, our assumption is that the performance difference between these two lies primarily in the larger amount of data presented to the BERTić model. (2) The improvements on the four tasks with the BERTić model seem to be

[4] Roughly half of the instances contain the other question: *What was the effect?*.

[5] The Croatian translator chose the second alternative, while in the original dataset the first alternative is chosen.

[6] http://hdl.handle.net/11356/1404

smaller on the morphosyntactic tagging task than the remaining three tasks that require more world and commonsense reasoning knowledge. (3) Except for the named entity recognition task on the Serbian non-standard dataset, we fail to observe greater improvements on Serbian tasks than on Croatian ones between `cseBERT` and `BERTić`, regardless the fact that the former has seen none and the latter has seen huge quantities of Serbian text, showing the irrelevance of minor language differences for performance of large transformer models. (4) While BiLSTM models are still close-to-competitive on the morphosyntactic tagging task, they cannot hold up on the named entity recognition task as it requires more common knowledge. Such knowledge transformer models manage to absorb to a much higher level than pre-trained static embeddings used by BiLSTMs.

The `BERTić` model is available from the HuggingFace repository at `https://huggingface.co/CLASSLA/bcms-bertic`.

Acknowledgments

This work has been supported by the Slovenian Research Agency and the Flemish Research Foundation through the bilateral research project ARRS N6-0099 and FWO G070619N "The linguistic landscape of hate speech on social media", the Slovenian Research Agency research core funding No. P6-0411 "Language resources and technologies for Slovene language", and the European Union's Rights, Equality and Citizenship Programme (2014-2020) project IMSyPP (grant no. 875263). We would like to thank the anonymous reviewers and Ivo-Pavao Jazbec for their useful feedback.

References

Vuk Batanović, Nikola Ljubešić, Tanja Samardžić, and Tomaž Erjavec. 2018. Training corpus SETimes.SR 1.0. Slovenian language resource repository CLARIN.SI.

Lukas Biewald. 2020. Experiment tracking with weights and biases. Software available from wandb.com.

Tom B Brown, Benjamin Mann, Nick Ryder, Melanie Subbiah, Jared Kaplan, Prafulla Dhariwal, Arvind Neelakantan, Pranav Shyam, Girish Sastry, Amanda Askell, et al. 2020. Language models are few-shot learners. *arXiv preprint arXiv:2005.14165*.

Damir Ćavar and Dunja Brozović Rončević. 2012. Riznica: the Croatian language corpus. *Prace filologiczne*, 63:51–65.

Kevin Clark, Minh-Thang Luong, Quoc V Le, and Christopher D Manning. 2020. Electra: Pre-training text encoders as discriminators rather than generators. *arXiv preprint arXiv:2003.10555*.

Alexis Conneau, Kartikay Khandelwal, Naman Goyal, Vishrav Chaudhary, Guillaume Wenzek, Francisco Guzmán, Edouard Grave, Myle Ott, Luke Zettlemoyer, and Veselin Stoyanov. 2019. Unsupervised cross-lingual representation learning at scale. *arXiv preprint arXiv:1911.02116*.

Jacob Devlin, Ming-Wei Chang, Kenton Lee, and Kristina Toutanova. 2018. Bert: Pre-training of deep bidirectional transformers for language understanding. *arXiv preprint arXiv:1810.04805*.

Mihaela Gaman, Dirk Hovy, Radu Tudor Ionescu, Heidi Jauhiainen, Tommi Jauhiainen, Krister Lindén, Nikola Ljubešić, Niko Partanen, Christoph Purschke, Yves Scherrer, et al. 2020. A report on the VarDial evaluation campaign 2020. In *Proceedings of the 7th Workshop on NLP for Similar Languages, Varieties and Dialects*. International Committee on Computational Linguistics.

Yinhan Liu, Myle Ott, Naman Goyal, Jingfei Du, Mandar Joshi, Danqi Chen, Omer Levy, Mike Lewis, Luke Zettlemoyer, and Veselin Stoyanov. 2019. Roberta: A robustly optimized bert pretraining approach. *arXiv preprint arXiv:1907.11692*.

Nikola Ljubešić. 2021. Choice of plausible alternatives dataset in Croatian COPA-HR. Slovenian language resource repository CLARIN.SI.

Nikola Ljubešić, Željko Agić, Filip Klubička, Vuk Batanović, and Tomaž Erjavec. 2018. Training corpus hr500k 1.0. Slovenian language resource repository CLARIN.SI.

Nikola Ljubešić and Kaja Dobrovoljc. 2019. What does neural bring? analysing improvements in morphosyntactic annotation and lemmatisation of Slovenian, Croatian and Serbian. In *Proceedings of the 7th Workshop on Balto-Slavic Natural Language Processing*, pages 29–34, Florence, Italy. Association for Computational Linguistics.

Nikola Ljubešić and Tomaž Erjavec. 2011. hrWaC and slWaC: Compiling web corpora for Croatian and Slovene. In *International Conference on Text, Speech and Dialogue*, pages 395–402. Springer.

Nikola Ljubešić, Tomaž Erjavec, Vuk Batanović, Maja Miličević, and Tanja Samardžić. 2019a. Croatian twitter training corpus ReLDI-NormTagNER-hr 2.1. Slovenian language resource repository CLARIN.SI.

Nikola Ljubešić, Tomaž Erjavec, Vuk Batanović, Maja Miličević, and Tanja Samardžić. 2019b. Serbian twitter training corpus ReLDI-NormTagNER-sr 2.1. Slovenian language resource repository CLARIN.SI.

Nikola Ljubešić and Filip Klubička. 2014. {bs, hr, sr} wac-web corpora of Bosnian, Croatian and Serbian. In *Proceedings of the 9th Web as Corpus Workshop (WaC-9)*, pages 29–35.

Louis Martin, Benjamin Muller, Pedro Javier Ortiz Suárez, Yoann Dupont, Laurent Romary, Éric Villemonte de la Clergerie, Djamé Seddah, and Benoît Sagot. 2019. Camembert: a tasty french language model. *arXiv preprint arXiv:1911.03894*.

Edoardo Maria Ponti, Goran Glavaš, Olga Majewska, Qianchu Liu, Ivan Vulić, and Anna Korhonen. 2020. XCOPA: A multilingual dataset for causal commonsense reasoning. In *Proceedings of the 2020 Conference on Empirical Methods in Natural Language Processing (EMNLP)*, pages 2362–2376, Online. Association for Computational Linguistics.

Peng Qi, Yuhao Zhang, Yuhui Zhang, Jason Bolton, and Christopher D Manning. 2020. Stanza: A Python natural language processing toolkit for many human languages. *arXiv preprint arXiv:2003.07082*.

Melissa Roemmele, Cosmin Adrian Bejan, and Andrew S Gordon. 2011. Choice of Plausible Alternatives: An Evaluation of Commonsense Causal Reasoning. In *AAAI Spring Symposium: Logical Formalizations of Commonsense Reasoning*, pages 90–95.

Yves Scherrer and Nikola Ljubešić. 2020. HeLju@ VarDial 2020: Social media variety geolocation with BERT models. In *Proceedings of the 7th Workshop on NLP for Similar Languages, Varieties and Dialects*, pages 202–211.

Matej Ulčar and Marko Robnik-Šikonja. 2020. FinEst BERT and CroSloEngual BERT. In *International Conference on Text, Speech, and Dialogue*, pages 104–111. Springer.

Wietse de Vries, Andreas van Cranenburgh, Arianna Bisazza, Tommaso Caselli, Gertjan van Noord, and Malvina Nissim. 2019. Bertje: A dutch BERT model. *arXiv preprint arXiv:1912.09582*.

RuSentEval: Linguistic Source, Encoder Force!

Vladislav Mikhailov[1,2], **Ekaterina Taktasheva**[2], **Elina Sigdel**[2], **Ekaterina Artemova**[2]
[1] SberDevices, Sberbank, Moscow, Russia
[2] HSE University, Moscow, Russia
Mikhaylov.V.Nikola@sberbank.ru
{etaktasheva, essigdel, elartemova}@hse.ru

Abstract

The success of pre-trained transformer language models has brought a great deal of interest on how these models work, and what they learn about language. However, prior research in the field is mainly devoted to English, and little is known regarding other languages. To this end, we introduce RuSentEval, an enhanced set of 14 probing tasks for Russian, including ones that have not been explored yet. We apply a combination of complementary probing methods to explore the distribution of various linguistic properties in five multilingual transformers for two typologically contrasting languages – Russian and English. Our results provide intriguing findings that contradict the common understanding of how linguistic knowledge is represented, and demonstrate that some properties are learned in a similar manner despite the language differences.

1 Introduction

Transformer language models (Vaswani et al., 2017) have achieved state-of-the-art results on a wide range of NLP tasks in multiple languages, demonstrated strong performance in zero-shot cross-lingual transfer (Pires et al., 2019), and even surpassed human solvers in NLU benchmarks such as SuperGLUE (Wang et al., 2019). The success has stimulated research in how these models work, and what they acquire about language. The majority of the introspection techniques are based on the concept of *probing tasks* (Adi et al., 2016; Shi et al., 2016; Conneau et al., 2018) which allow analyzing what linguistic properties are encoded in the intermediate representations. A rich variety of tasks has been introduced so far, ranging from token-level and sub-sentence probing (Liu et al., 2019; Tenney et al., 2019) to sentence-level probing (Alt et al., 2020). A prominent method to explore the inner workings of the models involves training a lightweight classifier to solve a probing task over features produced by them, and assess their knowledge by the classifier's performance. Recently, the methods have been greatly extended to latent subclass learning (Michael et al., 2020), correlation similarity measures (Wu et al., 2020), information-theoretic probing (Voita and Titov, 2020), investigation of individual neurons (Durrani et al., 2020; Suau et al., 2020), and many more.

Despite growing interest in the field, English remains the focal point of prior research (Belinkov and Glass, 2019; Rogers et al., 2021) leaving other languages understudied. To this end, several monolingual and cross-lingual probing suites have been assembled (see Section 2), with a few of them following SentEval toolkit (Conneau et al., 2018; Conneau and Kiela, 2018). However, most of them directly apply an English-oriented method which is not guaranteed to be universal across languages, or use the Universal Dependencies (UD) Treebanks (Nivre et al., 2016) which tend to be inconsistent (Alzetta et al., 2017; de Marneffe et al., 2017; Droganova et al., 2018).

This work proposes **RuSentEval**, a probing suite for evaluation of sentence embeddings for the Russian language. We adapted the method for English (Conneau et al., 2018) to complement the peculiarities of Russian. In contrast to closely related datasets (Ravishankar et al., 2019; Eger et al., 2020), RuSentEval is fully guided by linguistic expertise, relies on annotations obtained with the current state-of-the-art model for Russian morphosyntactic analysis (Anastasyev, 2020), and includes tasks that have not been explored yet.

The contributions are summarized as three-fold. First, we present an enhanced set of 14 probing tasks for Russian, organized by the type of linguistic properties. Second, we carry out a series of

Proceedings of the 8th BSNLP Workshop on Balto-Slavic Natural Language Processing, pages 43–65
April 20, 2021.

probing experiments on two typologically different languages: English, which is an analytic Germanic language, and Russian, which is a fusional Slavic one. Keeping in mind that the English (Conneau et al., 2018) and Russian datasets are combined from different annotation schemas, we introspect five multilingual transformer-based encoders, including their distilled versions. We apply several probing methods to conduct the analysis from different perspectives, and support the findings with statistical significance. Besides, we establish count-based and neural-based baselines for the tasks. Finally, RuSentEval is publicly available[1], and we hope it will be used for evaluation and interpretation of language models and sentence embeddings for Russian.

2 Related Work

Introspection of pre-trained language models for languages other than English, specifically Russian, is usually conducted in the cross-lingual setting. The primary goal of such experiments is to explore how particular linguistic properties are distributed in a given collection of multilingual embedding and language models. LINSPECTOR (Şahin et al., 2020) is one of the first probing suites that covers a wide range of linguistic phenomena in 24 languages. The benchmark uses UniMorph 2.0 (Kirov et al., 2018) to design the tasks since UD do not provide a sufficient amount of data for the considered languages. Despite this, UD Treebanks have become the main source for collection of multilingual probing tasks, limiting the scope to morphology and syntax (Krasnowska-Kieraś and Wróblewska, 2019). Other sources for the assembly include multilingual datasets created by means of machine translation, such as XNLI (Conneau et al., 2020b), or datasets that labelled with similar annotation schemes for named entity recognition (NER) and semantic role labelling (SRL) tasks (Şahin et al., 2020).

A few prior works (Ravishankar et al., 2019; Eger et al., 2020) that follow SentEval toolkit (Conneau and Kiela, 2018) directly apply the method designed for English to multiple typologically diverse languages, which raises doubts if such strategy is universal across languages that exhibit unique peculiarities, e.g. a free word order and rich inflectional morphology. This can lead to low quality of the datasets and unreliable experimental results, particularly for Russian. Consider a few examples for (**BShift**) task in Russian: ***Fedra zatem*** *povesilas', a Tesey uznal pravdu.* "**Phaedra later** hanged herself, and Theseus unraveled the truth." (Ravishankar et al., 2019), and *Shestoe –* ***zanimatsya nado*** *svoim obrazovaniem* "The sixth point is that you **to take care need** of your education" (Eger et al., 2020). The sentences are labelled as positive, meaning that they exhibit incorrect word order. While the word order changes can lead to the syntax perturbations for English, both sentences are still acceptable in terms of syntax for Russian. Moreover, the dataset sizes tend to be inconsistent across languages due to using UD Treebanks which makes it difficult to compare the results (Eger et al., 2020).

Another line of research includes probing machine translation models (Mareček et al., 2020) over multiple languages, and probing for cross-lingual similarity by utilizing paired sentences in mutually intelligible languages (Choenni and Shutova, 2020a,b). Last but not least, such benchmarks as XGLUE (Liang et al., 2020) and XTREME (Hu et al., 2020) allow evaluating the current state of language transferring methods.

3 Probing Tasks

Data The sentences for our probing tasks were extracted from the following publicly available resources: Russian Wikipedia articles[2] and news corpora such as Lenta.ru[3] and the news segment of Taiga corpus (Shavrina and Shapovalova, 2017). We used rusenttokenize library[4], a rule-based sentence segmenter for Russian, to split texts into sentences. Each sentence was tokenized with spaCy Russian Tokenizer[5]. The sentences were filtered by the 5-to-25 token range and annotated with the current state-of-the-art model for joint morphosyntactic analysis in Russian (Anastasyev, 2020). Besides, we performed two additional preprocessing steps. (1) We computed the IPM frequency of each sentence using the New Frequency Vocabulary of Russian Words (Lyashevskaya and Sharov, 2009) to control the word frequency distribution. The

[1] https://github.com/RussianNLP/rusenteval

[2] https://dumps.wikimedia.org/ruwiki/latest/

[3] https://github.com/yutkin/Lenta.Ru-News-Dataset

[4] https://pypi.org/project/rusenttokenize

[5] https://github.com/aatimofeev/spacy_russian_tokenizer

IPM values of each token lemma in the sentence (if present in the vocabulary) were averaged over a total number of token lemmas. The sentences with the IPM frequency of lower than 0.9 were filtered out. This allows discarding the majority of sentences that contain rare words, acronyms, abbreviations, or loanwords. (2) Syncretism is peculiar to fusional languages, that is, when a word can belong to multiple part-of-speech tags, or express multiple ambiguous morphosyntactic features (Baerman, 2007). Following (Şahin et al., 2020), we removed sentences in the semantic tasks (described below) where the target word has multiple part-of-speech tags. This step allows simplifying the probe interpretation and ensuring a fairer experimental setup in terms of the language comparison.

The total number of the annotated sentences after filtering is 3.6 mln, and they are publicly available. Each task consists of a 100k-sentence training set and 10k-sentence validation and test sets. There is no sentence overlap across the splits, and all sets are balanced by the number of instances per target class.

Surface properties tasks test if it is possible to recover information about surface properties from the contextualized representations. (**SentLen**) is a 6-way classification task aimed to predict a number of tokens given a sentence representation. Similar to (Adi et al., 2016; Conneau et al., 2018), we grouped sentences into 6 equal-width bins by length. The *word content* (**WC**) task tests if the information on the original words in a sentence can be inferred from its representation. We selected 1k lemmas from the source corpus vocabulary within the 1.5k-3k rank range when sorted by frequency, and sampled equal numbers of sentences that contain only one of these lemmas. The task is treated as a 1k-way classification that requires knowledge about lexical items and their inflectional paradigms.

Syntactic properties is a group of tasks that probe the encoder representations for syntactic properties. In the (**ConjType**) task, the sentences must be classified in terms of the type of connection between complex clauses. The objective of the classifier is to tell whether a sentence involves coordination or subordination.

(**ImpersonalSent**) is a binary classification task that aims to define if there is a lack of a grammatical subject in the main clause of a sentence. It is usually expressed by a singular third-person, reflexive, singular neuter, or invariable predicate form (*smerkaetsya* "it is getting dark"; *zharko* "it is hot"; *pora idti* "it is time to go"), an adverbial predicate phrase (*bylo sovershenno tikho* "it was absolutely quiet"), and intransitive verbs typically combined with a noun phrase in the instrumental (*zapahlo rozami* "it smells roses").

(**TreeDepth**) task tests whether the encoder representations store the information on the hierarchical and syntactic structure of sentences. Specifically, the goal is to probe for knowledge about the depth of the longest path from the root node to any leaf in the syntax tree. Similar to (Conneau et al., 2018), we obtained sentences where the tree depth and the sentence length are de-correlated. The tree depth values range from 5 to 9 which makes (**TreeDepth**) a 5-way classification task.

(**Gapping**) task deals with the detection of syntactic gapping that occurs in coordinated structures and elides a repeated predicate, typically from the second clause. We used data provided in the Shared Task on Automatic Gapping Resolution for Russian, or AGRR-2019 (Ponomareva et al., 2019). For instance, the sentence *Odin imel silu solntsa, drugoy – luny.* "One had the power of the Sun, the other ***(had the power of)*** the Moon." comprises an omission of a repeating predicate in the non-initial clause with its semantics remaining expressed.

The *N-gram shift* task (**NShift**) is analogous to SentEval's (**Bshift**) that tests the encoder's sensitivity to incorrect word order. As opposed to English, only specific cases of word inversion in Russian lead to syntax perturbation. We, therefore, perturbed N-grams that correspond to a set of predefined morphosyntactic patterns. We used TF-IDF method from scikit-learn library (Pedregosa et al., 2011) to build an N-gram feature matrix that was further applied for the word order perturbation. For instance, we reversed adjacent words in prepositional phrases, numeral phrases, compound noun phrases, etc. Below is an example where the head of the prepositional phrase *v schkolu* 'to school' is inverted with the dependent noun:

Segodnya on ne poshel **shkolu v**.
"He did not go **school to** today.'

Semantic properties tasks rely on both syntactic and semantic structure of a sentence to recover a higher-level property. (**SubjNumber**) and (**SubjGender**) probe for the number and gender features of the subject in the main clause. Similarly, (**ObjNumber**) and (**ObjGender**) focus on the number and gender of direct object in the main clause. In the following tasks, the aim is to probe for the morphosyntactic features of the predicate or the head of a predicative construction of the main clause: *predicate voice* (**PV**), *predicate aspect* (**PA**), and *predicate tense* (**PT**). The latter is analogous to SentEval's (**Tense**) task.

The semantic tasks test if the contextualized representations not only capture the morphosyntactic features but also encode higher-level, structural and syntactic-semantic information (namely, the syntax tree hierarchy and the actant structure of a predicate). Note that the boundary between the surface, syntactic and semantic tasks is relatively blurred.

4 Experimental Setup

4.1 Encoders

We run the experiments on the following 12-layer multilingual transformer encoders released by HuggingFace (Wolf et al., 2019):

M-BERT (Devlin et al., 2019) is trained on masked language modeling (MLM) and next sentence prediction tasks, over concatenated monolingual Wikipedia corpora in 104 languages.

XLM-R (Conneau et al., 2020a) is trained on 'dynamic' MLM task, over filtered CommonCrawl data in 100 languages (Wenzek et al., 2020).

MiniLM (Wang et al., 2020) is a distilled transformer of BERT architecture, but uses the XLM-RoBERTa tokenizer.

LABSE (Feng et al., 2020) employs a dual-encoder architecture that combines MLM and translation language modeling (Conneau and Lample, 2019).

M-BART (Liu et al., 2020) is a sequence-to-sequence transformer model with a BERT encoder, and an autoregressive GPT-2 decoder (Radford et al., 2019). We used only the encoder in the experiments.

4.2 Methods

Probing Classifiers We trained linear and non-linear classifiers over intermediate representations produced by the encoders[6], using categorical cross-entropy loss, and Adam optimizer (Kingma and Ba, 2015). For the non-linear classifier (MLP), we used the Sigmoid activation function, the number of hidden states of 250, and the dropout rate of 0.2. Training is run over 5 iterations with the L2-regularization parameter $\in [0.1, ..., 1e^{-5}]$ tuned on the validation set, and the best classifier selected. The performance is evaluated by accuracy score.

Individual Neuron Analysis Neuron-level introspection technique (Durrani et al., 2020) allows identifying *top neurons* that contribute most to a probing task and observe how these neurons are distributed across layers of the encoder. Similarly, we trained a linear probing classifier over concatenated sentence representations and used the weights to measure the importance of each neuron. The classifier is trained using Elastic-net regularization with L1 and L2 λ's $\in [0.1, \ldots, 1e^{-5}]$ tuned on the validation set. Refer to (Dalvi et al., 2019; Durrani et al., 2020) for more details.

Correlation Analysis Correlation-based analysis techniques posed in (Wu et al., 2020) allow measuring similarity of the encoder intermediate representations without any linguistic annotation. We apply neuron-level (`maxcorr`) and representation-level (`lincka`) similarity measures to investigate the encoders. `maxcorr` identifies pairs of neurons of the maximum correlation from two different layers. It is high when two layers have pairs of neurons with similar behavior. `lincka` provides a comparison of representations from different layers in a given collection of models. Two layers are assigned a high similarity if their representations behave similarly over all the neurons.

4.3 Baselines

We established a number of count-based and non-contextualized baseline features to train the probing classifiers as outlined in Section 4.2. We used N-gram range $\in [1, 4]$ and top-150k features in the vocabularies for each count-based baseline. The count-based features include **TF-IDF over character N-grams**, **TF-IDF over BPE tokens** (Sennrich et al., 2016), and **TF-IDF over SentencePiece tokens** (Kudo and Richardson, 2018). We applied multilingual BertTokenizer and XLMRobertaTokenizer by HuggingFace to segment sentences into BPE and SentencePiece tokens. The non-contextualized features are mean-pooled monolingual **fastText** sentence embeddings (Bojanowski et al., 2017). We used monolingual fastText models for English[7] and Russian. The latter was trained

[6]We used mean-pooled sentence representations to train the classifiers.

[7]`https://fasttext.cc/docs/en/crawl-vectors.html`

Probing Task	Language	M-BERT	LABSE	XLM-R	MiniLM	M-BART
Nshift	**Ru**	84.8 [8]	82.6 [5]	**86.9 [9]**	80.5 [9]	78.6 [12]
	En	81.8 [10]	84.4 [5]	**85.7 [10]**	79.3 [8]	83.8 [12]
ObjNumber	**Ru**	82.8 [6]	82.5 [2]	**83.7 [10]**	77.8 [10]	81.5 [7]
	En	**86.2 [6]**	85.4 [3]	86.0 [8]	85.2 [6]	85.9 [9]
SentLen	**Ru**	91.3 [2]	93.3 [1]	94.5 [2]	94.1 [2]	**96.2 [4]**
	En	96.3 [2]	96.6 [1]	95.8 [2]	96.1 [3]	**97.3 [3]**
SubjNumber	**Ru**	90.5 [7]	92.9 [3]	**94.9 [11]**	94.2 [12]	93.1 [10]
	En	87.8 [7]	**90.7 [12]**	86.9 [10]	85.6 [6]	87.3 [9]
Tense	**Ru**	99.5 [8]	**99.8 [5]**	**99.8 [5]**	98.2 [7]	99.6 [7]
	En	88.9 [8]	88.8 [6]	88.8 [9]	87.3 [5]	**89.1 [9]**
TreeDepth	**Ru**	44.7 [6]	46.1 [4]	**46.5 [5]**	44.8 [7]	45.8 [11]
	En	41.2 [5]	**42.7 [5]**	41.8 [7]	40.9 [7]	41.2 [12]
WC	**Ru**	84.8 [2]	85.8 [1]	82.6 [1]	72.8 [1]	**88.0 [1]**
	En	92.6 [1]	93.7 [1]	89.8 [1]	82.3 [1]	**93.8 [1]**

Table 1: Results of Logistic Regression classifier for each encoder over the shared English and Russian tasks. Languages: **Ru**=Russian, **En**=English.

over joint Russian Wikipedia and Lenta.ru news, and released by DeepPavlov (Burtsev et al., 2018).

5 Results

How is the linguistic knowledge of two contrasting languages distributed in pre-trained multilingual encoders? This section describes the results for shared English and Russian probing tasks, covering surface properties (**SentLen**, **WC**), syntax (**TreeDepth**, **NShift**), and semantics (**ObjNumber**, **SubjNumber**, and **Tense**). We also report the results for the remaining tasks and the baselines in Appendix B.

5.1 Layer-wise Supervised Probing

Table 1 presents the results of the linear classifier performance over the shared tasks. For the sake of space, we omit the results of the non-linear classifier and provide them in Appendix B. The best score for each task in each language is highlighted in grey, and the index number of the layer achieving the score is enclosed in square brackets. We observe that the surface and syntax tasks show similar trends for both languages, while a few semantic tasks reveal some differences. The overall pattern for the surface-level tasks (**SentLen**, **WC**) is that the probing curves[8] for both languages tend to be decaying after reaching the peak at the lower layers $[1-4]$. The exception is provided by **M-BART** which keeps the surface properties across the majority of layers. The baselines mostly perform on par with one another, with **fastText** and **TF-IDF Char** receiving the best score (see Appendix B).

(**Nshift**, **TreeDepth**) tasks demonstrate interesting distinctive features of **LABSE** and **M-BART** encoders with respect to the syntactic properties. Figure 1 depicts the probing curves over (**Nshift**) and (**Bshift**) tasks. First, **LABSE** is at most sensitive to the incorrect word order at the lower-to-middle layers $[2-8]$, as opposed to other encoders which distribute the information at the middle-to-higher layers $[8-12]$. Second, **M-BART** shows confident knowledge in **TreeDepth** task for both languages at the middle-to-higher layers $[7-12]$ and reaches the peak at layer 12, in contrast to the rest of the encoders which generally distribute the property at the middle layers $[5-7]$ (see Appendix B). The baselines performance varies from achieving a low score (**TreeDepth**) to being close to random choice (**Nshift**).

The probing curves for (**PT**) and (**Tense**) tasks illustrate that the models encode the property in a

[8]We refer to *probing curves* as to the performance trajectory of a probing classifier

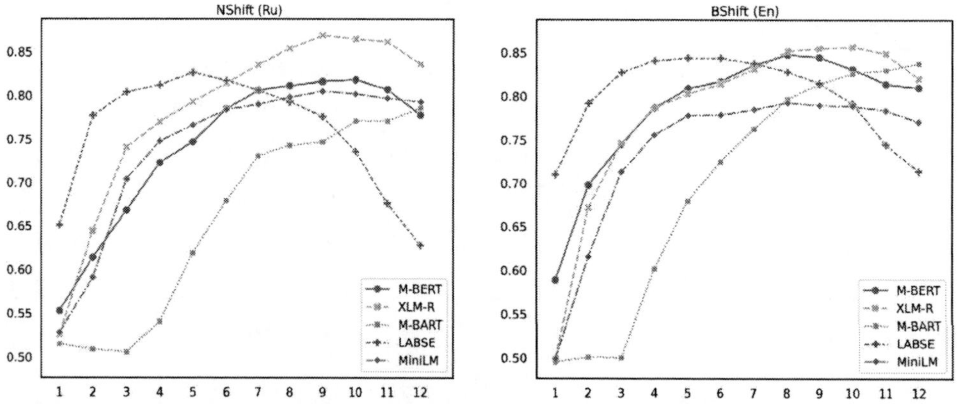

Figure 1: The probing results for each encoder on **NShift** (**Ru**, left) and **Bshift** (**En**, right) tasks. X-axis=Layer index number, Y-axis=Accuracy score.

very similar fashion, achieving the peak score at the middle layers [4, 5], and flattening the curves until the output layer (see Appendix B). In contrast, the behavior of the encoders on (**SubjNumber**) and (**ObjNumber**) is slightly different. The number of the subject for English is predominantly distributed at the middle-to-higher levels [5 − 12], while for Russian it is either at a steady pace from the very first layer (**M-BART**, **M-BERT**), or decaying at the lower and middle layers [3 − 5], and further increasing close to the higher levels [8−12] (**LABSE**, **MiniLM**). Other differences are found in the results for (**ObjNumber**) task. Specifically, the number of direct object for English is best inferred at the lower layers of **LABSE** [2, 3], as compared to the middle-to-higher layers of other encoders [6 − 9]. Despite this, the property is similarly distributed across the layers of the models. In the same manner as for English, **LABSE** concentrates the knowledge for the Russian task in layer 2 but decays once reaching the peak. However, the other models exhibit a distinct behavior as well, with the property best encoded at the middle layers [6, 7] (**M-BERT**, **M-BART**), or at layer 10 (**XLM-R**, **MiniLM**). Notably, the baselines receive a strong performance over the majority of the semantic tasks for both languages, meaning that they can be solved using sub-word features that can capture lexical, or morphosyntactic information.

Bootstrap We estimate statistical significance of the supervised probing by means of layer-wise bootstrap procedure (Berg-Kirkpatrick et al., 2012). Typically, we observe that when the probing curve rises, the layer-wise difference is statistically significant, while at the peak of the probing curve it turns insignificant. We can treat these observations in the following way: starting from the peak of the probing curve, the models acquire the knowledge needed for the task, and do not generally lose it in the higher layers.

5.2 Neuron-level Analysis

In contrast to layer-wise supervised probing (Section 5.1) which introspects each layer independently, individual neuron analysis allows exploring the distribution of top neurons selected from *the entire encoder*. This provides an alternative perspective to which layers contribute predominantly towards the probing tasks. Note that we trained distinct classifiers regularized with Elastic-net (Zou and Hastie, 2005) to estimate the importance of the neurons[9]. Figure 2 presents the results for (**SentLen**) tasks in Russian and English. Different from other models which predominantly capture the property by neurons at the lower layers [1 − 4], **M-BART** distributes the information across all the layers. Let us analyze the results with respect to some syntactic and semantic levels. A similar behavior of the encoders by language is observed over (**NShift**) and (**TreeDepth**) tasks (see Appendix C). **M-BERT**, **XLM-R**, and **MiniLM** generally capture the sensitivity to illegal word order by neurons at the middle and higher layers, while it is contributed by fewer layers of **LABSE** (**Ru**: [2 − 4]; **En**: [4 − 7]), and **M-BART** which surprisingly stores the property at layer 12 for each language. Another interesting finding is that the depth of the

[9]We selected top-20% neurons from each encoder using neuron ranking algorithm described in (Durrani et al., 2020)

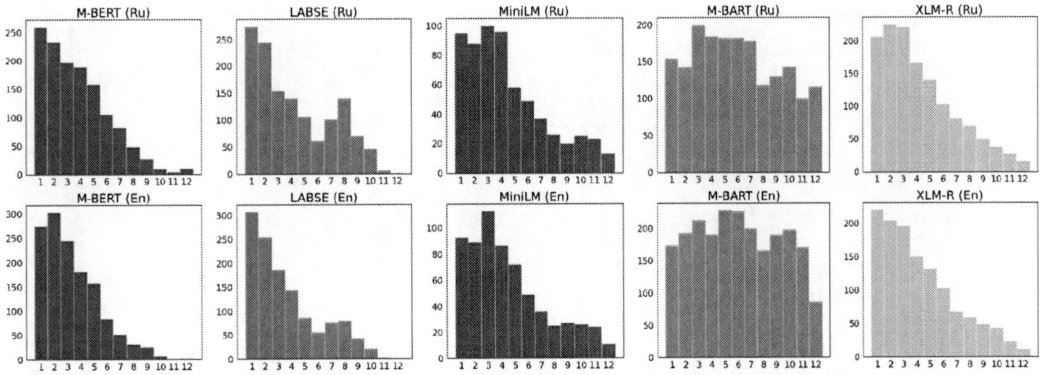

Figure 2: The distribution of top neurons over **SentLen** tasks for both languages: **Ru**=Russian, **En**=English. X-axis=Layer index number, Y-axis=Number of neurons selected from the layer.

syntax tree is typically spread across most of the layers of each encoder. An exception to this pattern is **M-BART** which locates the knowledge at the middle-to-higher layers $[7-11]$.

The neuron distributions for (**ObjNumber**) task are akin by language and slightly different by encoder, showing that the number of the direct object is learned by at least 5-7 layers of different encoder depth. At the same time, the properties for (**SubjNumber**) and (**PT**, **Tense**) tasks are captured differently by the encoders. **M-BERT**, **XLM-R** and **MiniLM** reveal similar behavior by task, whereas **LABSE** specializes the knowledge at either the lower layers (**Ru, SubjNumber**; and **En, Tense**: $[1-4]$), or the higher ones (**En, SubjNumber**; and **Ru, PT**: $[10-12]$). On the other hand, the most contributing neurons of **M-BART** are predominantly spread across all the layers.

5.3 Correlation Analysis

For analyzing the encoders by means of the correlation-based techniques, we used 1k stratified sentences from each test set of the shared tasks. We obtained the sentence representations and computed the measures applying the publicly-available code (Wu et al., 2020). Figure 3 shows heatmaps of similarities between layers of the encoders under neuron-level and representation-level measures for English. Notably, the heatmaps are very alike to the ones for Russian, which we enclose in Appendix D. `maxcorr` (Figure 3a) demonstrates that different layers of a single encoder have similar individual neurons, but the inter-encoder neuron similarities are greatly low. On the contrary, `lincka` (Figure 3b) induces considerably high similarities across the encoders, meaning that they produce similar sentence representations. However, **M-BERT** and **M-BART** show lower similarity with other encoders, particularly at the lower and higher layers (**M-BERT**: $[1-3]$, $[10-12]$; **M-BART**: $[10, 11]$). Besides, **M-BART** and **M-BERT** demonstrate low pairwise similarity, being fairly different at the lower-to-higher layers $[3-11]$.

6 Discussion

Three encoders exhibit similar behavior, but two other differ from them in capturing linguistic properties The most striking distinction based upon the results is that **M-BART** and **LABSE** exhibit different behavior for both languages, as opposed to **M-BERT**, **XLM-R**, and **MiniLM** (Section 5.1, 5.2). Specifically, **M-BART** generally tends to distribute the surface properties across all the layers, unlike other encoders where the information is specialized by the lower ones. The syntactic properties tend to be localized at the higher layers $[11-12]$ which is as well demonstrated in other Russian tasks (**Gapping**, **ImpersonalSent**). In contrast to other models that capture the semantic properties at the middle-to-higher layers, **LABSE** typically displays the knowledge at the lower-to-middle layers. The analysis of the understudied encoders contradicts the common findings on transformer models that syntactic information is stored at the middle layers, while semantic knowledge is most prominent at the higher layers (Rogers et al., 2021). Therefore, there is still room for exploring transformer-based models that differ by architecture type, or by a set of pre-training objectives.

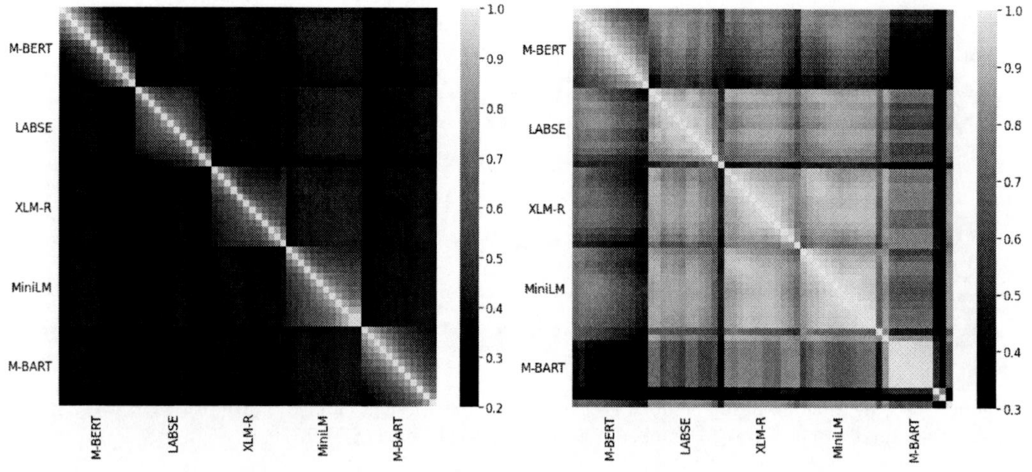

(a) `maxcorr` (b) `lincka`

Figure 3: Similarity heatmaps of layers in the encoders under neuron-level (`maxcorr`) and representation-level (`lincka`) measures.

MiniLM inherits linguistic properties from M-BERT Teacher models are usually compared with their distilled versions on a range of downstream tasks (Tsai et al., 2019), and little is explored on what language properties they bequeath to their students. We find that **MiniLM** is likely to mimic the behavior of **XLM-R** rather than of **M-BERT**, most probably due to using the same tokenization method. The similarity is most demonstrated by the individual neuron analysis (see Appendix C) and `lincka` (see Figure 3b). Along with that, the model receives comparative performance under layer-wise supervised probing (see Appendix B).

Surface and syntactic information is learned in a similar manner The probing curves demonstrate that the surface and semantic properties of the two languages are similarly distributed in the encoders. The surface properties are generally captured at the lower layers, and the pattern of the curves is decaying towards the output layer. The syntactic properties are predominantly inferred at the middle or higher layers, and the semantic tasks reveal a number of differences described in Section 5. Notably, the results obtained under layer-wise supervised probing (Section 5.1) are supported by the individual neuron analysis (Section 5.2), and the representation-level analysis (Section 5.3).

Encoders may have similar distributions of neurons by task, but different individual neurons Two neuron-level introspection methods allow drawing the following finding. Despite that top-neuron distributions in the encoder layers share similar patterns in the majority of probing tasks (Section 5.2), `maxcorr` induces high intra-encoder similarities and low inter-encoder similarities (Section 5.3). In other words, the neurons can similarly localize particular properties in the layers and yet behave differently across the models.

7 Conclusion

This paper introduces RuSentEval, an enhanced probing suite of 14 probing tasks that cover various linguistic phenomena of the Russian language. We explored five multilingual transformer encoders over the probing tasks on two typologically contrasting languages – Russian and English. The experiments are conducted using a combination of complementary probing methods, including layer-wise supervised probing, individual neuron-analysis, neuron- and representation-level similarity measures. Particularly, the behavior of the encoders under probing classifiers is reflected in distributions of top neurons with respect to a task, and the similarity is supported by linear centered kernel alignment method. We found that despite the language distinctions, the surface and syntactic properties are learned in a fairly similar manner, and the semantic knowledge is captured differently in a majority of tasks. We believe that the findings make the ongoing studies on cross-lingual transfer even more promising, specifically from English to Russian or vice versa. In contrast to prior works on how linguistic knowledge is represented in transformers, the analysis of the understudied models reveals that syntax and semantics can be differently represented across the layers. Besides, we found that different encoders often have similar distributions of neurons that contribute most to a probing task, and yet differ under neuron-level similarities. We also observed that distilled models inherit linguistic properties from their teachers, and receive comparative performance on a number of probing tasks. An exciting direction for future work is to investigate the correlation between probing and high-level downstream tasks, in order to identify which linguistic properties anticipate the behavior of a model in action.

Acknowledgments

Ekaterina Artemova works within the framework of the HSE University Basic Research Program.

References

Yossi Adi, Einat Kermany, Yonatan Belinkov, Ofer Lavi, and Yoav Goldberg. 2016. Fine-grained Analysis of Sentence Embeddings Using Auxiliary Prediction Tasks. *arXiv preprint arXiv:1608.04207*.

Christoph Alt, Aleksandra Gabryszak, and Leonhard Hennig. 2020. Probing Linguistic Features of Sentence-Level Representations in Relation Extraction. pages 1534–1545.

Chiara Alzetta, Felice Dell'Orletta, Simonetta Montemagni, and Giulia Venturi. 2017. Dangerous Relations in Dependency Treebanks. pages 201–210.

Daniil Anastasyev. 2020. Exploring Pretrained Models For Joint Morpho-syntactic Parsing of Russian.

Matthew Baerman. 2007. Syncretism. *Language and Linguistics Compass*, 1(5):539–551.

Yonatan Belinkov and James Glass. 2019. Analysis Methods in Neural Language Processing: a Survey. *Transactions of the Association for Computational Linguistics*, 7:49–72.

Taylor Berg-Kirkpatrick, David Burkett, and Dan Klein. 2012. An Empirical Investigation of Statistical Significance in NLP. pages 995–1005.

Piotr Bojanowski, Edouard Grave, Armand Joulin, and Tomas Mikolov. 2017. Enriching Word Vectors with Subword Information. *Transactions of the Association for Computational Linguistics*, 5:135–146.

Mikhail Burtsev, Alexander Seliverstov, Rafael Airapetyan, Mikhail Arkhipov, Dilyara Baymurzina, Nickolay Bushkov, Olga Gureenkova, Taras Khakhulin, Yurii Kuratov, Denis Kuznetsov, et al. 2018. DeepPavlov: Open-source Library for Dialogue Systems. pages 122–127.

Rochelle Choenni and Ekaterina Shutova. 2020a. Cross-neutralising: Probing for Joint Encoding of Linguistic Information in Multilingual Models. *arXiv e-prints*, pages arXiv–2010.

Rochelle Choenni and Ekaterina Shutova. 2020b. What Does it Mean to be Language-agnostic? Probing Multilingual Sentence Encoders for Typological Properties. *arXiv preprint arXiv:2009.12862*.

Alexis Conneau, Kartikay Khandelwal, Naman Goyal, Vishrav Chaudhary, Guillaume Wenzek, Francisco Guzmán, Édouard Grave, Myle Ott, Luke Zettlemoyer, and Veselin Stoyanov. 2020a. Unsupervised Cross-lingual Representation Learning at Scale. pages 8440–8451.

Alexis Conneau and Douwe Kiela. 2018. SentEval: An Evaluation Toolkit for Universal Sentence Representations.

Alexis Conneau, Germán Kruszewski, Guillaume Lample, Loïc Barrault, and Marco Baroni. 2018. What you Can Cram into a Single Vector: Probing Sentence Embeddings for Linguistic Properties. *arXiv preprint arXiv:1805.01070*.

Alexis Conneau and Guillaume Lample. 2019. Cross-lingual Language Model Pre-training. pages 7059–7069.

Alexis Conneau, Ruty Rinott, Guillaume Lample, Holger Schwenk, Ves Stoyanov, Adina Williams, and Samuel R Bowman. 2020b. XNLI: Evaluating Cross-lingual Sentence Representations. pages 2475–2485.

Fahim Dalvi, Nadir Durrani, Hassan Sajjad, Yonatan Belinkov, Anthony Bau, and James Glass. 2019. What is One Grain of Sand in the Desert? Analyzing Individual Neurons in Deep NLP Models. 33:6309–6317.

Jacob Devlin, Ming-Wei Chang, Kenton Lee, and Kristina Toutanova. 2019. BERT: Pre-training of Deep Bidirectional Transformers for Language Understanding. pages 4171–4186.

Kira Droganova, Olga Lyashevskaya, and Daniel Zeman. 2018. Data Conversion and Consistency of Monolingual Corpora: Russian UD Treebanks. pages 52–65.

Nadir Durrani, Hassan Sajjad, Fahim Dalvi, and Yonatan Belinkov. 2020. Analyzing Individual Neurons in Pre-trained Language Models. pages 4865–4880.

Steffen Eger, Johannes Daxenberger, and Iryna Gurevych. 2020. How to Probe Sentence Embeddings in Low-Resource Languages: On Structural Design Choices for Probing Task Evaluation. pages 108–118.

Fangxiaoyu Feng, Yinfei Yang, Daniel Cer, Naveen Arivazhagan, and Wei Wang. 2020. Language-agnostic BERT Sentence Embedding. *arXiv preprint arXiv:2007.01852*.

Junjie Hu, Sebastian Ruder, Aditya Siddhant, Graham Neubig, Orhan Firat, and Melvin Johnson. 2020. XTREME: A Massively Multilingual Multi-task Benchmark for Evaluating Cross-lingual Generalisation. pages 4411–4421.

Diederik P. Kingma and Jimmy Ba. 2015. Adam: A Method for Stochastic Optimization.

Christo Kirov, Ryan Cotterell, John Sylak-Glassman, Géraldine Walther, Ekaterina Vylomova, Patrick Xia, Manaal Faruqui, Sabrina J Mielke, Arya D McCarthy, Sandra Kübler, et al. 2018. UniMorph 2.0: Universal Morphology.

Katarzyna Krasnowska-Kieraś and Alina Wróblewska. 2019. Empirical Linguistic Study of Sentence Embeddings. pages 5729–5739.

Taku Kudo and John Richardson. 2018. SentencePiece: A Simple and Language Independent Subword Tokenizer and Detokenizer for Neural Text Processing. pages 66–71.

Yaobo Liang, Nan Duan, Yeyun Gong, Ning Wu, Fenfei Guo, Weizhen Qi, Ming Gong, Linjun Shou, Daxin Jiang, Guihong Cao, et al. 2020. XGLUE: A New Benchmark Datasetfor Cross-lingual Pre-training, Understanding and Generation. pages 6008–6018.

Nelson F Liu, Matt Gardner, Yonatan Belinkov, Matthew E Peters, and Noah A Smith. 2019. Linguistic Knowledge and Transferability of Contextual Representations. pages 1073–1094.

Yinhan Liu, Jiatao Gu, Naman Goyal, Xian Li, Sergey Edunov, Marjan Ghazvininejad, Mike Lewis, and Luke Zettlemoyer. 2020. Multilingual denoising pre-training for neural machine translation. *Transactions of the Association for Computational Linguistics*, 8:726–742.

Olga Lyashevskaya and Sergey Sharov. 2009. The Frequency Dictionary of Modern Russian Language. *Azbukovnik, Moscow*.

David Mareček, Hande Celikkanat, Miikka Silfverberg, Vinit Ravishankar, and Jörg Tiedemannb. 2020. Are Multilingual Neural Machine Translation Models Better at Capturing Linguistic Features? *The Prague Bulletin of Mathematical Linguistics*, (115):143–162.

Marie-Catherine de Marneffe, Matias Grioni, Jenna Kanerva, and Filip Ginter. 2017. Assessing the Annotation Consistency of the Universal Dependencies Corpora. pages 108–115.

Julian Michael, Jan A Botha, and Ian Tenney. 2020. Asking without Telling: Exploring Latent Ontologies in Contextual Representations. *arXiv preprint arXiv:2004.14513*.

Joakim Nivre, Marie-Catherine De Marneffe, Filip Ginter, Yoav Goldberg, Jan Hajic, Christopher D Manning, Ryan McDonald, Slav Petrov, Sampo Pyysalo, Natalia Silveira, et al. 2016. Universal Dependencies v1: A Multilingual Treebank Collection. pages 1659–1666.

Fabian Pedregosa, Gaël Varoquaux, Alexandre Gramfort, Vincent Michel, Bertrand Thirion, Olivier Grisel, Mathieu Blondel, Peter Prettenhofer, Ron Weiss, Vincent Dubourg, et al. 2011. Scikit-learn: Machine learning in Python. *the Journal of machine Learning research*, 12:2825–2830.

Telmo Pires, Eva Schlinger, and Dan Garrette. 2019. How Multilingual is Multilingual BERT? pages 4996–5001.

Maria Ponomareva, Kira Droganova, Ivan Smurov, and Tatiana Shavrina. 2019. AGRR 2019: Corpus for Gapping Resolution in Russian. pages 35–43.

Alec Radford, Jeffrey Wu, Rewon Child, David Luan, Dario Amodei, and Ilya Sutskever. 2019. Language Models are Unsupervised Multitask Learners. *OpenAI blog*, 1(8):9.

Vinit Ravishankar, Lilja Øvrelid, and Erik Velldal. 2019. Probing Multilingual Sentence Representations With XProbe. *ACL 2019*, page 156.

Anna Rogers, Olga Kovaleva, and Anna Rumshisky. 2021. A Primer in BERTology: What we Know about how BERT Works. *Transactions of the Association for Computational Linguistics*, 8:842–866.

Gözde Gül Şahin, Clara Vania, Ilia Kuznetsov, and Iryna Gurevych. 2020. Linspector: Multilingual Probing Tasks for Word Representations. *Computational Linguistics*, 46(2):335–385.

Rico Sennrich, Barry Haddow, and Alexandra Birch. 2016. Neural Machine Translation of Rare Words with Subword Units. pages 1715–1725.

Tatiana Shavrina and Olga Shapovalova. 2017. To the Methodology Corpus Construction for Machine Learning: "TAIGA" Syntax Tree Corpus and Parser. *CORPUS LINGUISTICS, 2017*, page 78.

Xing Shi, Inkit Padhi, and Kevin Knight. 2016. Does String-based Neural MT Learn Source Syntax? pages 1526–1534.

Xavier Suau, Luca Zappella, and Nicholas Apostoloff. 2020. Finding Experts in Transformer Models. *arXiv preprint arXiv:2005.07647*.

Ian Tenney, Patrick Xia, Berlin Chen, Alex Wang, Adam Poliak, R Thomas McCoy, Najoung Kim,

Benjamin Van Durme, Samuel R Bowman, Dipanjan Das, et al. 2019. What do you Learn from Context? Probing for Sentence Structure in Contextualized Word Representations. *arXiv preprint arXiv:1905.06316*.

Henry Tsai, Jason Riesa, Melvin Johnson, Naveen Arivazhagan, Xin Li, and Amelia Archer. 2019. Small and Practical BERT Models for Sequence Labeling. pages 3623–3627.

Ashish Vaswani, Noam Shazeer, Niki Parmar, Jakob Uszkoreit, Llion Jones, Aidan N Gomez, Łukasz Kaiser, and Illia Polosukhin. 2017. Attention is All You Need. pages 5998–6008.

Elena Voita and Ivan Titov. 2020. Information-Theoretic Probing with Minimum Description Length. *arXiv preprint arXiv:2003.12298*.

Alex Wang, Yada Pruksachatkun, Nikita Nangia, Amanpreet Singh, Julian Michael, Felix Hill, Omer Levy, and Samuel Bowman. 2019. SuperGLUE: A Stickier Benchmark for General-purpose Language Understanding Systems. pages 3266–3280.

Wenhui Wang, Furu Wei, Li Dong, Hangbo Bao, Nan Yang, and Ming Zhou. 2020. Minilm: Deep Self-attention Distillation for Task-agnostic Compression of Pre-trained Transformers. *arXiv preprint arXiv:2002.10957*.

Guillaume Wenzek, Marie-Anne Lachaux, Alexis Conneau, Vishrav Chaudhary, Francisco Guzmán, Armand Joulin, and Édouard Grave. 2020. CCNet: Extracting High Quality Monolingual Datasets from Web Crawl Data. pages 4003–4012.

Thomas Wolf, Lysandre Debut, Victor Sanh, Julien Chaumond, Clement Delangue, Anthony Moi, Pierric Cistac, Tim Rault, Rémi Louf, Morgan Funtowicz, et al. 2019. HuggingFace's Transformers: State-of-the-art Natural Language Processing. *ArXiv*, pages arXiv–1910.

John Wu, Yonatan Belinkov, Hassan Sajjad, Nadir Durrani, Fahim Dalvi, and James Glass. 2020. Similarity Analysis of Contextual Word Representation Models. pages 4638–4655.

Hui Zou and Trevor Hastie. 2005. Regularization and Variable Selection via the Elastic Net. *Journal of the royal statistical society: series B (statistical methodology)*, 67(2):301–320.

A Examples from RuSentEval Tasks

Table 2 provides with examples from RuSentEval tasks.

Task	Example	Label
ConjType	On otmetil , **chto** podobnyye progulki nebezopasny . *'He noted **that** such walks are unsafe.'*	**SCONJ**
Gapping	Ya yezdila dvazhdy , sestra – trizhdy . *'I went [there] twice, my sister [went there] three times'*	**1**
ImpersonalSent	Rabotal takzhe kak kontsertmeyster i lektor . *'[He] also worked as an accompanist and lecturer.'*	**0**
NShift	Kogda etogo **poluchilos' ne** , on ubezhal . *'When it **work out didn't**, he ran away'*	**I**
ObjGender	Rossiyskiy duet dopustil odnu **oshibku** . *'The Russian duo made one **mistake**.'*	**F**
ObjNumber	Serial poluchil neskol'ko prestizhnykh **nagrad** . *'The series has received several prestigious **awards**.'*	**NNS**
PA	On nikak ne **ob"yasnil** svoyu pozitsiyu . *'He did not **explain** his position in any way .'*	**PERF**
PT	Molodyye spetsialisty **poluchayut** yezhemesyachnuyu doplatu k zarplate . *'Young professionals **receive** a monthly supplement to their salary .'*	**PRES**
PV	Srok vozmozhnoy prem'yery lenty poka ne **nazyvayetsya** *'The date of a possible premiere of the film has not yet been **announced**.'*	**PASS**
SentLen	Ya ne videla boleye zlogo cheloveka . *'I haven't seen a more angry man.'*	**0**
SubjGender	**On** nosit beluyu dlinnuyu rubashku i dlinnyye seryye bryuki. *'**He** wears a white long shirt and long grey trousers.'*	**M**
SubjNumber	**On** byl lyubimtsem vsey moskovskoy i peterburgskoy aristokratii . *'**He** was a favorite of the entire Moscow and St. Petersburg aristocracy.'*	**NN**
TreeDepth	I vot v pervuyu ochered' my khoteli by pogovorit' ob etom . *'And first of all, we would like to talk about this.'*	**5**
WC	Proshluyu noch' ya sovsem ne **spal** . *'I didn't **sleep** at all last night.'*	**spat'** *'to sleep'*

Table 2: Examples from RuSentEval tasks.

B Layer-wise Supervised Probing

B.1 Results on All Tasks

The results reported in the main body of the paper are obtained with Logistic Regression classifier over the shared tasks (see Section 5.1). We present detailed results for both linear and non-linear classifiers on all Russian and English tasks in Tables 3–6. Tables 7–9 show the results of the baselines. Table 11 outlines statistical description of the tasks.

Probing Task	M-BERT	LABSE	XLM-R	MiniLM	M-BART
ConjType	98.8 [7]	**99.3 [4]**	**99.3 [6]**	98.6 [5]	98.8 [7]
Gapping	85.2 [7]	89.7 [8]	**94.1 [8]**	91.1 [9]	85.6 [12]
ImpersonalSent	91.6 [7]	92 [6]	**92.6 [4]**	88.4 [6]	85.7 [12]
NShift	81.8 [10]	82.6 [5]	**86.9 [9]**	80.5 [9]	78.6 [12]
ObjGender	70.1 [6]	70.4 [2]	69.4 [5]	64.1 [9]	**71.8 [1]**
ObjNumber	82.8 [6]	82.5 [2]	**83.7 [10]**	77.8 [10]	81.5 [7]
PA	91.2 [6]	93.8 [4]	94.4 [5]	89.4 [5]	**95.9 [10]**
PT	99.5 [8]	**99.8 [5]**	**99.8 [5]**	98.2 [7]	99.6 [7]
PV	77.5 [5]	76.3 [5]	76.8 [5]	71.4 [3]	**77.7 [3]**
SentLen	91.3 [2]	93.3 [1]	94.5 [2]	94.1 [2]	**96.2 [4]**
SubjGender	79.1 [9]	79.2 [2]	**79.4 [11]**	78.7 [10]	77.7 [7]
SubjNumber	90.5 [7]	92.9 [3]	**94.9 [11]**	94.2 [12]	93.1 [10]
TreeDepth	44.7 [6]	46.1 [4]	**46.5 [5]**	44.8 [7]	45.8 [11]
WC	84.8 [2]	85.8 [1]	82.6 [1]	72.8 [1]	**88.0 [1]**

Table 3: Results of Logistic Regression classifier by the encoder for RuSentEval tasks.

Probing Task	M-BERT	LABSE	XLM-R	MiniLM	M-BART
BShift	84.8 [8]	84.4 [5]	**85.7 [10]**	79.3 [8]	83.8 [12]
CoordInv	66.0 [8]	68.9 [8]	68.6 [8]	63.3 [8]	**69.4 [12]**
ObjNumber	**86.2 [6]**	85.4 [3]	86.0 [8]	85.2 [6]	85.9 [9]
SOMO	57.4 [8]	60.8 [7]	60.0 [8]	56.1 [9]	**62.3 [12]**
SentLen	96.3 [2]	96.6 [1]	95.8 [2]	96.1 [3]	**97.3 [3]**
SubjNumber	87.8 [7]	**90.7 [12]**	86.9 [10]	85.6 [6]	87.3 [9]
Tense	88.9 [8]	88.8 [6]	88.8 [9]	87.3 [5]	**89.1 [9]**
TopConst	**88 [6]**	79.9 [5]	78.5 [5]	76.5 [5]	79.5 [8]
TreeDepth	41.2 [5]	**42.7 [5]**	41.8 [7]	40.9 [7]	41.2 [12]
WC	92.6 [1]	93.7 [1]	89.8 [1]	82.3 [1]	**93.8 [1]**

Table 4: Results of Logistic Regression classifier by the encoder for SentEval tasks.

Probing Task	M-BERT	LABSE	XLM-R	MiniLM	M-BART
ConjType	98.6 [5]	**99.4 [4]**	99.2 [5]	98.9 [5]	98.8 [7]
Gapping	89.7 [10]	90.0 [9]	**96.0 [8]**	92.0 [11]	83.1 [9]
ImpersonalSent	**93.6 [7]**	90.9 [5]	92.4 [7]	88.7 [7]	89.4 [9]
NShift	81.5 [9]	82.7 [5]	**87.6 [9]**	81.1 [10]	78.8 [12]
ObjGender	69.1 [6]	70.1 [2]	69.5 [9]	65.1 [10]	**72.2 [1]**
ObjNumber	83.9 [6]	82.5 [2]	**84.8 [10]**	78.7 [10]	83.0 [7]
PA	90.9 [7]	93.5 [5]	94.6 [5]	89.7 [5]	**95.5 [8]**
PT	99.4 [4]	**99.9 [10]**	99.8 [5]	98.4 [6]	99.6 [9]
PV	77.7 [4]	76.5 [5]	78.4 [4]	72.5 [4]	**82.2 [1]**
SentLen	93.5 [2]	95.2 [1]	97.1 [2]	96.7 [1]	**98.2 [5]**
SubjGender	79.5 [9]	80.0 [2]	**81.0 [11]**	80.2 [12]	78.1 [7]
SubjNumber	90.3 [5]	93.0 [3]	**96.3 [12]**	95.8 [11]	94.5 [7]
TreeDepth	43.6 [6]	45.4 [4]	44.8 [7]	**46.7 [8]**	46.0 [7]
WC	80.8 [3]	82.7 [1]	78.5 [1]	69.9 [1]	**84.4 [1]**

Table 5: Results of MLP classifier by the encoder for RuSentEval tasks.

Probing Task	M-BERT	LABSE	XLM-R	MiniLM	M-BART
BShift	83.1 [8]	84.7 [6]	**85.8 [9]**	79.4 [7]	84.4 [12]
CoordInv	65.2 [8]	68.1 [8]	**68.8 [8]**	63.7 [8]	67.8 [10]
ObjNumber	86.5 [6]	86.4 [10]	86.4 [8]	85.0 [6]	**86.8 [8]**
SOMO	56.5 [8]	60.5 [7]	58.8 [8]	54.8 [9]	**61.7 [11]**
SentLen	97.0 [2]	98.4 [1]	98.0 [3]	98.5 [1]	**98.8 [4]**
SubjNumber	86.5 [10]	**90.9 [11]**	86.6 [6]	86.0 [6]	87.5 [9]
Tense	89.2 [9]	89.0 [6]	88.5 [10]	87.9 [5]	**89.4 [9]**
TopConst	**82.0 [7]**	80.6 [5]	79.5 [5]	77.8 [6]	80.6 [8]
TreeDepth	41.9 [6]	43.1 [5]	43.2 [7]	42.3 [6]	**45.3 [10]**
WC	91.2 [1]	92.7 [1]	88.9 [1]	80.3 [1]	**93.0 [1]**

Table 6: Results of MLP classifier by encoder for each SentEval task.

Probing Task	fastText	TF-IDF Char	TF-IDF BPE	TF-IDF SP
ConjType	88.1	**96.9**	95.4	95.5
Gapping	**84.1**	82.7	80.4	80.6
ImpersonalSent	**78.7**	69.4	53.8	56.3
NShift	**53.2**	53.0	51.0	50.5
ObjGender	70.1	**71.0**	35.4	38.9
ObjNumber	**82.3**	76.4	56.8	55.0
PA	**90.8**	80.7	53.4	54.2
PT	95.1	**97.7**	53.8	53.7
PV	69.2	**78.2**	36.0	37.0
SentLen	40.4	**64.0**	42.9	42.2
SubjGender	**78.7**	74.4	34.8	38.0
SubjNumber	**95.0**	90.4	63.7	64.4
TreeDepth	**35.7**	32.7	26.5	24.8
WC	**70.8**	49.2	22.0	13.0

Table 7: Results of Logistic Regression classifier by the baseline feature for each RuSentEval task.

Probing Task	fastText	TF-IDF Char	TF-IDF BPE	TF-IDF SP
BShift	50.0	**51.1**	49.9	50.1
CoordInv	52.2	**54.9**	50.2	50.1
ObjNumber	72.8	**79.4**	68.1	69.0
SOMO	49.9	49.9	**50.4**	49.7
SentLen	**65.2**	54.1	42.3	44.6
SubjNumber	76.6	**79.2**	68.1	71.6
Tense	81.2	**84.2**	70.8	74.2
TopConst	**59.8**	58.3	23.0	23.4
TreeDepth	**30.0**	28.3	23.3	23.2
WC	18.1	**47.3**	20.0	24.0

Table 8: Results of Logistic Regression classifier by the baseline feature for each SentEval task.

Probing Task	fastText	TF-IDF Char	TF-IDF BPE	TF-IDF SP
ConjType	88.4	**97.3**	95.6	95.5
Gapping	82.7	**86.1**	80.2	68.8
ImpersonalSent	**78.6**	70.5	52.9	56.6
NShift	**52.7**	**52.7**	50.0	50.6
ObjGender	70.0	**70.9**	35.1	37.2
ObjNumber	**82.8**	77.2	56.6	54.8
PA	**91.2**	80.9	51.8	53.5
PT	96.0	**97.6**	54.4	54.1
PV	68.5	**78.5**	35.3	36.8
SentLen	42.4	**73.7**	42.7	42.4
SubjGender	**80.0**	75.2	34.0	38.8
SubjNumber	**96.2**	90.8	61.8	64.4
TreeDepth	29.5	**35.6**	32.8	23.9
WC	**71.2**	53.8	20.0	11.0

Table 9: Results of MLP classifier by the baseline feature for each RuSentEval task.

Probing Task	fastText	TF-IDF Char	TF-IDF BPE	TF-IDF SP
BShift	48.2	**50.6**	50.0	49.3
CoordInv	50.1	**54.0**	50.0	51.7
ObjNumber	70.9	**77.1**	68.1	70.0
SOMO	50.1	49.9	**50.2**	**50.2**
SentLen	49.1	**62.5**	41.8	43.5
SubjNumber	72.8	**80.5**	66.4	71.3
Tense	74.7	**85.0**	70.5	73.8
TopConst	58.0	**59.7**	22.2	23.0
TreeDepth	23.0	**29.5**	23.0	22.1
WC	**63.3**	54.4	18.0	22.0

Table 10: Results of MLP classifier by the baseline feature for each SentEval task.

	RuSentEval				SentEval			
	Train	Dev	Test	Overall	Train	Dev	Test	Overall
	SentLen				**SentLen**			
sample size	100k	10k	10k	120k	100k	10k	10k	120k
tokens	1.45kk	144.8k	144.8k	1.74kk	1.66kk	165.4k	165.4k	1.99kk
unique tokens	116.7k	34.0k	33.7k	126.5k	34.8k	9.6k	10.0k	36.8k
tokens/sentence	14.47	14.48	14.48	14.47	16.59	16.54	16.55	16.59
label distribution	16.7/16.7/16.7/16.7/16.7/16.7				16.7/16.7/16.7/16.7/16.7/16.7			
	WC				**WC**			
sample size	100k	10k	10k	120k	100k	10k	10k	120k
tokens	1.19kk	117.9k	118.9k	1.43kk	1.5kk	149.2k	149.8k	1.8kk
unique tokens	106.6k	30.6k	30.8k	115.7k	37.4k	13.4k	13.4k	40.1k
tokens/sentence	11.89	11.79	11.89	11.88	15.02	14.92	14.98	15.00
label distribution	0.1/label, 1000 labels				0.1/label, 1000 labels			
	NShift				**BShift**			
sample size	100k	10k	10k	120k	100k	10k	10k	120k
tokens	1.49kk	125.0k	127.4k	1.74kk	1.38kk	137.4k	136.4k	1.65kk
unique tokens	138.2k	29.2k	29.6k	146.9k	36.2k	12.8k	12.7k	38.7k
tokens/sentence	14.88	12.74	12.51	14.51	13.78	13.74	13.64	13.77
label distribution	50/50				50/50			
	SubjNumber				**SubjNumber**			
sample size	100k	10k	10k	120k	100k	10k	10k	120k
tokens	1.04kk	99.9k	103.2k	1.25kk	1.41kk	140.3k	141.7k	1.7kk
unique tokens	100.3k	21.7k	23.1k	108.3k	38.5k	14.4k	14.5k	41.3k
tokens/sentence	10.42	9.99	10.32	10.38	14.14	14.03	14.17	14.13
label distribution	50/50				50/50			
	ObjNumber				**ObjNumber**			
sample size	100k	10k	10k	120k	100k	10k	10k	120k
tokens	946.7k	103.3k	100.2k	1.15kk	1.4kk	140.5k	139.9k	1.68kk
unique tokens	86.0k	23.8k	22.8k	95.7k	38.0k	14.3k	13.9k	40.9k
tokens/sentence	9.47	10.33	10.02	9.59	13.96	14.05	13.99	13.97
label distribution	50/50				50/50			
	PT				**Tense**			
sample size	100k	10k	10k	120k	100k	10k	10k	120k
tokens	1.13kk	112.8k	113.0k	1.36kk	1.32kk	131.1k	129.6k	1.58kk
unique tokens	114.5k	26.8k	26.7k	126.6k	35.9k	13.1k	13.2k	38.6k
tokens/sentence	11.30	11.28	11.30	11.30	13.20	13.11	12.96	13.17
label distribution	50/50				50/50			
	TreeDepth				**TreeDepth**			
sample size	100k	10k	10k	120k	100k	10k	10k	120k
tokens	1.57kk	157.2k	157.6k	1.88kk	1.35kk	135.0k	134.7k	1.62kk
unique tokens	150.3k	38.4k	38.3k	165.7k	34.8k	12.5k	12.6k	37.1k
tokens/sentence	15.72	15.72	15.76	15.73	13.47	13.50	13.47	13.47
label distribution	13.6/22.6/32.9/20.7/10.3				15.4/11.9/7.0/ 13.6/16.5/17.9/17.7			

Table 11: Comparative data statistics for the shared Russian and English probing tasks. Label distribution by target class is presented in %.

B.2 Probing Trajectories

Figures 4–9 show the probing curves of Logistic Regression classifier over the shared tasks (see Section 5.1). The results obtained with MLP classifier are pretty consistent with the ones presented in this Appendix.

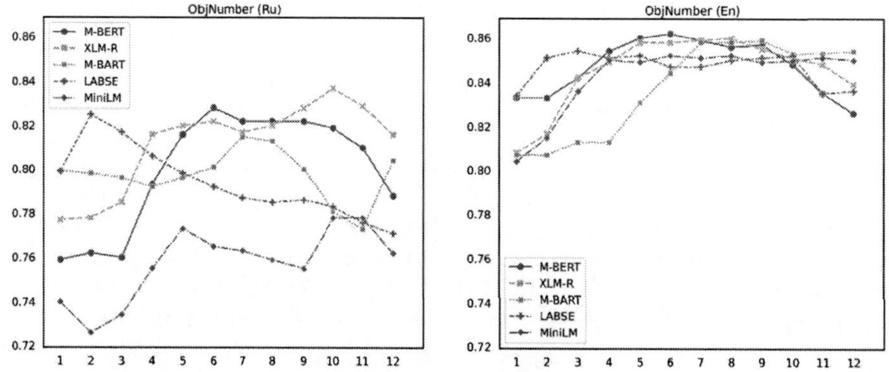

Figure 4: The probing results of Logistic Regression classifier for each encoder on **ObjNumber**. **Ru** is at the left; and **En** is at the right. X-axis=Layer number, Y-axis=Accuracy score.

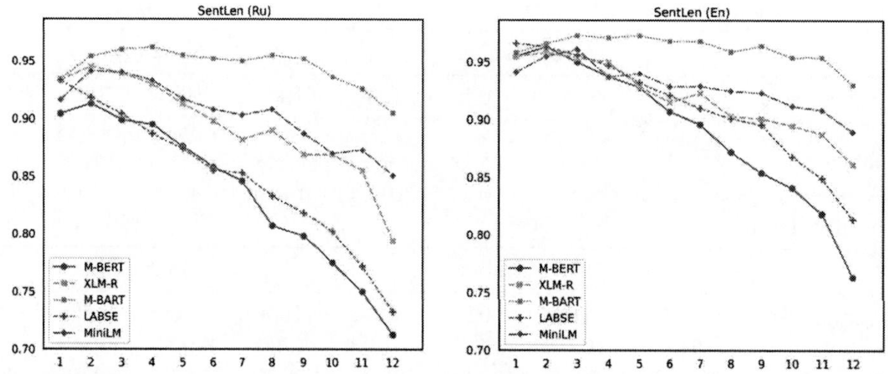

Figure 5: The probing results of Logistic Regression classifier for each encoder on **SentLen**. **Ru** is at the left; and **En** is at the right. X-axis=Layer number, Y-axis=Accuracy score.

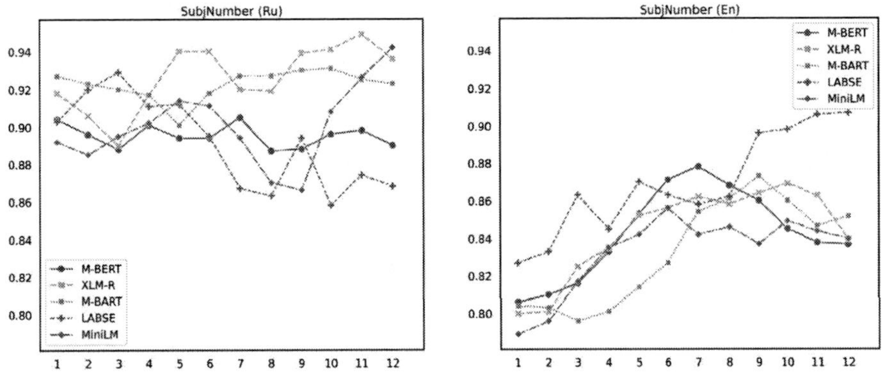

Figure 6: The probing results of Logistic Regression classifier for each encoder on **SubjNumber**. **Ru** is at the left; and **En** is at the right. X-axis=Layer number, Y-axis=Accuracy score.

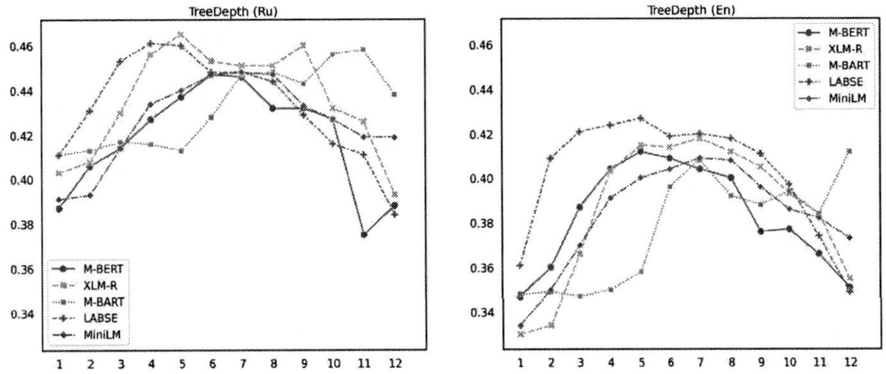

Figure 7: The probing results of Logistic Regression classifier for each encoder on **TreeDepth**. **Ru** is at the left; and **En** is at the right. X-axis=Layer number, Y-axis=Accuracy score.

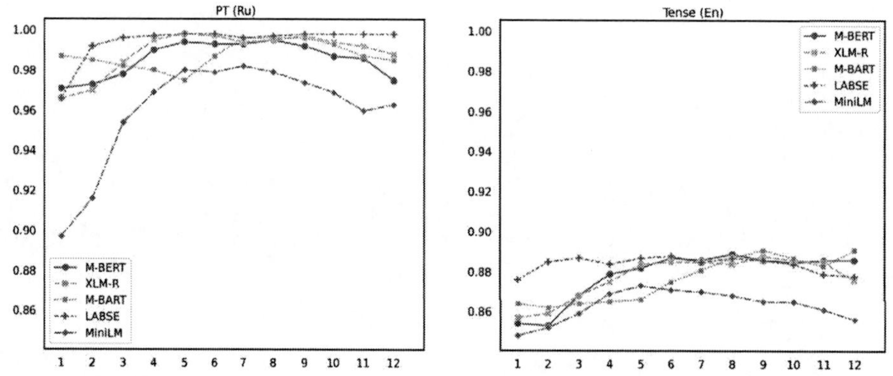

Figure 8: The probing results of Logistic Regression classifier for each encoder on **Tense**. **Ru** (**PT**) is at the left; and **En** (**Tense**) is at the right. X-axis=Layer number, Y-axis=Accuracy score.

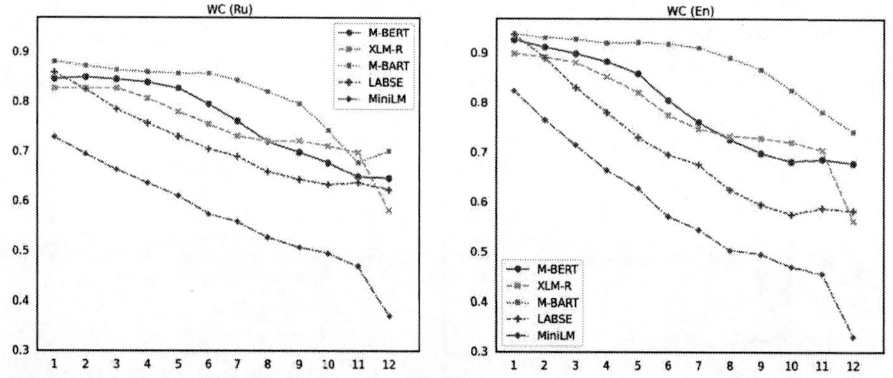

Figure 9: The probing results of Logistic Regression classifier for each encoder on **WC**. **Ru** is at the left; and **En** is at the right. X-axis=Layer number, Y-axis=Accuracy score.

C Individual Neuron Analysis

Figures 10–14 depict top neuron distributions for the tasks (see Section 5.2).

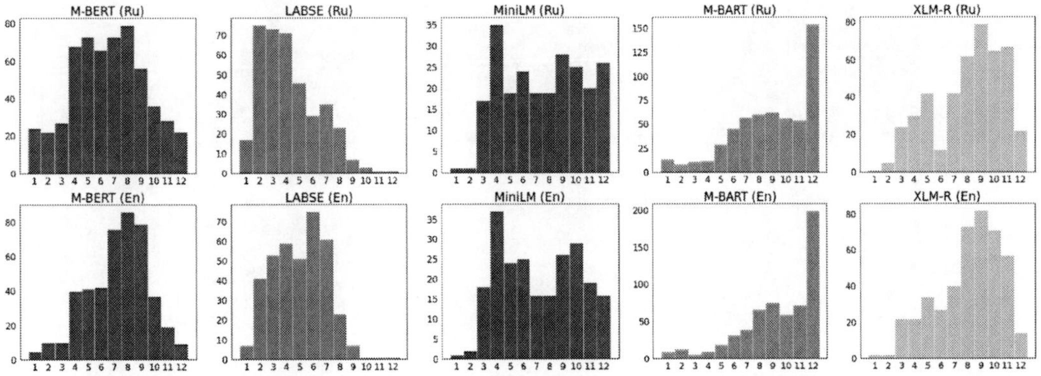

Figure 10: The distribution of top neurons over **NShift** tasks for both languages: **Ru**=Russian, **En**=English. X-axis=Layer index number, Y-axis=Number of neurons selected from the layer.

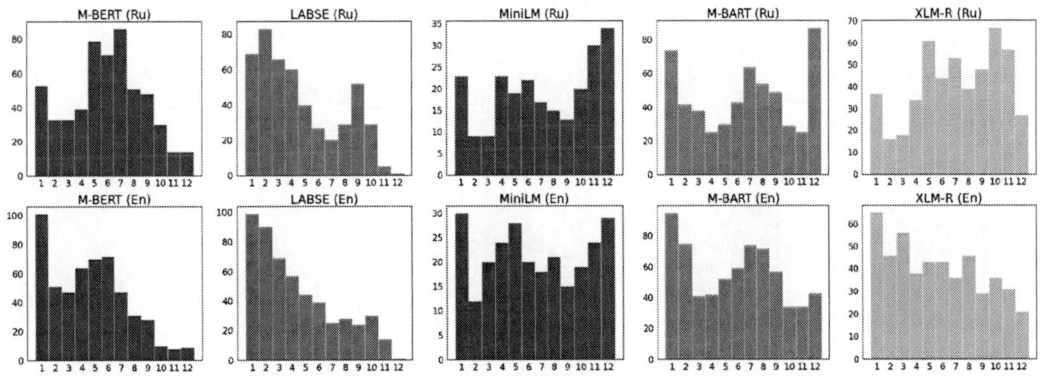

Figure 11: The distribution of top neurons over **ObjNumber** tasks for both languages: **Ru**=Russian, **En**=English. X-axis=Layer index number, Y-axis=Number of neurons selected from the layer.

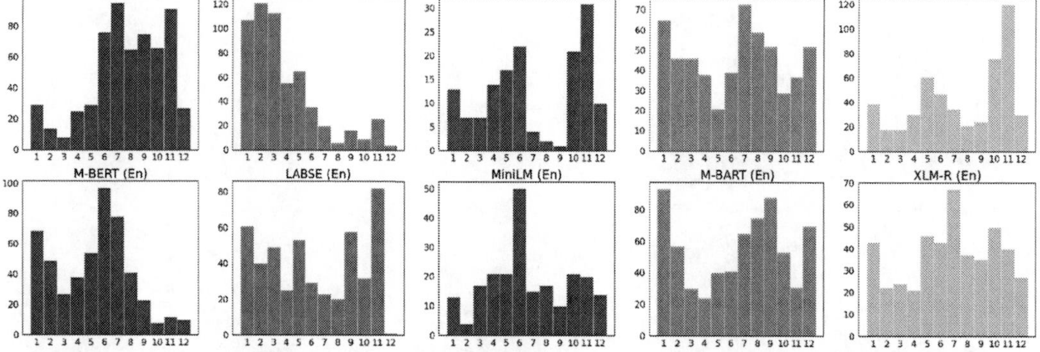

Figure 12: The distribution of top neurons over **SubjNumber** tasks for both languages: **Ru**=Russian, **En**=English. X-axis=Layer index number, Y-axis=Number of neurons selected from the layer.

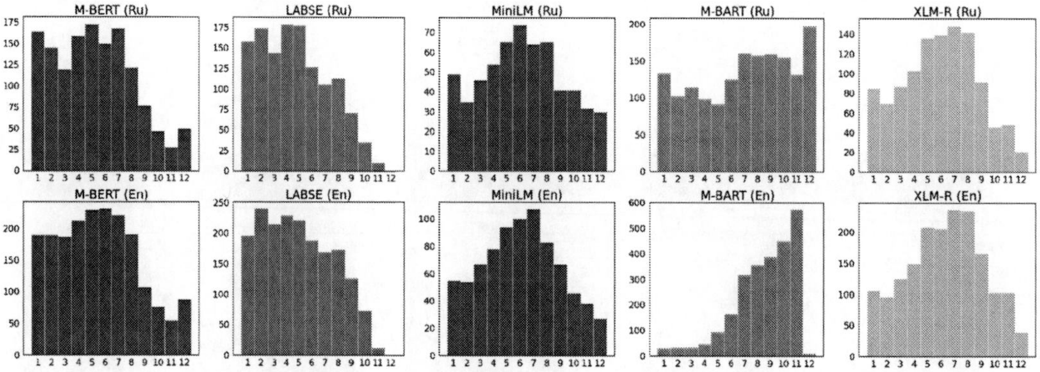

Figure 13: The distribution of top neurons over **TreeDepth** tasks for both languages: **Ru**=Russian, **En**=English. X-axis=Layer index number, Y-axis=Number of neurons selected from the layer.

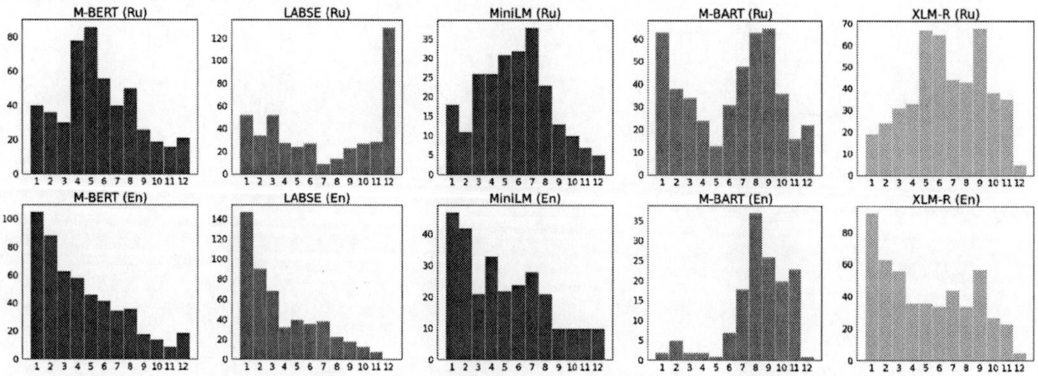

Figure 14: The distribution of top neurons over **Tense** tasks for both languages: **Ru**=Russian, **En**=English. X-axis=Layer index number, Y-axis=Number of neurons selected from the layer.

D Correlation Methods

Heatmaps (Figure 15) show similarities of the encoders under neuron-level and representation-level correlation-based similarity measures on the Russian tasks (see Section 5.3).

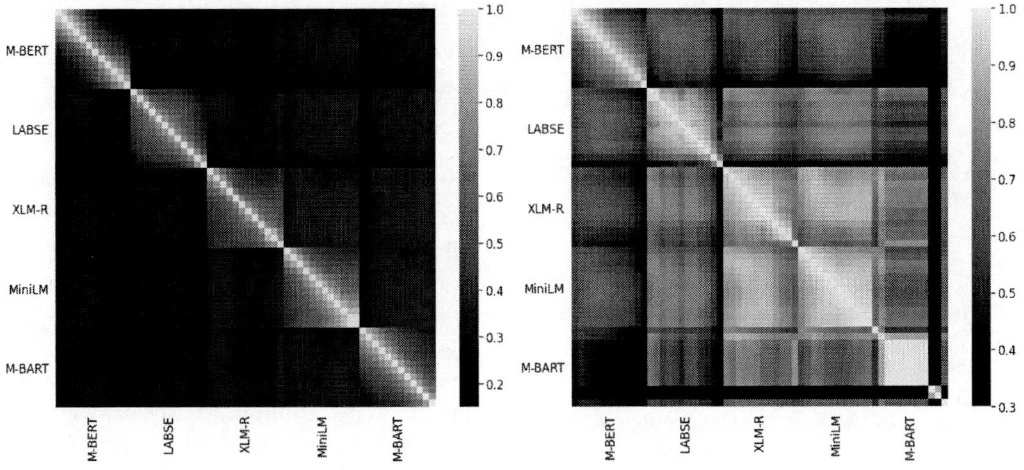

(a) `maxcorr` (b) `lincka`

Figure 15: Similarity heatmaps of layers in the encoders under neuron-level (`maxcorr`) and representation-level (`lincka`) measures for Russian.

Exploratory analysis of news sentiment using subgroup discovery

Anita Valmarska
Jožef Stefan Institute
Jamova cesta 39
and University of Ljubljana,
Faculty of Computer
and information science
Večna pot 113
Ljubljana, Slovenia
anita.valmarska@ijs.si

Luis Adrián Cabrera-Diego and **Elvys Linhares Pontes**
L3i laboratory
University of La Rochelle
La Rochelle, France
luis.cabrera_diego,
elvys.linhares_pontes
{@univ-lr.fr}

Senja Pollak
Jožef Stefan Institute
Jamova cesta 39
Ljubljana, Slovenia
senja.pollak@ijs.si

Abstract

In this study, we present an exploratory analysis of a Slovenian news corpus, in which we investigate the association between named entities and sentiment in the news. We propose a methodology that combines Named Entity Recognition and Subgroup Discovery - a descriptive rule learning technique for identifying groups of examples that share the same class label (sentiment) and pattern (features - Named Entities). The approach is used to induce the positive and negative sentiment class rules that reveal interesting patterns related to different Slovenian and international politicians, organizations, and locations.

1 Introduction

Traditionally, sentiment analysis refers to the use of natural language processing to systematically identify, extract, quantify, and study affective states and subjective information. Most frequently, it is used as a predictive technique used to model social media (Beigi et al., 2016), more specifically to predict or summarize opinions, attitudes and emotions in tweets, comments, online reviews etc., where the main focus is on predicting attitudes expressed towards a specific entity (Mejova, 2009). Another line of research applies sentiment analysis on news text, where the focus has shifted from analyzing sentiment towards a specific target to analyzing the intrinsic mood of the text itself (Pelicon et al., 2020). Authors aimed to model feelings (positive, negative, or neutral) that readers feel while reading a certain piece of news (Bučar et al., 2018; Liu, 2012; Pelicon et al., 2020), also in relation to news covering Covid-19 (Aslam et al., 2020), modelled news sentiment in relation to stock market and economic conditions (Van de Kauter et al., 2015; Bowden et al., 2019; Rambaccussing and Kwiatkowski, 2020). Sentiment analysis has been also used in fake news identification (Bhutani et al., 2019) and in media bias analysis (El Ali et al., 2018).

In the current trend of natural language processing research (Rogers and Augenstein, 2020), the main focus is on improving the predictive performance over state-of-the art especially using deep learning-based methods. The drawback of these models is in their very limited interpretability. In contrast, several data and text mining techniques have been developed to improve domain understanding and support exploratory analysis of data, with focus on explainable models, which is crucial e.g. in medical applications, but also interesting for interdisciplinary research in the field of digital humanities and digital social sciences. Our research falls under this line of research.

The aim of our study is to gain better understanding into news sentiment by analysis of named entities in a manually annotated corpus of Slovenian news articles (Bučar, 2017). More specifically, our aim is to identify groups of topics with negative or positive sentiment in Slovenian news, where topics are identified by named entities and their interaction forms the context of the reported stories. We propose the employment of subgroup discovery — a descriptive rule learning technique for identification of groups of examples sharing the same class label (sentiment) and same pattern (features). The task of subgroup discovery is the combination of predictive and descriptive rule induction. The result of subgroup discovery is to provide understandable descriptions of subgroups of individuals which share a common target property of interest. Subgroup discovery methods have traditionally be successfully applied to in different medical applications (e.g. detecting of groups of patients at risk for atherosclerotic cardiovascular disease (Gamberger and Lavrač, 2002), supporting factors for brain ischemia (Gamberger and Lavrač, 2007), and psychiatric emergency (Carmona et al.,

Proceedings of the 8th BSNLP Workshop on Balto-Slavic Natural Language Processing, pages 66–72
April 20, 2021.

2011), but only rarely applied to model textual data. The closest to our study is the work by (Vavpetič et al., 2013) using the subgroup discovery system Hedwig for analyzing news articles about Portugal focusing on interesting vocabulary patterns that reflect credit default swap. The authors focused on financial entities, geographical entities and a specialized vocabulary of the European sovereign debt crisis.

The main contributions of this paper are two fold. First, we propose a novel approach using named entity recognition and linking in a subgroup discovery setting. Next, we apply the method on the Slovenian news dataset, getting new insights into Slovenian news reporting in terms of news sentiment and showcase the potential of our approach for digital social science research.

The paper is structured as follows: in Section 2, we present the data used in the experimental work. Section 3 presents a short outline of the employed methodology. In Section 4 and Section 5, we present our results and offer our conclusions and ideas for further work.

2 Data

In our experiments, we used the manually sentiment annotated Slovenian news corpus SentiNews 1.0 (Bučar et al., 2018; Bučar, 2017)[1]. The corpus consists of Slovene web-crawled news containing more than 250,000 documents with political, business, economic and financial content from five Slovene media resources on the web. The data covers the period between 1 September 2007 to 31 December 2013. Data used in the experiments is a manually sentiment annotated stratified random sample of 10,427 documents from news portals 24ur, Dnevnik, Finance, Rtvslo, and Žurnal24. Data was independently annotated by 2-6 annotators, using the five-level Lickert scale (1 – very negative, 2 – negative, 3 – neutral, 4 – positive, and 5 – very positive) on three levels of granularity, i.e. on document, paragraph, and sentence level. The sentiment of an instance is defined as the average of the sentiment scores given by the different annotators, where an instance labeled as negative has received an average score less than or equal to 2.4 and an instance labeled as positive has received an average score to 3.6. Instances with an average score in-between were labeled as neutral. The analysis of the agreement between annotators is available in (Bučar et al., 2018). The value of annotators agreement on document level as measured by the Cronbach's alpha is 0.903.

In this paper we are interested only in documents with either positive or negative sentiment, which corresponds to 1665 positive and 3337 negative articles, respectively. Note that the dataset is thus imbalanced towards the negative class (which is also matching the observations of media researchers that attention to negative news is disproportionate (e.g. (Van der Meer et al., 2019; Soroka et al., 2019)).

3 Methodology

The methodology for named entity-based sentiment subgroup discovery consists of three steps.

3.1 Named entity recognition and linking

For each document from the corpora, we perform named entity recognition (NER) and named entity linking (NEL) using the approaches described in Boros et al. (2020)[2] and Linhares Pontes et al. (2020)[3], respectively. Specifically, for the NER system we fine-tuned CroSloEngual BERT (Ulčar and Robnik-Šikonja, 2020) with two staked Transformer blocks on the top. For the NEL system we used the architecture founded on the Multilingual End-to-End Entity Linking with match correction and candidate filtering. Both systems, NER and NEL, were trained using the Slovene WikiANN dataset (Pan et al., 2017). The dataset was split in three partitions, train, development and test. The evaluation on the test partition, showed that the NER system has a micro F-score of 0.954, while the NEL system has an F-score of 0.705.

In SentiNews 1.0, we identified 914 person names, 699 organizations and 476 locations with assigned NEL identifiers. We used the NEL codes to extract the nominative case of the named entities from the the Slovenian Wikipedia.

3.2 Data transformation

As the state-of-the-art algorithms for subgroup discovery work on structured data, the second step of the methodology is to transform the discovered (and linked) named entities from step 1 into a tabular form suitable for subgroup discovery. The resulting tables were constructed by representing

[1] Data is available on https://www.clarin.si/repository/xmlui/handle/11356/1110

[2] Code available at: https://github.com/EMBEDDIA/stacked-ner

[3] Code available at: https://github.com/EMBEDDIA/multilingual_entity_linking

each non-neutral sentiment document from the corpora as a row in a table. The documents are described by the values of the identified entities, *yes* if the respective entity was identified in the document and *no* if the entity was not present in the document. The document's sentiment represent the class label.

The result of data transformation is a table with 2645 rows (i.e. documents with positive or negative class label, and identified linked named entity) and 2089 columns (i.e. named entities corresponding to person, organisation and location names) as attributes. In our order to reduce the number of columns and improve the chances of the subgroup discovery algorithm of discovering good subgroups, we chose to proceed only with top *n* (with n=20) most frequent entities from each entity group: person, organization, and location.[4] As we are only interested into entities mentioned in the articles, we removed all documents without any identified entity, thus resulting in a table with 1703 rows and 60 columns i.e. entities, with the positive and negative sentiment class distribution (560, 1143), which is similar to the dataset distribution before preprocessing).

Table 1 presents the 20 most frequent persons, organizations, and locations identified in the corpora. Entities are ordered according to their frequency, the most popular entities are written on top.

Persons	Organizations	Locations
Borut Pahor	Ljubljanska borza	Združeno kraljestvo
Janez Janša	Evropska komisija	Luka Koper
Dow Jones	Evropska unija	New York
Danilo Türk	Telekom Slovenije	Nova Gorica
Igor Bavčar	Košarkarski klub Zlatorog	Murska Sobota
Karl Erjavec	Radiotelvizija Slovenija	Ljubljanska borza
Gregor Virant	Newyorška borza	Slovenj Gradec
Alenka Bratušek	Luka Koper	Mestna občina Ljubljana MOL
Katarina Kresal	Adria Airways	Slovenija
Nogometni klub Koper	Dow Jones	Črna gora
Mitja Gaspari	Nova Ljubljanska banka NLB	Novo mesto
Angela Merkel	Wall Street	Škofja Loka
Goldman Sachs	Svetovna banka	Kranjska Gora
Gregor Golobič	Pop TV	Bosna in Hencegovina
Nicolas Sarkozy	General Motors	Bela krajina
Ivo Sanader	Lehman Brothers	Južna Koreja
Dimitrij Rupel	Bank of America	Hrvaška
Andrej Bajuk	Republika Slovenija	Mestna občina Maribor MOM
Janeza Drnovška	Standard & Pool	Nova Zelandija
Barack Obama	Deutsche Bank	Grad Brdo pri Kranju

Table 1: Twenty most frequent persons, organizations, and locations in SentiNews1.0.

3.3 Subgroup discovery

The third step of the methodology is the identification of subgroups via subgroup discovery. Subgroup discovery is a descriptive induction technique that learns descriptive rules from labeled data. The task of subgroup discovery is to find interesting subgroups in the population, i.e. subgroups that have a significantly different class distribution than the entire population (Klösgen, 1996; Wrobel, 1997). The result of subgroup discovery is a set of individual rules, where the rule consequence is a class label. An important characteristic of subgroup discovery is that its task is a combination of predictive and descriptive rule induction. It provides understandable descriptions of subgroups of individuals which share a common target property of interest.

We performed subgroup discovery using the DoubleBeam-SD algorithm (Valmarska et al., 2017)[5]. The DoubleBeam-SD subgroup discovery algorithm combines separate refinement and selection heuristics with the beam search. Inverted m-estimate is used as the heuristics in the rule refinement phase while m-estimate is the rule selection heuristics. The width of the beam was set to 100. The algorithm was set to extract up to 10 best rules for each class.

4 Results

Table 2 presents the rules describing groups of documents with positive or negative sentiment. The prefixes *PER_*, *ORG_*, and *LOC_* denote a person, an organization or a location respectively. For example, the interpretation of the first rule, `LOC_Nova_Gorica = no AND PER_Igor_Bavčar = yes AND LOC_Grad_Brdo_pri_Kranju = no → negative` is as follows: articles that talk about the person Igor Bavčar and do not talk about the locations *Nova_Gorica* and *Grad_Brdo_pri_Kranju* (corresponding to Brdo pri Kranju, the location of

[4]The number of most frequent named entities (*n*) from each category was set arbitrarily.

[5]The code of the DoubleBeam-SD algorithm is available on `https://github.com/bib3rce/RL_SD`.

Slovenian government's main venue for diplomatic meetings) are articles with *negative* sentiment. This rule covers 28 documents, out of which 26 are actually labeled with *negative* sentiment, while 2 are annotated with positive sentiment.

Rules describing articles with *negative* sentiment concern articles written about Igor Bavčar, a Slovenian politician and manager. As politician, he played an important role during the Slovenian independence period (he acted as minister of internal affairs in the beginning of the 90s and later as Slovenian minister for European affairs) (Plut-Pregelj et al., 2018). In 2002, he withdraw from politics to engage in the private sector and was connected to financial affairs, which explains the negative sentiment association in our corpus. Bavčar became the chairman of the Istrabenz holding company in 2002. On 31 March 2009 Bavčar resigned as the President of Istrabenz due to poor business performance as the company was forced into financial restructuring. Bavčar was indicted for disputed trading in Istrabenz shares in 2017, when he attempted to take over the company. He was arrested in financial fraud investigation and released after 10 hours.[6]

The discovered subgroups of articles with *positive* sentiment contain articles talking either about Slovenia's former president, Danilo Türk, or the city of New York, *New Yorku*. Danilo Türk is a Slovenian diplomat, professor of international law, human rights expert, and political figure who served as President of Slovenia from 2007 to 2012. Note that the rules of discovered subgroups have a low precision (as the distribution of true positive and false positive is 53% vs. 47%). However one should take into account that the dataset is very imbalanced — with only 33% of articles annotated with a positive sentiment class label. These rules also show the main objective of subgroup discovery — discovering and describing groups of examples with significantly different class distribution to the the population class distribution rather than prediction.

It is interesting that the positive sentiment for New York is connected to the absence of other named entities, closely related to New York including the former president of the United States, Barack Obama. Another entity whose omission in news articles strengthens the positive sentiment associated with New York is the investment bank Lehman Brothers. On September 15, 2008, Lehman Brothers Holdings, Inc. sought Chapter 11 protection, initiating the largest bankruptcy proceeding in United States (U.S.) history. It declared $639 billion in assets and $613 billion in debts. At the time, Lehman was the fourth-largest U.S. investment bank. Despite being thought "too big to fail", the federal government did not employ extraordinary measures to save Lehman, such as the enabling financing it had facilitated for J.P. Morgan Chase's purchase of a failing Bear Stearns just six months earlier. Lehman's demise was a seminal event in the financial crisis that began in the U.S. subprime mortgage industry in 2007, spread to the credit markets, and then burned through the world's financial markets. The crisis resulted in significant and wide losses to the economy. (Wiggins et al., 2014)

Other rules of positive sentiment with named entity New York, also include the absence of Standard & Poor's, an American credit rating agency and a division of S&P Global (*ORG_Standard_&_Pools*) that publishes financial research and analysis on stocks, bonds, and commodities, and the Bank of America (*ORG_Bank_of_America*).

The positive sentiment of Danilo Türk is related to the omission of the above mentioned politician involved in financial affairs, Igor Bavčar. The quality of the rules presented in Table 2 is presented in Table 3 in the appendix.

5 Conclusions

In this paper, we presented a sentiment subgroup discovery approach through the lenses of named entities. Experiments were performed on a corpora of Slovene news data, manually labeled with positive and negative sentiment. Our approach utilizes the fact that the sentiment in news articles is tied-up to their discussed named entities. We identified groups of news articles with negative and positive sentiment.

The identified groups of articles were described by rules containing only one positive condition, confirming the presence of a named entity in an article. Many of the identified subgroups for a chosen sentiment focus on the same entity. One of the key person entities associated with negative sentiment is Igor Bavčar - a polarizing Slovenian politician and manager, whose presence in the news from 2009 is accompanied by negative sentiment due to

[6] `https://en.wikipedia.org/wiki/Igor_Bav%C4%8Dar`, Last accessed: 8 February 2021.

R.nr.	Rule	Sentiment	TP	FP
N1	LOC_Nova_Gorica = no AND PER_Igor_Bavčar = yes AND LOC_Grad_Brdo_pri_Kranju = no	→ negative	26	2
N2	PER_Igor_Bavčar = yes AND ORG_Telekom_Slovenije = no AND LOC_Grad_Brdo_pri_Kranju = no AND PER_Dimitrij_Rupel = no	→ negative	26	2
N3	LOC_Hrvaška = no AND PER_Igor_Bavčar = yes AND LOC_Grad_Brdo_pri_Kranju = no AND PER_Dimitrij_Rupel = no	→ negative	26	2
N4	PER_Ivo_Sanader = no AND PER_Igor_Bavčar = yes AND LOC_Grad_Brdo_pri_Kranju = no	→ negative	26	2
N5	PER_Igor_Bavčar = yes AND LOC_Grad_Brdo_pri_Kranju = no AND PER_Mitja_Gaspari = no AND PER_Dimitrij_Rupel = no	→ negative	26	2
N6	PER_Igor_Bavčar = yes AND ORG_Bank_of_America = no	→ negative	26	2
N7	PER_Igor_Bavčar = yes AND LOC_Grad_Brdo_pri_Kranju = no AND LOC_New_York = no	→ negative	26	2
N8	LOC_Nova_Zelandija = no AND PER_Igor_Bavčar = yes AND LOC_Grad_Brdo_pri_Kranju = no AND PER_Dimitrij_Rupel = no	→ negative	26	2
N9	LOC_Slovenija = no AND PER_Igor_Bavčar = yes AND LOC_Grad_Brdo_pri_Kranju = no	→ negative	26	2
N10	PER_Ivo_Sanader = no AND PER_Igor_Bavčar = yes	→ negative	26	2
P1	ORG_Nova_Ljubljanska_banka_NLB = no AND PER_Angela_Merkel = no AND LOC_New_York = yes	→ positive	57	51
P2	PER_Barack_Obama = no AND ORG_Evropska_komisija = no AND LOC_New_York = yes	→ positive	57	51
P3	ORG_Nova_Ljubljanska_banka_NLB = no AND PER_Igor_Bavčar = no AND PER_Danilo_Türk = yes	→ positive	24	18
P4	ORG_Lehman_Brothers = no AND ORG_Evropska_komisija = no AND LOC_New_York = yes	→ positive	57	51
P5	PER_Igor_Bavčar = no AND PER_Angela_Merkel = no AND LOC_New_York = yes	→ positive	57	51
P6	ORG_Standard_&_Pool = no AND ORG_Evropska_komisija = no AND LOC_New_York = yes	→ positive	57	51
P7	ORG_Nova_Ljubljanska_banka_NLB = no AND PER_Igor_Bavčar = no AND ORG_Košarkarski_klub_Zlatorog = no AND PER_Danilo_Türk = yes	→ positive	24	18
P8	ORG_Košarkarski_klub_Zlatorog = no AND PER_Angela_Merkel = no AND LOC_New_York = yes	→ positive	57	51
P9	ORG_Bank_of_America = no AND ORG_Evropska_komisija = no AND LOC_New_York = yes	→ positive	57	51
P10	ORG_Nova_Ljubljanska_banka_NLB = no AND PER_Igor_Bavčar = no AND PER_Danilo_Türk = yes AND ORG_Združeno_kraljestvo = no	→ positive	57	51

Table 2: List of rules describing subgroups of articles with *negative* and *positive* sentiment.

financial affairs. We are also able to identify a generally positive sentiment towards another Slovenian politician and a location.

In future work we will adapt the used algorithm for subgroup discovery to identify subgroups that are not overlapping, thus potentially involving multiple entities.

Acknowledgments

This work was supported by the Slovenian Research Agency (ARRS) grants for the programmes, Knowledge technologies (P2-0103) and Artificial intelligence and inteligent systems (P2-0209), the project Computer-assisted multilingual news discourse analysis with contextual embeddings (CANDAS, J6-2581), as well as the European Union's Horizon 2020 research and innovation programme under grant agreement No 825153, project EMBEDDIA (Cross-Lingual Embeddings for Less-Represented Languages in European News Media).

References

Faheem Aslam, Tahir Mumtaz Awan, Jabir Hussain Syed, Aisha Kashif, and Mahwish Parveen. 2020. Sentiments and emotions evoked by news headlines of coronavirus disease (covid-19) outbreak. *Humanities and Social Sciences Communications*, 7(1):1–9.

Ghazaleh Beigi, Xia Hu, Ross Maciejewski, and Huan Liu. 2016. An overview of sentiment analysis in social media and its applications in disaster relief. *Sentiment analysis and ontology engineering*, pages 313–340.

Bhavika Bhutani, Neha Rastogi, Priyanshu Sehgal, and Archana Purwar. 2019. Fake news detection using sentiment analysis. In *2019 Twelfth International Conference on Contemporary Computing (IC3)*, pages 1–5. IEEE.

Emanuela Boros, Ahmed Hamdi, Elvys Linhares Pontes, Luis Adrián Cabrera-Diego, Jose G. Moreno, Nicolas Sidere, and Antoine Doucet. 2020. Alleviating Digitization Errors in Named Entity Recognition for Historical Documents. In *Proceedings of the 24th Conference on Computational Natural Language Learning (CoNLL)*, pages 431–441, Online. Association for Computational Linguistics.

James Bowden, Andrzej Kwiatkowski, and Dooruj Rambaccussing. 2019. Economy through a lens: Distortions of policy coverage in uk national newspapers. *Journal of Comparative Economics*, 47(4):881–906.

Jože Bučar. 2017. Manually sentiment annotated slovenian news corpus SentiNews 1.0. Slovenian language resource repository CLARIN.SI.

Jože Bučar, Martin Žnidaršič, and Janez Povh. 2018. Annotated news corpora and a lexicon for sentiment analysis in slovene. *Language Resources and Evaluation*, 52(3):895–919.

Cristóbal J Carmona, Pedro González, María José del Jesus, Mercedes Navío-Acosta, and Luís Jiménez-Trevino. 2011. Evolutionary fuzzy rule extraction for subgroup discovery in a psychiatric emergency department. *Soft Computing*, 15(12):2435–2448.

Abdallah El Ali, Tim C Stratmann, Souneil Park, Johannes Schöning, Wilko Heuten, and Susanne CJ Boll. 2018. Measuring, understanding, and classifying news media sympathy on twitter after crisis events. In *Proceedings of the 2018 CHI Conference on Human Factors in Computing Systems*, pages 1–13.

Dragan Gamberger and Nada Lavrač. 2007. Supporting factors in descriptive analysis of brain ischaemia. In *Conference on Artificial Intelligence in Medicine in Europe*, pages 155–159. Springer.

Dragan Gamberger and Nada Lavrač. 2002. Expert-guided subgroup discovery: Methodology and application. *Journal of Artificial Intelligence Research*, 17:501–527.

Marjan Van de Kauter, Diane Breesch, and Véronique Hoste. 2015. Fine-grained analysis of explicit and implicit sentiment in financial news articles. *Expert Systems with applications*, 42(11):4999–5010.

Willi Klösgen. 1996. Explora: A multipattern and multistrategy discovery assistant. In *Advances in Knowledge Discovery and Data Mining*, pages 249–271. AAAI/MIT Press.

Nada Lavrač, Branko Kavšek, Peter Flach, and Ljupco Todorovski. 2004. Subgroup discovery with cn2-sd. *J. Mach. Learn. Res.*, 5(2):153–188.

Elvys Linhares Pontes, Luis Adrián Cabrera-Diego, Jose G. Moreno, Emanuela Boros, Ahmed Hamdi, Nicolas Sidère, Mickaël Coustaty, and Antoine Doucet. 2020. Entity Linking for Historical Documents: Challenges and Solutions. In *Proceedings of the 22nd International Conference on Asia-Pacific Digital Libraries (ICADL 2020)*, pages 215–231, Kyoto, Japan. Springer International Publishing.

Bing Liu. 2012. Sentiment analysis and opinion mining. *Synthesis lectures on human language technologies*, 5(1):1–167.

Toni GLA Van der Meer, Anne C Kroon, Piet Verhoeven, and Jeroen Jonkman. 2019. Mediatization and the disproportionate attention to negative news: The case of airplane crashes. *Journalism Studies*, 20(6):783–803.

Yelena Mejova. 2009. Sentiment analysis: An overview. *University of Iowa, Computer Science Department*.

Xiaoman Pan, Boliang Zhang, Jonathan May, Joel Nothman, Kevin Knight, and Heng Ji. 2017. Cross-lingual Name Tagging and Linking for 282 Languages. In *Proceedings of the 55th Annual Meeting of the Association for Computational Linguistics (Volume 1: Long Papers)*, pages 1946–1958, Vancouver, Canada. Association for Computational Linguistics.

Andraž Pelicon, Marko Pranjić, Dragana Miljković, Blaž Škrlj, and Senja Pollak. 2020. Zero-shot learning for cross-lingual news sentiment classification. *Applied Sciences*, 10(17):5993.

Leopoldina Plut-Pregelj, Gregor Kranjc, Žarko Lazarević, and Carole Rogel. 2018. *Historical Dictionary of Slovenia (Historical Dictionaries of Europe)*. Rowman & Littlefield Publishers.

Dooruj Rambaccussing and Andrzej Kwiatkowski. 2020. Forecasting with news sentiment: Evidence with uk newspapers. *International Journal of Forecasting*, 36(4):1501–1516.

Anna Rogers and Isabelle Augenstein. 2020. What can we do to improve peer review in nlp? *arXiv preprint arXiv:2010.03863*.

Stuart Soroka, Patrick Fournier, and Lilach Nir. 2019. Cross-national evidence of a negativity bias in psychophysiological reactions to news. *Proceedings of the National Academy of Sciences*, 116(38):18888–18892.

Matej Ulčar and Marko Robnik-Šikonja. 2020. FinEst BERT and CroSloEngual BERT. In *Text, Speech, and Dialogue*, pages 104–111, Cham. Springer International Publishing.

Anita Valmarska, Nada Lavrač, Johannes Fürnkranz, and Marko Robnik-Šikonja. 2017. Refinement and selection heuristics in subgroup discovery and classification rule learning. *Expert Systems with Applications*, 81:147–162.

Anže Vavpetič, Petra Kralj Novak, Miha Grčar, Igor Mozetič, and Nada Lavrač. 2013. Semantic data mining of financial news articles. In *International Conference on Discovery Science*, pages 294–307. Springer.

Rosalind Wiggins, Thomas Piontek, and Andrew Metrick. 2014. The Lehman Brothers bankruptcy a: Overview. *Yale program on financial stability case study*.

Stefan Wrobel. 1997. An algorithm for multi-relational discovery of subgroups. In *Proceedings of the First European Symposium on Principles of Data Mining and Knowledge Discovery, PKDD 1997*, pages 78–87.

A Appendix. Quality of subgroup rules

Table 3 presents the quality measures of rules describing subgroups presented in Table 2. Note that the purpose of these experiments is exploratory analysis, not a prediction classification task and that the results are reported on the entire dataset, without any train-test data split. In addition to the traditional measures of precision, accuracy and recall, we also present values of *weighted relative accuracy* (WRACC).

R.nr	Precision	Accuracy	Recall	WRACC
N1—N10	0.929	0.685	0.023	0.004
P1—P2	0.528	0.332	0.102	0.013
P3	0.571	0.332	0.043	0.006
P4—P6	0.528	0.332	0.102	0.013
P7	0.571	0.332	0.043	0.006
P8—P10	0.528	0.332	0.102	0.013

Table 3: Quality of the rules describing subgroup presented in Table 2.

Lavrač et al. (2004) argue that WRACC, also referred to as *unusualness*, is the most important measure of subgroup discovery rules. WRACC for a chosen rule is defined as follows

$$WRACC = \frac{TP + FP}{P + N}\{\frac{TP}{TP + FP} - \frac{P}{P + N}\}, \quad (1)$$

where TP is the number of *true positive* examples covered by the rule, FP is the number of *false positive* examples covered by the rule, while P and N are the number of positive and negative examples, respectively, in the population. WRACC reflects both the rule significance and rule coverage, as subgroup discovery is interested in rules with significantly different class distribution than the prior class distribution that covers many instances.

Creating an Aligned Russian Text Simplification Dataset from Language Learner Data

Anna Dmitrieva
Department of Digital Humanities
University of Helsinki
Helsinki, Finland;
HSE University
Moscow, Russia
annadmitrieva252@gmail.com

Jörg Tiedemann
Department of Digital Humanities
University of Helsinki
Helsinki, Finland
jorg.tiedemann@helsinki.fi

Abstract

Parallel language corpora where regular texts are aligned with their simplified versions can be used in both natural language processing and theoretical linguistic studies. They are essential for the task of automatic text simplification, but can also provide valuable insights into the characteristics that make texts more accessible and reveal strategies that human experts use to simplify texts. Today, there exist a few parallel datasets for English and Simple English, but many other languages lack such data. In this paper we describe our work on creating an aligned Russian-Simple Russian dataset composed of Russian literature texts adapted for learners of Russian as a foreign language. This will be the first parallel dataset in this domain, and one of the first Simple Russian datasets in general.

1 Introduction

Automatic text simplification is a task of natural language processing aimed at making texts more readable and accessible to a broader audience. Nowadays, this task is most often viewed as a neural machine translation problem (Xu et al., 2015). Much like cross-lingual machine translation, intralingual neural text simplification requires a substantial amount of data in order to be able to train and test appropriate models.

Currently there are multiple datasets to choose from for English text simplification, such as Simple PPDB (Pavlick and Callison-Burch, 2016), Simple Wiki (Kauchak, 2013) and Newsela (Xu et al., 2015). However, not a lot of simplification-specific datasets are available for other languages. A few exceptions are, for example, the Spanish version of the Newsela dataset and the Alector parallel Simplified French corpus (Gala et al., 2020). For Russian, there are currently very limited options for publicly available simplification corpora. One such example is the dataset for one of the Dialogue Evaluation tasks (RuSimpleSentEval)[1]. However, this dataset consists mainly of texts from the WikiLarge corpus (Zhang and Lapata, 2017) that were translated into Russian automatically and parallel data from the Russian paraphrase corpus (Gudkov et al., 2020). Only the texts from the development and test set have been simplified by human experts. We will, instead, produce a corpus of Russian texts adapted by human experts for language learners, a unique resource for further work on Russian text simplification.

Creating a new dataset for text simplification poses quite a few challenges. First of all, there needs to be a source of such data. Possible options include simplified Wikipedia articles like Simple English Wikipedia or Vikidia[2], a French website intended for young people with more accessible articles than in Wikipedia, both in terms of language and content (Brouwers et al., 2014). Other possible sources could be texts simplified for children or second language learners, since not many languages actually have a simplified Wikipedia equivalent. There is also an option of simplifying some texts manually with the help of human experts, like it was done in Newsela or Alector, but this is expensive and slow.

Another issue that gathering simplified data poses is the fact that there is no one simple language. Simplified texts can vary in complexity levels and intended target audience: for example, texts adapted for second language learners or children typically become more complex as the reader's age or L2 proficiency increases. The comprehensibility of the reading materials for users of easy language is typically higher than for plain language users (Maaß, 2019). Therefore, it is important to

[1] https://github.com/dialogue-evaluation/RuSimpleSentEval
[2] http://fr.vikidia.org

Proceedings of the 8th BSNLP Workshop on Balto-Slavic Natural Language Processing, pages 73–79
April 20, 2021.

remember that it is impossible for one dataset to satisfy the needs of all simplified language users.

In this paper, we will describe the process of creating a Russian-Simple Russian parallel dataset made out of adapted Russian literature texts intended for learners of Russian as a foreign language (RaaFL). The corpus we produced is aligned on the paragraph level.

2 Data sources

The contents of the dataset described here are simplified Russian books and their original versions. The simplified books were adapted by professional RaaFL writers. They have been provided by the Zlatoust publishing house[3] for the purposes of this research.

The books and short stories in our dataset are all works by Russian writers, most of them being classical literature, such as novels by A. S. Pushkin, F. M. Dostoevsky, and A. P. Chekhov. There are also more modern works by writers like B. Akunin and V. Pelevin. Among the books provided for this dataset are 6 collections of novels and 16 separate books.

Most of the books and collections of novels are aimed at readers with an intermediate level of Russian, with some of them being aimed at lower and higher levels. All together, there are 2 books in this dataset dedicated for A2 level, 2 for levels A2-B1, 11 for B1, 1 for B1-B2, 3 for B2, and 3 collections of novels that fall between B1 and C1 levels.

For evaluation and as an additional reference, we have also created a smaller dataset that is made of 300 adapted texts from textbooks for children who are learners of Russian as a native language (1-4 school grades). Those are short texts from exercises that we manually aligned with their original versions.

At the moment, we are negotiating the possibility of giving open access for research purposes to parts of the collection. We aim at publishing a large portion of the parallel data with permissive licenses depending on the agreement we can establish. We will make that part available on GitHub or similar websites.

3 Data collection and preprocessing

The original format of the books and novel collections that were used for this dataset is PDF. Extracting the text from PDF files creates the first challenge in our process. The conversion was done with the help of the Apache Tika software[4] that allowed us to turn PDF documents into accessible XML files. After that, the texts were further cleaned and normalized to remove unnecessary line breaks, diacritics and other noisy symbols with the help of a dedicated Python script. The original texts that were downloaded from open sources were also processed in the same way and all texts were then stored in plain text files for further analysis and subsequent alignment.

While studying the characteristics of simplified texts, we performed word and sentence tokenization and, in certain cases, lemmatization on our dataset. For lemmatization, we used pymystem3[5], a wrapper for Yandex Mystem 3.1, which is a morphological analyzer for Russian (Segalovich, 2003). It is a dictionary-based algorithm, which has been proven to achieve up to 96,43% accuracy on POS tagging (Dereza et al., 2016), and up to 82,08% accuracy on lemmatization (Akhmetov et al., 2020). We also relied on Mystem for word tokenization, considering only words that it recognizes as tokens. Therefore, for, example, digits and punctuation were not considered words (tokens). For sentence tokenization, we used the NLTK sentence tokenizer for Russian which is based on ru_punkt[6]. It is important to note that these instruments were used only for obtaining dataset statistics and not during text alignment or neural text simplification.

4 Characteristics of the simplified texts

First of all, we wanted to see how different the adapted texts are compared to the corresponding original versions. In this study, we focus on automatic measures to provide essential properties of the texts and we leave a deeper analysis of the simplification level to future work. We looked at a number of metrics that are commonly used for determining the complexity of texts for RaaFL learners (Laposhina et al., 2018). The results are listed in Table 1, where we also list some dataset statistics. Some of the scores are weighted: for example, when computing average paragraph length in the whole dataset, average paragraph length in each text is weighted by the number of paragraphs in this text. For Flesch-Kincaid grade level (FKGL) we used a formula with constants that were adapted

[3] http://zlat.spb.ru/

[4] https://tika.apache.org/

[5] https://github.com/nlpub/pymystem3

[6] https://github.com/Mottl/ru_punkt

Metric	Original	Adapted
Words	885167	268409
Unique words	89318	32762
Sentences	69737	29003
Par length / text*	250.45	180.29
Punctuation / sent*	2.40	1.66
Sentences / par*	3.15	3.19
Average TTR	0.42	0.43
Words / par*	39.06	28.70
Word length / text*	5.08	4.89
Average FKGL	6.04	4.49

Table 1: Characteristics of adapted and original texts. Sent = sentence, par = paragraph. * - weighted average.

for Russian texts[7]. In this formula, the number of vowels in the word is considered to be the number of syllables.

It can be seen that original and adapted texts vary in length with the originals having more words on average. However, the number of sentences per paragraph stays almost the same. Average word length and sentence complexity (approximated by the average number of punctuation characters per sentence) are slightly bigger in the original versions. Adapted texts also have higher readability according to the Flesch-Kincaid grade level. Nevertheless, the degree of lexical variation does not seem to change drastically according to the type-token ratio (TTR).

We also calculated the number of words in the texts that are supposed to be known to the reader on a certain level of language acquisition. There are established lexical minimums with appropriate vocabulary to every level of RaaFL (see Andryushina and Kozlova (2012), Andryushina and Kozlova (2011), Andryushina et al. (2018), Andryushina et al. (2019a), and Andryushina et al. (2019b)). These lists consist of lemmatized words, so the texts were also lemmatized before counting the percentages of known words. We also considered people's names (that is, first names, surnames and patronymics) and location names to be known to the reader, since in literature the audience quickly becomes acquainted with characters and the places where the plot is set up. We identified those words with the help of pymystem3. For example, in Table 2 A1 vocab is the percentage of words in the text that are supposed to be in an A1 level speaker of

[7]https://github.com/infoculture/plainrussian

Level	Original	Adapted
A1	57.48	62.97
A2	65.62	71.81
B1	74.3	80.69
B2	81.82	87.24
C1	89.67	92.97

Table 2: Mean amount of known vocabulary (percentage of words in the lexical minimum).

Russian's vocabulary. Because most of our texts have more experienced readers as their target audience, the amount of known vocabulary for A1 and A2 levels is lower on average.

We can see that even at the C1 level, an average speaker will most likely not recognize all words even in the adapted versions of texts. However, the percentage of known words is higher in the adapted books at all levels.

5 Text alignment

Further analysis and the use of the data for training automatic text simplification tools require an explicit alignment between original and simplified text segments. Many alignment algorithms and tools have been proposed for the creation of parallel corpora mainly in the context of machine translation research.

We used multiple alignment approaches ranging from semi-automatic to fully automatic tools. First of all, we tried InterText (Vondřička, 2014) - an editor for managing parallel texts. It has multiple options for automatic pre-alignment of the text that can then be adjusted using a graphical interface. In our work, we tried Hunalign (Varga et al., 2007). This aligner turned out to have some shortcomings, especially in aligning big texts where one version is significantly longer than the other. This is not a surprise as Hunalign (as most of the other algorithms) is developed for cross-lingual sentence alignment and not for linking texts in the same language but different levels of complexity. Nevertheless, the InterText interface provides a convenient tool that enabled a semi-automatic alignment of a smaller dataset that we can use for the evaluation of fully automatic alignment algorithms later on. Using this method we created a gold standard of 302 aligned segments taken from textbook exercises.

We tested two methods to align the entire collection of books and novels, Bleualign (Sennrich and Volk, 2010) and CATS-Align: a tool for customised

Data	Words	Vocab	Sents
Bleualign orig	345779	52010	32593
Bleualign adapt	254000	31831	30553
CATS orig	589715	55380	50673
CATS adapt	268396	32746	32382

Table 3: Alignment statistics. Vocab = vocabulary, sents = sentences, orig = original versions, adapt = adapted versions.

alignment of text simplification corpora[8] (Stajner et al., 2017). Bleualign[9] is designed for sentence-to-sentence alignment of parallel texts used for training machine translation models. The alignment is performed based on the modified BLEU score between source sentences translated into the target language and the original target language sentences. The principle of matching sentences in the same language suits our needs very well and in the case of simplified language alignment we can, therefore, skip the translation step.

CATS-Align is a tool developed specifically for aligning simplification datasets, particularly for Newsela. It offers multiple options for similarity strategies, alignment levels, alignment strategies and other parameters. Our choices were the character trigram similarity strategy that uses the log TF-IDF weighting and compares vectors with the cosine similarity, paragraph alignment level, and closest similarity alignment strategy.

As mentioned above, we chose paragraph alignment for our texts. We believe that text simplification should not consider isolated sentences only but also look at additional context. We are interested in cases where larger portions of the text are removed, sentences are merged or split or even some information is expanded. Also, creating sentence alignments out of an existing paragraph alignment is more effective and reliable than just aligning sentences from texts (Stajner et al., 2017). Hence, we can easily extend the dataset with additional linking between individual sentences later on.

Using Bleualign on our data resulted in 7452 aligned paragraphs, and 9352 with CATS-Align. Other statistics, such as total numbers of word tokens, sentences, and the number of unique words (vocabulary) can be found in Table 3.

Among the CATS alignments, multiple original

[8]https://github.com/neosyon/SimpTextAlign

[9]https://github.com/rsennrich/Bleualign

Aligner	Strict F1	Lax F1
Bleualign	0.90	0.90
CATS	0.98	0.98

Table 4: Alignment evaluation.

paragraphs end up being aligned with more than one different adapted paragraph, and vice versa. Therefore, we only have 7671 unique original paragraphs and 9202 unique adapted paragraphs. However, sometimes having multiple simplified options for one paragraph can be helpful. And, if needed, the cosine similarity scores that CATS provides for each pair of paragraphs can help choose between multiple versions of one paragraph alignment (that is, the pair with the highest score can be chosen from multiple pairs with good scores). With Bleualign, non-unique alignments happen only with paragraphs that are repeated in the original and adapted texts - for example, the word "Pause." in plays.

In order to evaluate the alignment quality, we employed strict and relaxed (lax) F1 scores, as in Sennrich and Volk (2010). We considered precision to be the number of correct alignments per the number of proposed alignments, and recall to be the number of correct alignments per the number of alignments in the reference corpus. However, for strict F1 score we only considered an alignment correct if it matched the reference alignment exactly, and for lax F1 score an alignment was considered correct if both sides overlapped with the original paragraph pair. We used the small, hand-aligned dataset for alignment evaluation. The results are presented in Table 4.

As can be seen, although both aligners showed good results, CATS-Align performed better on hand-aligned data. When investigating the errors of Bleualign, we found out that most of the erroneous alignments happen because the aligner takes some additional sentences from the next paragraphs. This seems to only happen with adapted paragraphs. One possible reason is the size mismatch between original and adapted texts. However, when aligning longer books and novels, this might be appropriate, since sometimes longer paragraphs from the original texts are split into multiple paragraphs during adaptation, so it can be good to grab additional adapted paragraphs during alignment to match a longer original one.

To study the impact of different aligners on

downstream applications, we then decided to compare the performance on simplification models when using different alignment tools (see below).

6 Neural text simplification

In order to evaluate the impact of alignment, we built neural text simplification models from the collected training data. We chose the architecture based on (Nisioi et al., 2017), which has proven to perform well on English-Simple English data. This architecture is openly available online[10] and has some modifications that have further improved its performance (Cooper and Shardlow, 2020). We used OpenNMT-py (Klein et al., 2017) to build our models.

Similar to the original paper, we used an architecture with 2 LSTM layers with hidden states of 500 and 500 hidden units. The dropout probability was set to 0.3. SGD was used as an optimizer, and global attention and input feeding were employed. We also employed the default learning rate of 1.0 with the decay of 0.7. The vocabulary size was set to 50000, which also happen to suit our needs, since, as can be seen from Table 3, the vocabularies of the original paragraphs only slightly exceed this number, and the adapted vocabularies are even smaller.

For evaluation, we used the BLEU and SARI metrics from the EASSE library (Alva-Manchego et al., 2019) and the aforementioned Flesch-Kincaid Grade Level score with constants optimized for Russian. We evaluated our models on both test sets that consisted of data from the same books and novels but which the models have not seen during training, and the small hand-crafted dataset used for alignment evaluation, which consists predominantly of excerpts from children's literature. The test and development set sizes for the dataset aligned with Bleualign were both 1000 paragraphs, and for the data aligned with CATS - 1500 paragraphs. The best results for each system on larger test sets can be seen in Table 5.

Because there are no state-of-the-art Russian automatic text simplification systems yet, we don't have anything to compare these scores to. In the original paper, the highest BLEU score was 87.50, and the highest SARI was 38.59. FKGL scores were not reported. However, this system was built for a different language and trained on a bigger corpus with sentence-level alignment.

Aligner	BLEU	SARI	FKGL
Bleualign	21.68	42.97	2.82
CATS	14.69	40.94	2.82

Table 5: Simplification evaluation – larger automatically aligned test sets.

Aligner	BLEU	SARI	FKGL
Bleualign	10.86	35.53	3.33
CATS	7.51	33.84	2.72

Table 6: Simplification evaluation – small manually aligned test set.

As can be seen, models trained on the data aligned with Bleualign tend to have higher BLEU scores. However, the SARI scores for both datasets are close, and the outputs are equally readable according to FKGL.

As for the performance on completely unseen out-of-domain data, both kinds of models did not show great results. The best results for each system on the small test set are presented in Table 6. It can be seen that, although the BLEU scores halve compared to the bigger test set, the SARI and FKGL scores do not show such a rapid decline. In fact, the change in readability is very little in comparison to Table 5.

Clearly, the models need further work to be able to perform well on new domains. However, the performance on larger test sets indicates that our data can be used for neural text simplification, perhaps not only as a single dataset, but also as material for fine-tuning existing models.

7 Conclusions

We have described the process of creating a parallel Russian-Simple Russian dataset made of literature texts adapted by human experts. This dataset is still a work in progress. For now, we have described some linguistic properties of our texts and established differences between various alignment strategies. We also provide initial tests on the use of the data for neural text simplification. In the future we plan to add sentence alignments and further improvements to the automatic text simplification derived from the data. Data and models will be publicly released if copyrights permit.

[10] https://github.com/senisioi/NeuralTextSimplification

References

Iskander Akhmetov, Alexander Krassovitsky, Irina Ualiyeva, Alexander Gelbukh, and Rustam Mussabayev. 2020. An open-source lemmatizer for russian language based on tree regression models. *Research in Computing Science*, 149:147–153.

Fernando Alva-Manchego, Louis Martin, Carolina Scarton, and Lucia Specia. 2019. EASSE: Easier automatic sentence simplification evaluation. In *Proceedings of the 2019 Conference on Empirical Methods in Natural Language Processing and the 9th International Joint Conference on Natural Language Processing (EMNLP-IJCNLP): System Demonstrations*, pages 49–54, Hong Kong, China. Association for Computational Linguistics.

N. P. Andryushina and T. V. Kozlova. 2011. *Lexical minimum for Russian as a foreign language. Base level.* Zlatoust Publishing House, Russia, Saint Petersberg.

N. P. Andryushina and T. V. Kozlova. 2012. *Lexical minimum for Russian as a foreign language. Elementary level.* Zlatoust Publishing House, Russia, Saint Petersberg.

Natalia Andryushina, Irina Afanaseva, Galina Bitekhtina, Liubov Klobukova, and Irina IAtsenko. 2019a. *Lexical minimum for Russian as a foreign language. Second certification level.* Zlatoust Publishing House, Russia, Saint Petersberg.

Natalia Andryushina, Irina Afanaseva, Larisa Dunaeva, Liubov Klobukova, Lidiia Krasilnikova, and Irina IAtsenko. 2019b. *Lexical minimum for Russian as a foreign language. Third certification level.* Zlatoust Publishing House, Russia, Saint Petersberg.

Natalia Andryushina, Galina Bitekhtina, Liubov Klobukova, Larisa Noreiko, and Irina Odintsova. 2018. *Lexical minimum for Russian as a foreign language. First certification level.* Zlatoust Publishing House, Russia, Saint Petersberg.

Laetitia Brouwers, Delphine Bernhard, Anne-Laure Ligozat, and Thomas François. 2014. Syntactic sentence simplification for French. In *Proceedings of the 3rd Workshop on Predicting and Improving Text Readability for Target Reader Populations (PITR)*, pages 47–56, Gothenburg, Sweden. Association for Computational Linguistics.

Michael Cooper and Matthew Shardlow. 2020. CombiNMT: An exploration into neural text simplification models. In *Proceedings of the 12th Language Resources and Evaluation Conference*, pages 5588–5594, Marseille, France. European Language Resources Association.

Oksana Dereza, Dmitry Kayutenko, and Alyona Fenogenova. 2016. Automatic morpho-logical analysis for russian: A comparative study. In *Proceedings of the International Conference Dialogue 2016. Computational linguistics and intellectual technologies. Student session (online publication).*

Núria Gala, Anaïs Tack, Ludivine Javourey-Drevet, Thomas François, and Johannes C. Ziegler. 2020. Alector: A parallel corpus of simplified French texts with alignments of misreadings by poor and dyslexic readers. In *Proceedings of the 12th Language Resources and Evaluation Conference*, pages 1353–1361, Marseille, France. European Language Resources Association.

Vadim Gudkov, Olga Mitrofanova, and Elizaveta Filippskikh. 2020. Automatically ranked Russian paraphrase corpus for text generation. In *Proceedings of the Fourth Workshop on Neural Generation and Translation*, Online. Association for Computational Linguistics.

David Kauchak. 2013. Improving text simplification language modeling using unsimplified text data. In *Proceedings of the 51st Annual Meeting of the Association for Computational Linguistics (Volume 1: Long Papers)*, pages 1537–1546, Sofia, Bulgaria. Association for Computational Linguistics.

Guillaume Klein, Yoon Kim, Yuntian Deng, Jean Senellart, and Alexander Rush. 2017. OpenNMT: Open-source toolkit for neural machine translation. In *Proceedings of ACL 2017, System Demonstrations*, pages 67–72, Vancouver, Canada. Association for Computational Linguistics.

Antonina Laposhina, Tatiana Veselovskaya, Mariia Lebedeva, and Olga Kupreshchenko. 2018. Automated text readability assessment for Russian second language learners. In *Komp'juternaja Lingvistika i Intellektual'nye Tehnologii*, pages 396–406.

Christiane Maaß. 2019. Easy language and beyond: How to maximize the accessibility of communication. pages 1 – 41, Hildesheim.

Sergiu Nisioi, Sanja Štajner, Simone Paolo Ponzetto, and Liviu P. Dinu. 2017. Exploring neural text simplification models. In *Proceedings of the 55th Annual Meeting of the Association for Computational Linguistics (Volume 2: Short Papers)*, pages 85–91, Vancouver, Canada. Association for Computational Linguistics.

Ellie Pavlick and Chris Callison-Burch. 2016. Simple PPDB: A paraphrase database for simplification. In *Proceedings of the 54th Annual Meeting of the Association for Computational Linguistics (Volume 2: Short Papers)*, pages 143–148, Berlin, Germany. Association for Computational Linguistics.

Ilya Segalovich. 2003. Fast morphological algorithm with unknown word guessing induced by a dictionary for a web search engine. In *Proceedings of the International Conference on Machine Learning; Models, Technologies and Applications)*, pages 73–280, Las Vegas, Nevada, USA.

Rico Sennrich and Martin Volk. 2010. MT-based sentence alignment for OCR-generated parallel texts. In *Proceedings of AMTA 2010.*

Sanja Stajner, Marc Franco-Salvador, Simone Paolo Ponzetto, Paolo Rosso, and Heiner Stuckenschmidt. 2017. Sentence alignment methods for improving text simplification systems. In *Proceedings of the 55th Annual Meeting of the Association for Computational Linguistics, ACL 2017, Vancouver, Canada, July 30 - August 4, Volume 2: Short Papers*, pages 97–102.

Dániel Varga, Péter Halácsy, András Kornai, Viktor Nagy, László Németh, and Viktor Trón. 2007. Parallel corpora for medium density languages. *Recent Advances in Natural Language Processing IV*.

Pavel Vondřička. 2014. Aligning parallel texts with InterText. In *Proceedings of the Ninth International Conference on Language Resources and Evaluation (LREC'14)*, pages 1875–1879, Reykjavik, Iceland. European Language Resources Association (ELRA).

Wei Xu, Chris Callison-Burch, and Courtney Napoles. 2015. Problems in current text simplification research: New data can help. *Transactions of the Association for Computational Linguistics*, 3:283–297.

Xingxing Zhang and Mirella Lapata. 2017. Sentence simplification with deep reinforcement learning. In *Proceedings of the 2017 Conference on Empirical Methods in Natural Language Processing*, pages 584–594, Copenhagen, Denmark. Association for Computational Linguistics.

Multilingual Named Entity Recognition and Matching Using BERT and Dedupe for Slavic Languages

Marko Prelevikj
Laboratory for Data Technologies,
University of Ljubljana,
Ljubljana, Slovenia
marko.prelevikj@gmail.com

Slavko Žitnik
Laboratory for Data Technologies,
University of Ljubljana,
Ljubljana, Slovenia
slavko.zitnik@fri.uni-lj.si

Abstract

This paper describes the University of Ljubljana (UL FRI) Group's submissions to the shared task at the Balto-Slavic Natural Language Processing (BSNLP) 2021 Workshop. We experiment with multiple BERT-based models, pre-trained in multi-lingual, Croatian-Slovene-English and Slovene-only data. We perform training iteratively and on the concatenated data of previously available NER datasets. For the normalization task we use Stanza lemmatizer, while for entity matching we implemented a baseline using the Dedupe library. The performance of evaluations suggests that multi-source settings outperform less-resourced approaches. The best NER models achieve 0.91 F-score on Slovene training data splits while the best official submission achieved F-scores of 0.84 and 0.78 for relaxed partial matching and strict settings, respectively. In multi-lingual NER setting we achieve F-scores of 0.82 and 0.74.

1 Introduction

Natural Language Processing (NLP) has recently become more popular, especially due to advancements in deep learning that helped to achieve superior results for various NLP tasks. One of the main issues - adaptation of models to low-resourced languages has been nicely addressed by multi-lingual and large pretrained models. Languages such as English, German, Spanish are very well developed, with a lot of resources, while on the other hand, under-developed languages, such as the Slavic languages, have less annotated resources. Still, research may show that highly inflected languages contain more semantic information that could be exploited using NLP in the future.

In this paper we explore existing resources for Slavic languages, more particularly, Slovene. We use novel BERT-based approaches (Devlin et al., 2018) and pretrained models, such as the CroSlo-Engual BERT (Ulčar and Robnik-Šikonja, 2020). We especially focused into how well they perform for the NER task which takes part in BSNLP 2021, and how we can improve its performance with pre-existing data sets, such as ssj500k (Krek et al., 2019) and BSNLP 2017 datasets.

Additionally, we provide a simple strategy for training the Dedupe method (Gregg and Eder, 2019) as part of the Entity Matching task. The strategy is based on choosing positive and negative examples for Dedupe, which manages to outperform the baseline of assigning a single cluster to all entities on a language level. Finally, we utilize NLP pipelines to perform PoS tagging of the documents and bring the named entities in a normalized form.

The paper is organized as follows. We first describe the Shared Task (Section 2), then present our method variations for named entity recognition and matching (Section 3). We conclude the paper with a subset of results and discussion (Section 4).

2 Task Description

2.1 Tasks

The BSNLP 2021 challenge consists of the three tasks: (a) Named Entity Detection and Classification, also known as Named Entity Recognition (NER), (b) Name Lemmatization (NL), and (c) Entity Matching (EM). The NER task focuses on detection and classification of named entities (NEs) in 5 classes: persons (PER), organizations (ORG), locations (LOC), events (EVT), and products (PRO). The purpose of the NL task is to compute the normal form of the detected named entities. Finally, the EM task connects all NE mentions that refer to the same entity with a unique identifier across the data set. The identifier should be the same on document-level, language-level, and cross-

Proceedings of the 8th BSNLP Workshop on Balto-Slavic Natural Language Processing, pages 80–85
April 20, 2021.

language level.

2.2 Data

The provided data sets consist of two sets of data: (a) the raw documents retrieved from the Web, and (b) the annotations for each document, respectively. Further details about the data can be found on the BSNLP 2021 shared task official web page[1].

The data sets focus on various topics, such as Donald Trump, European Commission, Nord Stream, etc. Topics cover a variety of named entities, and thus it is worth exploring and comparing how the mentions are occurring across different languages.

2.3 Our Work

We have made an effort to participate in all of the described tasks. We detect and extract the NEs from the raw documents, normalize them, and try to link the mentions which correspond to the same entity. However, our focus lies within the scope of the NER task. More specifically, we are interested in the performance of our models on the Slovene part of the data sets, as our group specializes on improving the tools for digitization of the Slovene language.

3 Methods

In this section we describe the methodology we used to obtain our submission results. To do so, we built a pipeline which first pre-processes the provided data in a format, appropriate for training. Pre-processed data is then used to train NER models, normalize the NE occurrences, and find matches among them. In the last step we merge all the obtained results to create a BSNLP-compatible output.

3.1 Data Preprocessing and Entity Normalization

The provided data consists of two distinct parts: the raw documents, and the annotations for the corresponding documents. The first part of our pipeline merges both parts together. To do so, we tokenize the contents of the raw documents and detect the annotations of the NE within the tokens. The NE annotations are following the widely used IOB2 format (Ratnaparkhi, 1998). The tokenizers split the documents into sentences with corresponding words (tokens). So, in the end we obtain the tokens, the sentence they are a part of, and the ground truth annotation of the NEs.

We use the CLASSLA[2](Ljubešić, 2020) NLP pipeline, which we applied to the Slovene and Bulgarian parts of the provided data sets. For the rest of the languages we use Stanza library (Qi et al., 2020). These tokenizers are related: CLASSLA is a fork of the Stanza project, which specializes in Balkan languages. The tokenizers also provide processors for lemmatization of the tokens, and Part of Speech (PoS) taggers. Since our focus is the NER task, we used the lemmatization provided from the tokenizers as our NL submission. The PoS information is later used for the EM task.

3.2 Named Entity Recognition

As previously mentioned, we focused our efforts in exploring the performance of NER models for the Slovene language. Furthermore, we were interested in the performance of contemporary BERT (Devlin et al., 2018) and RoBERTa (Liu et al., 2019) based models. We further trained the pre-trained models for the NER downstream task.

From the large set of BERT-based models we used (a) the BERT-Base Multilingual-Cased[3] (M-Cased) and (b) BERT-Base Multilingual-Uncased[4] (M-Uncased) models which are both pre-trained by the original BERT authors (Devlin et al., 2018) on multiple languages. Additionally, we use (c) the CroSloEngual BERT[5] (Ulčar and Robnik-Šikonja, 2020), which is pre-trained on the Croatian, Slovene, and English languages and (d) the recently published SloBERTa 1.0[6] and (e) SloBERTa 2.0[7] models, which are pre-trained for the Slovene language only.

We use the following hyper-parameters for all of the models:

- epochs: 5,
- batch size: 32,
- maximum sentence size: 128 tokens,
- AdamW Optimizer learning rate: $3e-5$, and
- AdamW Optimzer epsilon: $1e-8$.

[1]http://bsnlp.cs.helsinki.fi/shared-task.html (Accessed: March 6, 2021).

[2]https://github.com/clarinsi/classla-stanfordnlp

[3]https://huggingface.co/bert-base-multilingual-cased

[4]https://huggingface.co/bert-base-multilingual-uncased

[5]http://hdl.handle.net/11356/1330

[6]http://hdl.handle.net/11356/1387

[7]http://hdl.handle.net/11356/1397

We trained multiple bundles of models, which we further describe in Appendix A. We use the standard F_1 based evaluation metrics, proposed in the BSNLP shared task guidelines: Relaxed Partial (RP), Relaxed Exact (RE), and Strict (S). Additionally, we use the Seqeval's (Nakayama, 2018) micro F_1 score to perform evaluation of the models as we are training them.

3.3 Entity Matching

For the entity matching task, we used the Dedupe (Gregg and Eder, 2019) library, which links the NEs based on provided positive and negative examples. The Dedupe takes into account additional attributes, apart from the NE mention. In our case, we use the lemma and the PoS tag obtained by the tokenizer.

Since the Dedupe approach is very memory greedy, we first group all the mentions by their first character. Then, we group all of the ground-truth mentions by their EM identifier, from which we sample $K = 3$ random chosen occurrences which are used as positive examples. The more demanding part is generating negative samples, which can grow exponentially when computing all of the possible combinations of non-matching NEs. To reduce this number, we toss a fair coin ($P(Heads) = P(Tails) = \frac{1}{2}$), in order to determine whether to keep the combination or not. Whenever the coin determines to keep the negative example, we use the same procedure for generating the negative examples as we do for the positive examples.

4 Results and Discussion

The training of the NER models is divided into multiple training bundles (see Appendix A). First we evaluated our models for all languages on a test set from each language - Table 1. The second training bundle focuses on the performance of the models on each (unseen) data set. The models were trained on three topics in a corpus and evaluated on the fourth one - the results are shown in Table 2. All these models were fine tuned based on M-Cased model as it is case-sensitive and it covers all of the languages from the BSNLP 2021 shared task.

The Slovene-based bundles try to identify the best model for the NER task. With the Slovene-All bundle we establish a baseline for the performance of the chosen models on the Slovene portion of the BSNLP 2021 data set. The results for the Slovene-

Lang	RP	RE	S	N
all	0.96	0.92	0.93	0.93
bg	0.97	0.95	0.95	0.95
cs	0.97	0.93	0.94	0.94
pl	0.96	0.92	0.93	0.93
ru	0.94	0.88	0.88	0.88
sl	0.92	0.86	0.89	0.89
uk	0.94	0.87	0.89	0.89
all	0.82	0.74	0.74	0.45
bg	0.85	0.80	0.78	0.22
cs	0.83	0.78	0.77	0.43
pl	0.86	0.81	0.82	0.49
ru	0.79	0.68	0.68	0.47
sl	0.84	0.76	0.78	0.42
uk	0.81	0.75	0.75	0.55

Table 1: Results for the Multilingual training bundle per language. All of the models were trained in FF mode. The language notation means that the corresponding model was trained and tested on that portion of the BSNLP 2021 data set. The table also contains the Normalization (N) score for the Name Lemmatization task. The bottom part shows official shared task results.

Set	RP	RE	S	N
N.Stream	0.95	0.92	0.93	0.93
Ryanair	0.92	0.88	0.88	0.88
Brexit	0.92	0.85	0.87	0.87
A.Bibi	0.89	0.81	0.82	0.82

Table 2: Results for the "Leave-One-Out" training bundle for all languages. We trained the M-Cased model in FF training mode for all data sets, except the one we tested. The table also contains the Normalization (N) score for the Name Lemmatization task.

Model	Mode	RP	RE	S
CroSloEngual	FC	**0.93**	0.87	0.90
SloBERTa 1.0	FF	0.93	**0.88**	0.90
SloBERTa 2.0	FC	0.93	0.87	0.89
SloBERTa 2.0	FF	0.93	0.87	0.89
CroSloEngual	FF	0.93	0.88	**0.90**
SloBERTa 1.0	FC	0.93	0.87	0.89
M-Cased	FF	0.93	0.87	0.89
M-Cased	FC	0.92	0.88	0.90
M-Uncased	FF	0.76	0.65	0.66
M-Uncased	FC	0.76	0.64	0.65

Table 3: Results for the Slovene-All training bundle.

Model	M	P	R	F_1
SloBERTa 1.0	FF	0.90	**0.88**	**0.89**
CroSloEngual	FC	0.90	0.87	0.88
SloBERTa 1.0	FC	0.90	0.86	0.88
M-Cased	FC	**0.91**	0.85	0.88
CroSloEngual	FF	0.89	0.86	0.88
M-Cased	FF	0.88	0.84	0.86
SloBERTa 2.0	FF	0.87	0.82	0.84
SloBERTa 2.0	FC	0.87	0.82	0.84
M-Uncased	FC	0.88	0.79	0.83
M-Uncased	FF	0.87	0.78	0.83

Table 4: Results for the Slovene Miscellaneous Only training bundle after applying the best SMO model. Training on the Slovene part of the BSNLP 2021 data set only on the EVT and PRO NE categories.

All bundle are presented in Table 3 which suggest that the CroSloEngual or the SloBERTa models are the best models to be used, which significantly outperform the M-Cased and M-Uncased models, which we take as a baseline in our case.

The most "complex" training bundle is the Slovene-Miscellaneous bundle is trained two-fold: first on 4-category data sets, and then uses an additional model to split the MISC class into PRO and EVT. For this purpose, we first explored the performance of the MISC classifier using the Slovene-Miscellaneous-Only training bundle. The results of the SMO bundle are shown in Table 4. Later we use only the best model from the SMO bundle to predict the MISC class of the models in the SM bundle. The results for the SM bundle are shown in Table 5.

The results from Table 5 also display the impact of additional data sets when training a Slovene model for the BSNLP data sets. The best-performing model (SloBERTa 1.0) is trained on all available BSNLP documents (a union of the 2017 and 2021 data sets), which suggests that more data can lead to better results. The rest of the trained models listed in Table 5 use the additionally introduced data set - ssj500k. Note that in this setting we show results for all 5 NE categories. We trained the models in two settings: (a) *Combination* setting takes all data at one and trains the model, while (b) *Iterative* first trains the model on one dataset, then continues training on another, etc. The models in Table 5 are first trained on 4 NE classes and then additional model is employed to further classify MISC classes into PRO and EVT (using best model from SMO bundle) to get the results.

By comparing the results from Table 3 and Table 5 we can notice that the two-step prediction (i.e. 4 NEs first and then additionally classifying PRO and EVT) of the NEs can be beneficial as it increases the strict matching F_1 score. Still, the increase does not seem to be significant, so in practice it can also be omitted to utilize less computing resources.

For the EM task, we obtained the results shown in Table 7. We have managed to improve over the 2 out of 3 metrics of the baseline. The baseline in our case is a single entity ID for all NE occurrences. We notice that with our approach we greatly improve the precision, but fail to identify many of the related entities, i.e., very low recall score.

For the participation in the Shared Task we submitted 5 system responses - one multi-language and others only for the Slovene language. In Table 6 we show results of the best performing system. Other systems achieved similar results with up to 1% difference, so there were no significant differences among them. The bottom part of Table 1 and Table 7 contain results of a M-Cased model, trained in a FF setting. We observe that the results of a multi-lingual model are much lower than our initial results. Also in the shared task data, results for the US election 2020 data set are in general better (i.e. 5-10%) than for Covid-19 dataset.

The code to reproduce the experiment results and re-train the models is publicly available in our public GitHub repository[8].

5 Conclusion

We have built a pipeline that addresses the BSNLP 2021 shared task. The pipeline normalizes the in-

[8]https://github.com/UL-FRI-Zitnik/BSNLP-2021-Shared-Task

Model	Training data sets				Train	Metrics		
	ssj500k	2017	2021	2017 & 2021		RP	RE	S
SloBERTa 1.0				X	Comb	0.94	0.89	0.91
CroSloEngual	X		X		Iter	0.93	0.88	0.91
SloBERTa 2.0	X		X		Iter	0.93	0.88	0.90
M-Cased	X			X	Iter	0.91	0.88	0.89
M-Uncased	X			X	Comb	0.78	0.68	0.69

Table 5: Results for the Slovene-Miscellaneous training bundle. The shown results are for the models trained in the FF learning mode. These results show the best training combinations per the RP metric of each used pre-trained model. The 2017, 2021 refer to BSNLP data sets.

SloBERTa 1.0 2017 & 2021 Comb FF	US Election 2020				Covid 2019				All Slovene data			
	RP	RE	S	N	RP	RE	S	N	RP	RE	S	N
	0.89	0.82	0.85	0.44	0.78	0.69	0.68	0.40	0.84	0.76	0.78	0.42

Table 6: Official results for the Slovene part of BSNLP 2021 Shared Task data. Apart from the model in the table, the following models were evaluated and performed similarly: (a) CroSloEngual ssj500k + 2021 Iter FC, (b) CroSloEngual ssj500k + 2021 Iter FF and (c) SloBERTa 2.0 ssj500k + 2021 Iter FF.

	Level	P	R	F_1
Baseline	Document	0.15	0.91	0.26
	Language	0.13	0.82	0.22
	Cross-Lang	0.11	0.81	0.19
Dedupe	Document	0.76	0.24	0.37
	Language	0.88	0.55	0.68
	Cross-Lang	0.83	0.09	0.17
Shared Task results	Document	0.72	0.20	0.32
	Language	0.76	0.14	0.24
	Cross-Lang	0.61	0.00	0.01

Table 7: Results for the EM task. The baseline consists of a single cluster for all of the entities.

puts, builds NER models, builds EM models, and persists the results. All the source code is publicly available. Furthermore, we have explored multiple options on how to improve the Slovene language models using more data and selecting specialized models for the targeted language. Finally, we present a simple strategy for Entity Matching which can be used for Language-Level linking of NEs.

References

Jacob Devlin, Ming-Wei Chang, Kenton Lee, and Kristina Toutanova. 2018. BERT: pre-training of deep bidirectional transformers for language understanding. *CoRR*, abs/1810.04805.

Forest Gregg and Derek Eder. 2019. Dedupe. `https://github.com/dedupeio/dedupe`.

Simon Krek, Kaja Dobrovoljc, Tomaž Erjavec, Sara Može, Nina Ledinek, Nanika Holz, Katja Zupan, Polona Gantar, Taja Kuzman, Jaka Čibej, Špela Arhar Holdt, Teja Kavčič, Iza Škrjanec, Dafne Marko, Lucija Jezeršek, and Anja Zajc. 2019. Training corpus ssj500k 2.2. Slovenian language resource repository CLARIN.SI.

Yinhan Liu, Myle Ott, Naman Goyal, Jingfei Du, Mandar Joshi, Danqi Chen, Omer Levy, Mike Lewis, Luke Zettlemoyer, and Veselin Stoyanov. 2019. Roberta: A robustly optimized BERT pretraining approach. *CoRR*, abs/1907.11692.

Nikola Ljubešić. 2020. The CLASSLA-StanfordNLP model for lemmatisation of non-standard slovenian 1.1. Slovenian language resource repository CLARIN.SI.

Hiroki Nakayama. 2018. seqeval: A python framework for sequence labeling evaluation. Software available from https://github.com/chakki-works/seqeval.

Peng Qi, Yuhao Zhang, Yuhui Zhang, Jason Bolton, and Christopher D. Manning. 2020. Stanza: A Python natural language processing toolkit for many human languages. In *Proceedings of the 58th Annual Meeting of the Association for Computational Linguistics: System Demonstrations*.

Adwait Ratnaparkhi. 1998. Maximum entropy models for natural language ambiguity resolution.

Matej Ulčar and Marko Robnik-Šikonja. 2020. Finest bert and crosloengual bert: less is more in multilingual models.

A NER Training Strategy

Training of the NER models depends on a number of factors which include the base model used, the data sets used for training and the target language for training. The provided data is split into 20% testing data, and 80% training data. The training data is further split into 10% (8% of all data) for validation, leaving 72% of all data for training.

Base Model We use 5 distinct BERT-based models for the training process. The majority of the models are focused towards the Slovene language.

Training Mode We differentiate between propagating the changes only in the fully-connected layer (FC learning), while the pre-trained model is intact, and fully fine-tuning the entire model in addition to training the fully-connected layer on top (FF learning).

Training Data Used The BSNLP shared task data is split per years when the challenge was held: 2017, 2019, and 2021. The data from 2017 has 4 classes (PER, ORG, LOC, and miscellaneous - MISC) which is inconsistent with the 2019 and 2021 data. The data from 2019 is a subset of the data from 2021, so we do not take the 2019 subset explicitly into account. Additionally, we enrich BSNLP's Slovene corpus with the ssj500k corpus (Krek et al., 2019), which is annotated consistently with the data from the BSNLP 2017 shared task.

Training Data Union Due to having multiple training sets, we also explore how they impact the performance of the trained models. In addition to training on a single data set, we train on unions of the data sets: sequentially training on multiple data sets, e.g., training first on ssj500k, and then BSNLP 2017, or combining the data sets first and learning on all data at once, e.g. training the model on the union of the ssj500k and BSNLP 2017 data sets.

A.1 Training bundles

We trained a significant amount of models in order to explore the effects of all aforementioned factors.

Multilingual (M) Trained only on the Multilingual Cased and Uncased models, in FF learning modes. The training and testing is performed on each language subset of the BSNLP 2021 data. We also train a model on all available languages.

Leave-One-Out (L1O) Training only on the Multilingual-Cased model in FF learning mode. In this mode we train the model in a leave-one-out-cross-validation fashion, where we rotate the excluded data set on which we evaluate the performance of the model.

Slovene-All (SA) Trained on all 5 models, in both learning modes. The training and testing data sets include only the Slovene portion of the BSNLP 2021 data set.

Slovene-Miscellaneous-Only (SMO) Trained on all 5 models, in both learning modes. The training and testing data sets include only the Slovene portion of the BSNLP 2021 data set which is reduced to only annotations for EVT and PRO classes. We build these models as an extension of the SM training bundle, in order to classify the MISC class into either EVT or PRO.

Slovene-Miscellaneous (SM) Training is performed on all 5 models, in both learning modes, including all possible combinations of the Slovene training data sets. The testing is performed on all available data sets having the EVT and PRO categories merged into MISC. Then we employ best model from the SMO bundle to further differentiate EVT and PRO classes from MISC predictions. In the end we built 100 distinct models, having 400 evaluations of the testing data sets.

Priberam Labs at the 3rd Shared Task on SlavNER

Pedro Ferreira, Rúben Cardoso, Afonso Mendes
Priberam Labs / Portugal
{pedro.ferreira, ruben.cardoso, amm}@priberam.pt

Abstract

This document describes our participation at the 3rd Shared Task on SlavNER, part of the 8th Balto-Slavic Natural Language Processing Workshop, where we focused exclusively in the Named Entity Recognition (NER) task. We addressed this task by combining multi-lingual contextual embedding models, such as XLM-R (Conneau et al., 2020), with character-level embeddings and a biaffine classifier (Yu et al., 2020). This allowed us to train down-stream models for NER using all the available training data. We are able to show that this approach results in good performance when replicating the scenario of the 2nd Shared Task.

1 Introduction

This document describes our participation at the 3rd Shared Task on SlavNER, part of the 8th Balto-Slavic Natural Language Processing Workshop, held in conjunction with the 16th Conference of the European Chapter of the Association for Computational Linguistics (EACL). It includes three different subtasks: Named Entity Recognition (NER), including detection and classification, lemmatization, and cross-lingual entity linking. The differentiating feature of this shared task is the focus on six Slavic languages: Bulgarian (BG), Czech (CS), Polish (PL), Russian (RU), Slovene (SL), and Ukrainian (UK).

We focus our participation exclusively on the task of NER, and we base ourselves on recent developments that show that cross-lingual embeddings produce good results for a wide range of languages and tasks (Pires et al., 2019; Hu et al., 2020).

Our overall approach is heavily based in Yu et al. (2020), and uses both contextual and character-level embeddings as input to a sequence of models which culminates in a biaffine classifier. Due to the multilingual nature of this task we explore multilingual contextual embedding models, such as Multilingual BERT (Devlin et al., 2019) and XLM-RoBERTa (Conneau et al., 2020), as a way of leveraging all the available training data at once. It differs from the approaches presented in the previous edition of the shared task (Piskorski et al., 2019) in the following aspects: (i) we explore more contextual embedding approaches; (ii) we further finetune the contextual embedding model while training the downstream model; (iii) we use the same topics in our train and development sets; and (iv) we use a different classifier architecture.

Our approach resulted in strong performance when replicating the scenario of the 2nd Shared Task on SlavNER.

2 Related Work

Named Entity Recognition corresponds to the task of both finding and classifying named entities in text. Some of the most common approaches to tackle NER that make use of neural networks involve combining models such as Conditional Random Fields (CRFs, Lafferty et al. 2001), bidirectional Long-Short-Term-Memory Neural Networks (biLSTMs, Schuster and Paliwal 1997), and Convolutional Neural Networks (CNNs, LeCun et al. 1989). Two examples of such approaches are Chiu and Nichols (2016) and Ma and Hovy (2016), which use biLSTMs and CNNs to build both word- and character-level features, diverging in the fact that the latter performs decoding with a CRF, while the former uses a linear layer.

With the development of better pre-trained embedding models, transfer-learning became a significant part of approaches that tackle NER. This technique implies using a pre-trained model in order to obtain an embedding for each word of the input. These representations are then used as input to a model that is able to solve the desired downstream task. In terms of pre-trained embeddings we

Proceedings of the 8th BSNLP Workshop on Balto-Slavic Natural Language Processing, pages 86–92
April 20, 2021.

highlight ELMo embeddings (Peters et al., 2018), which are trained using a bidirectional language model, the Flair embeddings (Akbik et al., 2018), trained with a character-level language model, and finally embeddings retrieved from Transformer-based models (Vaswani et al., 2017), such as BERT (Devlin et al., 2019), and RoBERTa (Liu et al., 2019). Any combination of these embeddings can be used as input to a model that is able to predict entity classes, such as a LSTM-CRF (Straková et al., 2019), a biaffine-classifier (Yu et al., 2020), or a linear layer (Devlin et al., 2019).

Particularly relevant to this work is the possibility of using pre-trained cross-lingual embeddings, such as multilingual BERT (Devlin et al., 2019) and XLM-RoBERTa (Conneau et al., 2020), both covering a high-number of languages with different scripts. Such models have been shown to perform well on different tasks and languages (Pires et al., 2019; Lewis et al., 2020; Hu et al., 2020).

In the previous edition of the SlavNER shared task (Piskorski et al., 2019) multiple submissions used multilingual BERT to retrieve cross-lingual representations. In particular, Tsygankova et al. (2019) used both word- and character-embeddings as input to a biLSTM-CRF, Arkhipov et al. (2019) further pretrained multilingual BERT on the four target Slavic languages of last shared task's edition and combined its representations with a word-level CRF, and the submission by IIUWR.PL used a combination of different embeddings, where BERT and Flair were included.

3 Approach

Our approach makes use of three key components: a multilingual contextual embedding model, a character-level embedding model, and a biaffine classifier model.

In terms of multilingual contextual embedding models we have explored three options:

1. Multilingual BERT model, which covers 104 languages, and follows the configuration of the BERT-base model (Devlin et al., 2019).

2. XLM-RoBERTa (XLM-R) model (Conneau et al., 2020), trained on 100 languages. We use the large version of the model.

3. Slavic BERT model (Arkhipov et al., 2019), which corresponds to the Multilingual BERT-model further finetuned using resources for Bulgarian, Czech, Polish and Russian. Furthermore, it also rebuilds the original vocabulary to better match these languages.

Besides finetuning the the top-layers of the contextual embedding model during training, we complement these representations with character-level embeddings, obtained with a single-layer CNN.

The biaffine classifier model follows the work by Yu et al. (2020). In particular, the token- and character-level embeddings are concatenated and fed into a Highway BiLSTM (Zhang et al., 2016) which yields a representation for each token. These representations are given to two individual Feed-Forward Neural Networks (FFNNs), responsible for creating a representation that models whether a token is the start/end of a span. Finally, these are passed to a biaffine model, which returns a *scores tensor* with all possible start-end combinations with shape $n \times n \times c$, where n is the number of tokens and c is the number of NER classes plus one, corresponding to the no-entity prediction. This scores tensor masks non-valid spans, i.e., spans where the end position is lower than the start position.

A series of heuristics is then applied to the scores tensor in order to predict spans. First, all the valid spans are retrieved and matched with the corresponding highest-scoring label. Then, all spans whose highest-scoring label corresponds to an entity are sorted by score, from highest to lowest, and are evaluated sequentially. All predicted spans are kept, unless they clash with some of the spans already validated for that input, i.e., unless they overlap with entities that were given an higher score. One of the advantages of this model is that it can model both flat and nested entities, based upon the heuristics we apply.

The model is optimized with the softmax cross-entropy loss.

4 Experimental Setup

4.1 Task

The 3rd edition of the SlavNER Shared Task includes three subtasks: Named Entity Recognition, lemmatization, and cross-lingual entity linking. The available data for this edition adds two extra languages (Slovene and Ukrainian) to the four languages covered in the 2nd edition of the shared task (Bulgarian, Czech, Polish, and Russian).

Our work targets exclusively the subtask of NER, for which there are five types of entities: persons (PER), locations (LOC), organizations (ORG), events (EVT), and products (PRO).

The evaluation of this subtask is case-insensitive, and since the goal is to correctly identify a "*bag-of-mentions*" in a document, it uses three specific metrics, two "relaxed" and one "strict":

- *Relaxed Partial Matching* (RPM) and *Relaxed Exact Matching* (REM), where the system only needs to identify at least one of the forms of a given entity to count a match (e.g. it would only need to identify *Alexandr Kogan* for both *Alexandr Kogan* and *Alexandra Kogana* to be matched). The difference between partial and strict is that the former requires matching only a part of the named entity, while the latter requires an exact match (e.g. in the previous example, matching *Kogan* would be enough for the partial metric).

- *Strict Matching* (SM), where the system has to identify each unique form of a named entity present in a given document (i.e. in the previous example both *Alexandr Kogan* and *Alexandra Kogana* would have to be predicted).

4.2 Data

The train data for the 3rd edition of the SlavNER shared task (SLAVNER2021) includes four topics and covers a total of six languages. The four topics: ASIA_BIBI, BREXIT, NORD_STREAM, and RYANAIR, were part of the data used in the 2nd edition of the SlavNER shared task (SLAVNER2019), apart from minor revisions and two extra languages, Slovene and Ukrainian. Furthermore, there is also an additional generic topic this year, OTHER, which includes only Slovene data. The two added languages have the smallest amount of documents available, 279 and 159 respectively for Slovene and Ukrainian. The other languages have more data available, ranging from 571 in the case of Russian to 918 in the case of Bulgarian.

This edition's test data includes two topics, *"Covid-19"* and *"US_election_2020"*, which are particularly challenging due to the their very specific vocabulary. The most represented language is Slovene, with 333 documents, and the least represented language is Ukrainian, with 168 documents.

Similarly to Tsygankova et al. (2019), we consider data from the 1st edition of the SlavNER shared task, which we will refer to as SLAVNER2017. It includes two topics, EU and TRUMP, and covers seven languages: Czech, Croatian, Polish, Russian, Slovak, Slovene, and Ukrainian. Despite the different set of tags, the extra data can improve the overall performance (Tsygankova et al., 2019).

We use an internal tokenizer that is able to split sentences and also words from punctuation. The data was processed in order to match the format expected by our internal framework used to train NER models, on a sentence-by-sentence basis. This requires matching the document-level annotations, as provided by the organizers of the shared task, with all the individual occurrences in the text. As mentioned in Tsygankova et al. (2019), this leads to two possible errors: matching occurrences of words that do not correspond to entities, and the opposite. The relative difference between the expected number of entities at the document-level and our number of annotations is between 0.78% and 1.6%. Besides the two aforementioned errors, we found the most common mismatches to be related with typos in entities, encoding errors of Latin-text annotations in Cyrillic documents, and errors due to our tokenization.

To make our predictions match the expected format we keep only the unique (case-insensitive) predicted entities, and remove the ones tagged as MISC, obtained when using SLAVNER2017 data.

Unless otherwise noted, train and development data use the same topics and are split by using the top 5% of sentences as development data and the remainder 95% as training data. This split is performed at the level of each topic + language, so that the original ratio of data is kept. SLAVNER2017 data is not included by default.

4.3 Training

We implement our approach using PyTorch (Paszke et al., 2019). The contextual embedding models use the Hugging-Face Transformers library (Wolf et al., 2019), and our biaffine classifier implementation mostly follows the original one[1]. Further training details can be seen in Appendix A.

5 Results

5.1 Preliminary Experiments

Our first set of experiments was conducted using SLAVNER2019 and SLAVNER2021 data. We keep NORD_STREAM and RYANAIR as test topics, and the remainder as train topics. These

[1]https://github.com/juntaoy/biaffine-ner

	Model	F1 - All RPM	REM	SM	F1 - SM - All CS	RU	BG	PL	UK	SL
2nd ST	Best Reported Scores	90.94	86.40	85.66	84.07	**88.52**	88.25	82.03	-	-
	Multilingual BERT	92.26	88.06	88.62	91.56	84.91	84.12	91.62	-	-
	Slavic BERT	**95.07**	**91.73**	**91.75**	**94.01**	87.14	**91.69**	**93.52**	-	-
	XLM-R Large	94.91	90.68	91.07	93.98	87.11	89.15	92.83	-	-
3rd ST	Multilingual BERT	93.32	88.69	89.32	92.68	85.00	88.28	91.47	**85.05**	89.99
	Slavic BERT	93.54	88.86	89.48	93.38	**87.14**	**92.51**	**93.04**	77.91	85.34
	XLM-R Large	**94.04**	**89.73**	**90.18**	**93.88**	86.14	89.33	92.76	82.86	**90.64**

Table 1: Results obtained for the topics NORD_STREAM and RYANAIR using SLAVNER2019 data (**2nd ST**) and SLAVNER2021 data (**3rd ST**).

Base	F1 - All - Score Diff RPM	REM	SM
XLM-RoBERTa-Large	94.04	89.73	90.18
- Finetune Layers	-1.10	-0.94	-1.21
- Both Topics	-2.97	-3.67	-3.38
- Char Embeds	+0.08	+0.13	+0.18
+ 2017 Data	-0.31	-0.34	-0.31

Table 2: Difference in performance obtained for the NORD_STREAM and RYANAIR topics of the SLAVNER2021 when modifying our approach.

experiments have the following goals: (i) compare our approach's performance with the official SLAVNER2019 scores; and (ii) evaluate the impact of the added languages for the same topics in SLAVNER2021.

For the SLAVNER2019 experiments we used the original test set data. As for the train data, we noticed a mismatch between the number of documents in the original data available for download and the information reported in Piskorski et al. (2019). Since the equivalent data (i.e., the same topics and languages) in this year's data matched both the expected number of documents and entities, we used it instead. For the SLAVNER2021 experiments we use the available data with the aforementioned topic splits.

The obtained results can be seen in Table 1. The impact of further finetuning Multilingual BERT with the four SLAVNER2019 languages in Slavic BERT is noticeable and it results in the best overall scores for that edition's data. However, the extra finetuning step degrades considerably the performance for the two added language in SLAVNER2021, where the model performs worse than any other. This finetune mismatch might partially explain the fact why XLM-R outperforms Slavic BERT in the overall metrics of SLAVNER2021, as opposed to what is observed for SLAVNER2019. Another key aspect for XLM-R's performance is the fact this contextual embedding model is much larger than its BERT-base counterparts (300M vs 120M parameters).

Overall, all models trained with SLAVNER2019 largely outperformed the best scores reported for the 2nd edition of the shared task[2]. We hypothesize these differences are due to: (i) a larger multilingual contextual embedding model, such as XLM-R Large; (ii) a biaffine approach which has been shown to outperform CRF approaches (Yu et al., 2020); (iii) finetuning the top layers of the contextual embedding model during training, which has a positive impact over simple feature extraction (Sun et al., 2019); and (iv) train/development sets using all non-test available topics.

The first hypothesis matches what we have observed in the results presented in Table 1. In particular, the increased model capacity of XLM-R helps to mitigate the multilingual language model tradeoff highlighted by Conneau et al. (2020), "*for a fixed-size model, the per-language capacity decreases as we increase the number of languages*".

The last two hypotheses can be discussed together with the results presented in Table 2, where we perform a simple ablation study. We can observe that not finetuning the top-layers of the contextual embedding model hurts performance. It is plausible to attribute this to the unique characteristics of the languages and entities of the task at hand, where making part of the parameters trainable allows the model to learn better contextual representations for the NER task.

Using both topics as train and development data has a large impact in terms of performance, when compared with using BREXIT as training data and ASIA_BIBI as development data. Even though the scores obtained for the development data are artificially larger, it appears that the model's ability to generalize to new topics is not affected.

The two last results of Table 2 provide us interesting insights. First, it is noticeable that adding SLAVNER2017 data degrades performance. This was something we observed for all SLAVNER2021

[2]http://bsnlp.cs.helsinki.fi/bsnlp-2019/final_ranking.pdf

	Model	CE	2017	F1 - All RPM	REM	SM	F1 - SM - All BG	CS	PL	RU	SL	UK
(S1)	XLM-R	-	-	85.24	79.51	78.92	78.94	**82.10**	84.83	73.48	83.80	76.84
(S2)	XLM-R	x	-	**85.66**	**80.07**	**79.34**	79.94	81.43	**85.38**	**73.65**	**84.24**	**77.95**
(S3)	XLM-R	-	x	84.78	79.51	78.83	**80.00**	80.69	84.76	73.39	83.46	76.27
(S4)	XLM-R	x	x	83.77	78.03	77.82	77.61	80.03	82.92	72.90	82.35	76.67
(S5)	XLM-R/Slavic BERT	-/-	x/-	84.29	78.51	77.99	77.67	80.98	82.94	72.57	83.46	76.27

Table 3: Results obtained for the test set of the 3rd edition of the shared task. **CE** - Includes contextual embeddings. **2017** - Includes SLAVNER2017 data.

Model	F1 - SM - All PER	LOC	ORG	PRO	EVT
S1	**90.88**	90.30	70.17	52.00	**11.63**
S2	90.69	90.67	**70.68**	**54.27**	10.46
S3	90.69	**90.79**	69.74	43.35	05.13
S4	90.55	90.37	69.06	39.62	07.28
S5	89.55	89.75	69.16	50.40	06.11

Table 4: Entity-level results for the test set of the 3rd edition of the shared task.

experiments, and for all SLAVNER2019 experiments excluding the one that used Multilingual BERT. Secondly, removing the character-level embeddings seems to have an almost negligible impact. However, we noticed some variance in scores among runs with regard to this change.

5.2 3rd SlavNER Shared Task Submissions

We have made a total of five submissions to this year's shared task, as detailed in Appendix B. Following the scores reported in Table 1, and the corresponding discussion in Subsection 5.1, we have decided to use XLM-R in most of our submissions. The first four submissions correspond to a XLM-R with all the possible combinations with/without character embeddings and including/not including the SLAVNER2017 data in the training data. We selected these combinations due to the observed variance of scores when using character embeddings, and due to the fact that both Ukrainian and Slovene are part of the SLAVNER2017 data. The fifth submission is an hybrid approach, where the Ukrainian and Slovene documents are predicted with a model trained with a XLM-R using both SLAVNER2021 and SLAVNER2017 data, and the predictions for the remaining languages were obtained with a Slavic BERT model.

Our submissions' scores can be seen in Table 3. The second submission, which uses a XLM-R with character embeddings, scored the highest in terms of F1 for the overall metrics and in four of the six languages in terms of strict matching F1. It is noticeable that adding the SLAVNER2017 data to the training data had a negative impact, and that the impact of character embeddings is variable. The hybrid approach (S5) did not yield the expected scores, since using Slavic BERT as the contextual embedding model did not improve performance for BG/CS/PL/RU, as opposed to what we observed in our preliminary experiments.

With regard to the entity-level results, as observed in Table 4, our scores for PRO and EVT seem subpar. After analyzing the error-log files, we noticed some common mistakes: (i) We miss some quotation marks, e.g., we predict *abcd* instead of *«abcd»*; (ii) Covid-19 related tags are mostly erroneously classified as PRO and not as EVT; and (iii) we miss topic-specific vocabulary. Some of the most common wrong/missed target predictions for the *"covid-19"* topic are *EVT-Covid-19*, *EVT-Pandemic*, and *ORG-BioNTech*, and for the *"us_election_2020"* topic are *PRO-CNN*, *ORG-The-White-House*, and *ORG-Republican-Party-USA*.

At the time of writing this document we do not yet have access to the overall results, and therefore cannot comment on our relative performance.

6 Conclusion

We have proposed a multilingual approach to the 3rd SlavNER Shared Task, where we can make use of a single model trained with multiple source languages to predict NER tags. In particular, we have shown that using a large model, such as XLM-R, coupled with character-level embeddings and a biaffine classifier is able to perform well when replicating the scenario of the 2nd Shared Task on SlavNER, as well as for the languages added to this year's edition of the SlavNER shared task.

Acknowledgments

This work is supported by the EU H2020 SELMA project (grant agreement No 957017) and the Lisbon Regional Operational Programme (Lisboa 2020), under the Portugal 2020 Partnership Agreement, through the European Regional Development Fund (ERDF), within project TRAINER (Nº045347).

References

Alan Akbik, Duncan Blythe, and Roland Vollgraf. 2018. Contextual string embeddings for sequence labeling. In *Proceedings of the 27th international conference on computational linguistics*, pages 1638–1649.

Mikhail Arkhipov, Maria Trofimova, Yurii Kuratov, and Alexey Sorokin. 2019. Tuning multilingual transformers for language-specific named entity recognition. In *Proceedings of the 7th Workshop on Balto-Slavic Natural Language Processing*, pages 89–93.

Jason PC Chiu and Eric Nichols. 2016. Named entity recognition with bidirectional lstm-cnns. *Transactions of the Association for Computational Linguistics*, 4:357–370.

Alexis Conneau, Kartikay Khandelwal, Naman Goyal, Vishrav Chaudhary, Guillaume Wenzek, Francisco Guzmán, Édouard Grave, Myle Ott, Luke Zettlemoyer, and Veselin Stoyanov. 2020. Unsupervised cross-lingual representation learning at scale. In *Proceedings of the 58th Annual Meeting of the Association for Computational Linguistics*, pages 8440–8451.

Jacob Devlin, Ming-Wei Chang, Kenton Lee, and Kristina Toutanova. 2019. Bert: Pre-training of deep bidirectional transformers for language understanding. In *Proceedings of the 2019 Conference of the North American Chapter of the Association for Computational Linguistics: Human Language Technologies, Volume 1 (Long and Short Papers)*, pages 4171–4186.

Junjie Hu, Sebastian Ruder, Aditya Siddhant, Graham Neubig, Orhan Firat, and Melvin Johnson. 2020. Xtreme: A massively multilingual multi-task benchmark for evaluating cross-lingual generalisation. In *International Conference on Machine Learning*, pages 4411–4421. PMLR.

Diederik P Kingma and Jimmy Ba. 2015. Adam: A method for stochastic optimization. In *ICLR (Poster)*.

John Lafferty, Andrew McCallum, and Fernando CN Pereira. 2001. Conditional random fields: Probabilistic models for segmenting and labeling sequence data.

Yann LeCun, Bernhard Boser, John S Denker, Donnie Henderson, Richard E Howard, Wayne Hubbard, and Lawrence D Jackel. 1989. Backpropagation applied to handwritten zip code recognition. *Neural computation*, 1(4):541–551.

Patrick Lewis, Barlas Oguz, Ruty Rinott, Sebastian Riedel, and Holger Schwenk. 2020. Mlqa: Evaluating cross-lingual extractive question answering. In *Proceedings of the 58th Annual Meeting of the Association for Computational Linguistics*, pages 7315–7330.

Yinhan Liu, Myle Ott, Naman Goyal, Jingfei Du, Mandar Joshi, Danqi Chen, Omer Levy, Mike Lewis, Luke Zettlemoyer, and Veselin Stoyanov. 2019. Roberta: A robustly optimized bert pretraining approach. *arXiv preprint arXiv:1907.11692*.

Xuezhe Ma and Eduard Hovy. 2016. End-to-end sequence labeling via bi-directional lstm-cnns-crf. In *Proceedings of the 54th Annual Meeting of the Association for Computational Linguistics (Volume 1: Long Papers)*, pages 1064–1074.

Adam Paszke, Sam Gross, Francisco Massa, Adam Lerer, James Bradbury, Gregory Chanan, Trevor Killeen, Zeming Lin, Natalia Gimelshein, Luca Antiga, Alban Desmaison, Andreas Kopf, Edward Yang, Zachary DeVito, Martin Raison, Alykhan Tejani, Sasank Chilamkurthy, Benoit Steiner, Lu Fang, Junjie Bai, and Soumith Chintala. 2019. Pytorch: An imperative style, high-performance deep learning library. In H. Wallach, H. Larochelle, A. Beygelzimer, F. d'Alché-Buc, E. Fox, and R. Garnett, editors, *Advances in Neural Information Processing Systems 32*, pages 8024–8035. Curran Associates, Inc.

Matthew Peters, Mark Neumann, Mohit Iyyer, Matt Gardner, Christopher Clark, Kenton Lee, and Luke Zettlemoyer. 2018. Deep contextualized word representations. In *Proceedings of the 2018 Conference of the North American Chapter of the Association for Computational Linguistics: Human Language Technologies, Volume 1 (Long Papers)*, pages 2227–2237.

Telmo Pires, Eva Schlinger, and Dan Garrette. 2019. How multilingual is multilingual bert? In *Proceedings of the 57th Annual Meeting of the Association for Computational Linguistics*, pages 4996–5001.

Jakub Piskorski, Laska Laskova, Michał Marcińczuk, Lidia Pivovarova, Pavel Přibáň, Josef Steinberger, and Roman Yangarber. 2019. The second cross-lingual challenge on recognition, normalization, classification, and linking of named entities across slavic languages. In *Proceedings of the 7th Workshop on Balto-Slavic Natural Language Processing*, pages 63–74.

Mike Schuster and Kuldip K Paliwal. 1997. Bidirectional recurrent neural networks. *IEEE transactions on Signal Processing*, 45(11):2673–2681.

Jana Straková, Milan Straka, and Jan Hajic. 2019. Neural architectures for nested ner through linearization. In *Proceedings of the 57th Annual Meeting of the Association for Computational Linguistics*, pages 5326–5331.

Chi Sun, Xipeng Qiu, Yige Xu, and Xuanjing Huang. 2019. How to fine-tune bert for text classification? In *China National Conference on Chinese Computational Linguistics*, pages 194–206. Springer.

Tatiana Tsygankova, Stephen Mayhew, and Dan Roth. 2019. Bsnlp2019 shared task submission: Multi-source neural ner transfer. In *Proceedings of the 7th Workshop on Balto-Slavic Natural Language Processing*, pages 75–82.

Ashish Vaswani, Noam Shazeer, Niki Parmar, Jakob Uszkoreit, Llion Jones, Aidan N Gomez, Łukasz Kaiser, and Illia Polosukhin. 2017. Attention is all you need. In *Proceedings of the 31st International Conference on Neural Information Processing Systems*, pages 6000–6010.

Thomas Wolf, Lysandre Debut, Victor Sanh, Julien Chaumond, Clement Delangue, Anthony Moi, Pierric Cistac, Tim Rault, Rémi Louf, Morgan Funtowicz, et al. 2019. Huggingface's transformers: State-of-the-art natural language processing. *arXiv preprint arXiv:1910.03771*.

Juntao Yu, Bernd Bohnet, and Massimo Poesio. 2020. Named entity recognition as dependency parsing. In *Proceedings of the 58th Annual Meeting of the Association for Computational Linguistics*, pages 6470–6476.

Yu Zhang, Guoguo Chen, Dong Yu, Kaisheng Yaco, Sanjeev Khudanpur, and James Glass. 2016. Highway long short-term memory rnns for distant speech recognition. In *2016 IEEE International Conference on Acoustics, Speech and Signal Processing (ICASSP)*, pages 5755–5759. IEEE.

A Training Details

We implement our approach using PyTorch (Paszke et al., 2019). We train models for 60 epochs, evaluating the model twice per epoch, and stop training early if NERC F1 does not improve in the development set after 24 validation steps. All models are optimized with Adam (Kingma and Ba, 2015), with a batch size of 32 and a maximum grad norm of 5. We keep the model with the highest NERC F1 score in the development set. Using scores from 33 experiments we have calculated Pearson Correlation Coefficient values of 0.89/0.79/0.84 between the NERC F1 test set values and the official RPM/REM/SM metrics. Despite the mismatch, the correlation values show that NERC F1 is a good approximation of the official metrics.

The character embeddings are learned during training, and the contextual embedding model, implemented using Hugging-Face Transformers library (Wolf et al., 2019), is further finetuned. In particular, until otherwise mentioned, we freeze all parameters of the contextual embedding model apart from the embedding-layer and the top-4 layers. Moreover, an embedding pooler learns a weighted average of the contextual embedding model's top-4 layers for each token. We have not observed gains from either finetuning more layers, nor using more layers when pooling the representation for a given token. Following Devlin et al. (2019) we represent each token by its first subtoken. Both embeddings models use a learning rate of 5e-5, with a linear scheduler where the maximum value occurs after 10% of the training steps.

All the contextual embedding models are available in the HuggingFace Transformers library, under the names BERT-BASE-MULTILINGUAL-CASED (Multilingual BERT), XLM-ROBERTA-LARGE (XLM-R Large), and DEEPPAVLOV/BERT-BASE-BG-CS-PL-RU-CASED (Slavic BERT). Both multilingual BERT and XLM-R cover all the six languages that are part of this shared task.

Our implementation of the biaffine classifier model mostly follows the original implementation[3]. It uses a learning rate of 1e-3 with a exponential scheduler, implemented from its TensorFlow version[4]. We follow Yu et al. (2020) choice of hyperparameters, as described in Table 5.

Hyperparameter	Value
Char Embeddings Dimension	8
Char Embeddings Filter Size	50
Char Embeddings Filter Width	3,4,5
Embeddings Dropout	0.5
BiLSTM Hidden Dimension	200
BiLSTM Number of Layers	3
BiLSTM Dropout	0.4
FFNN Hidden Dimension	150
FFNN Dropout	0.2
Scheduler Decay Step	100
Scheduler Decay Rate	0.999
Scheduler Staircase	True

Table 5: Classifier hyperparameters.

B Submissions Details

Submission	Details
Submission 1	XLM-R w/o CE w/o 2017
Submission 2	XLM-R w/ CE w/o 2017
Submission 3	XLM-R w/o CE w/ 2017
Submission 4	XLM-R w/ CE w/ 2017
Submission 5	UK/SL: XLM-R w/o CE w/ 2017 Other: Slavic BERT w/o CE w/o 2017

Table 6: Submission details including or not Char Embeddings (CE) and SLAVNER2017 data (2017).

[3] https://github.com/juntaoy/biaffine-ner

[4] See tf.keras.optimizers.schedules.ExponentialDecay

BSNLP Shared Task 2021 submission: Multilingual Slavic Named Entity Recognition

Rinalds Vīksna
Tilde
Faculty of Computing,
University of Latvia
rinalds.viksna@tilde.lv

Inguna Skadiņa
Tilde
Faculty of Computing,
University of Latvia
inguna.skadina@tilde.lv

Abstract

Named entity recognition, in particular for morphological rich languages, is challenging task due to the richness of inflected forms and ambiguity. This challenge is being addressed by SlavNER Shared Task. In this paper we describe system submitted to this task. Our system uses pre-trained multilingual BERT Language Model and is fine-tuned for six Slavic languages of this task on texts distributed by organizers. Our multilingual NER model achieves 83.7 F1 score on all corpora, with best result for Polish (88.8) and worst for Russian (79.1). Entity linking module achieved F1 score of 48.8 as evaluated by bsnlp2021 organizers.

1 Introduction

Named entity recognition, in particular for morphological rich languages, is challenging task due to the richness of inflected forms and their ambiguity. Evaluation results are usually lower for these languages, when compared to morphologically simpler languages. For instance, for Finnish language Virtanen et al. (2019) reports the F1 score of 92.4 on in-domain data and 81.47 on out of domain data, for Latvian state-of-the-art NER system (Znotiņš and Barzdins, 2020) achieves the F1 score 82.6, while for English LUKE model (Yamada et al., 2020) achieves F1 score of 94.3 on CoNLL-2003 dataset.

In this paper we present our submission to the SlavNER Shared Task on the analysis of Named Entities in multilingual Web documents in Slavic languages. Our submission implements modular architecture, consisting of three modules that correspond to the tasks of the Shared task - named entity recognition, entity normalization and multilingual entity linking.

Results of the previous challenges on named entity recognition show that fine-tuning of a large language model leads to the best overall result. Using this approach in previous Shared task the best result was achieved by Arkhipov et al. (2019), allowing to reach 87.2 F1 score for Bulgarian, 87.3 F1 for Russian, 93.2 F1 for Polish and 93.9 F1 score for Czech.

For Named Entity linking task we use a dynamic knowledge base, which is built at run-time using identified entity mentions and their embeddings, similar to Yamada et al. (2016). Our model uses pre-trained LaBSE model (Feng et al., 2020) to obtain aligned embeddings in different languages. We achieve average F1 score of 48.8 (us election 2020 dataset F1 score 51.98 and covid-19 dataset F1 score 42.3).

2 Data Preparation

We use data provided by Shared Task organizers to train the named entity recognition (NER) component. The data consists of raw text documents with some metadata (language, source, title, date, file-id) and annotation documents. Each annotation file contains a file-id linking it to the respective text document and list of Named Entities present in document.

In order to train NER, we transformed data into conll2003 like format. At first, raw documents were split into sentences using nltk library (Bird et al., 2009). Language specific nltk models were used for sentence segmentation where they were available and Russian model was applied when language specific models were not available.

Each token in sentence is labeled as either belonging to one of the named entity classes used in this task or labeled with label "O". Although in this dataset documents are categorized into 5 topics - "asia-bibi", "brexit", "nord-stream", "ryanair" and "other", we train single model for all topics.

As an additional data for training, we ex-

Proceedings of the 8th BSNLP Workshop on Balto-Slavic Natural Language Processing, pages 93–97
April 20, 2021. ©2021 Association for Computational Linguistics

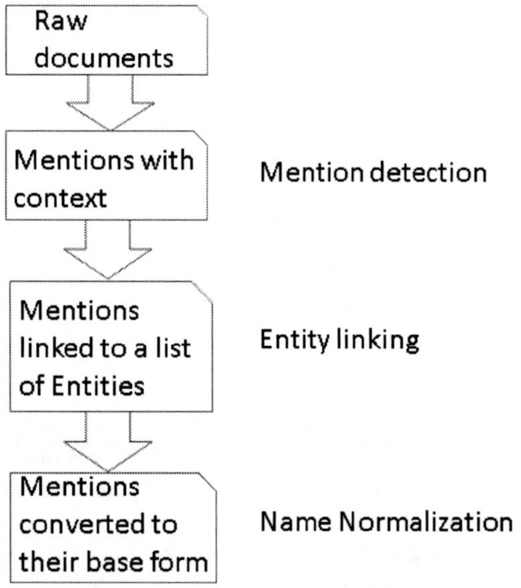

Figure 1: Overall System Architecture

plored various data sets in languages covered by bsnlp2021, however, in our opinion none of publicly available data sets match entity types required in this task. We found a data set in Latvian (Znotiņš, 2015), which includes the same entities as this task (person, location, organization, event and product). Since Latvian is also a morphologically rich inflected language, we decided to train a NER system using this data in addition to the data provided by shared task organizers.

3 Architecture and Modules

The architecture of our system is modular, consisting of three modules (Figure 1). At first, NER component identifies candidate entity mentions. Then, entity mentions are linked to already found entity mentions or added as new entity to a list. Finally, a base form for a given entity mention is obtained.

3.1 Mention Detection

We consider mention detection as sequence labeling problem aiming at labeling each token of the sequence. In our implementation we modify BERT (Devlin et al., 2019) model by adding dense layer and CRF layer on top of BERT model for Named Entity detection. We use multilingual BERT[1] provided by Google to fine-tune a single model for all six languages (Bulgarian,Czech,Polish,Russian, Slovene and Ukrainian) covered by the shared task.

[1] https://github.com/google-research/bert/blob/master/multilingual.md

	bg	cs	pl	ru	sl	uk
EVT	96.7	98.5	96.1	84.9	94.0	89.3
LOC	98.6	96.7	98.4	88.2	94.3	95.9
ORG	96.5	92.5	94.4	95.4	83.5	95.0
PER	97.3	96.1	96.6	95.2	92.0	96.9
PRO	85.6	94.9	89.2	61.5	66.6	66.6
ALL	96.8	95.4	96.0	87.3	89.4	95.3

Table 1: Internal evaluation results.

Provided data were split into 90% training dataset and 10% test set. We train single NER model using data from all 6 languages and evaluate for each language separately. Results of this internal evaluation are summarized in Table 1. This named entity mention recognition model achieved average F1 score of 93.

We expected that the test data for shared task will be crawled from Web and thus input may be noisy and include lowercase, uppercase and mixed case named entity mentions. Knowing that state-of-the-art NER models demonstrate good performance on grammatically correct datasets, while performing poorly on noisy data, in particular, data containing capitalization errors (Mayhew et al., 2020), we augmented training data with their noisy copies. To minimize impact of noisy data on NER performance, we augment training data using method described by Bodapati et al. (2019), i.e., using uppercased and lower-cased text variants. We prepared four datasets for training:

- original data (TLD1),
- original data augmented with casing variants (TLD2),
- original data + Latvian (TLD3),
- original data + Latvian and augmented with casing variants (TLD4).

We trained four corresponding systems which were used in final evaluation (Table 2). The best performing system was TLD1. System TLD3 was trained using additional Latvian corpus, which allowed to detect Event and Person entities better, however this was not enough to reach better overall result. Systems TLD2 and TLD4 were trained on datasets augmented with their lower-cased and upper-cased versions. The augmentation with noisy data lead to performance decrease by 2.6 F1 points for both systems, apparently because there are few casing errors in the test data. Detection of Product and Event

	TLD1	TLD2	TLD3	TLD4
PER	92.0	91.0	**92.3**	91.4
LOC	**92.9**	90.9	92.6	91.1
ORG	**78.7**	75.1	77.8	75.3
PRO	**59.3**	51.0	58.1	48.2
EVT	26.2	24.1	**31.6**	20.6
All	**83.7**	81.1	83.5	80.9

Table 2: Four systems evaluated on shared task test data (Relaxed partial matching)

	bg	cs	pl	ru	sl	uk
PER	89.3	95.7	93.9	87.6	95.5	96.5
LOC	94.5	93.5	96.4	91.2	91.4	95.1
ORG	79.7	86.6	83.7	72.7	81.7	81.0
PRO	61.1	66.8	75.7	51.4	64.3	52.6
EVT	23.6	18.0	37.5	21.2	41.8	09.8
All	83.9	85.7	88.8	79.1	87.1	82.7

Table 3: Evaluation results for TLD1 system on shared task test data (Relaxed partial matching)

entities is poor for all systems, as they mostly failed to detect unseen events and products (e.g., covid, sputnik, coronavirus, inauguration, election).

Table 3 provides more detailed evaluation results of TLD1 system. The system performs better on Slovene, Polish and Czech texts which have Latin script, while for Bulgarian, Russian and Ukrainian which use Cyrillic script results are lower, still acceptable. For all languages Event type is poorly identified. It could be explained by entities from medicine domain (e.g., covid-19) which were not part of the training data and thus were the most challenging for our recognizer. Relatively poor results for Product and Event detection in Russian and Ukrainian can be partially explained by the fact that evaluation script rejected entities without quotation marks (e.g. Sputnik V is considered wrong, since "Sputnik V" is expected).

3.2 Entity Linking

The goal of the entity linking task is to associate entity mentions found in a text with corresponding entries in a Knowledge Base (KB) (Zheng et al., 2010). Entity linking consists of three sub-tasks: candidate generation, candidate ranking and unlinkable mention prediction (Shen et al., 2015). When performed without a knowledge base, entity linking reduces to entity coreference resolution, where entity mentions across one or multiple documents are clustered into multiple clusters, each representing specific entity, based on the entity mention and context. For entity linking we use mention-ranking model (Rahman and Ng, 2009) to decide whether or not an active mention is coreferent with a candidate antecedent.

	Recall	Precision	F score
PER	38.491	88.832	53.710
LOC	64.654	79.818	71.440
ORG	22.625	51.409	31.421
PRO	12.924	34.134	18.749
EVT	00.516	40.675	01.019
All	35.563	77.994	48.851

Table 4: Entity linking results evaluated on SlavNER test data (Document level, system TLD3)

For each entity mention we obtain embedding using language-agnostic BERT sentence embedding LaBSE. Each candidate mention is compared with entities already in a linked entities list by calculating cosine similarity score. We use entity type information as a hard consistency check (which filters out mentions which do not have the same type) (Khosla and Rose, 2020).

We use two similarity thresholds as hyperparameters: one for early stopping if cosine similarity is over 0.95 and second for unlinkable entity detection, set at 0.6. Entity having similarity score higher than early stopping value, is considered to be the same entity as candidate antecedent and no further comparison is needed. Entity with lower similarity score than unlinkable threshold for any antecedent, is considered as new and added to a list of entities found. For entities with similarity scores between these two hyperparameters, the most similar entity is selected and linked as correct entity.

The best results in entity linking task achieved TLD3 system. Evaluation results for this system are summarized in Table 4. Since this task depends on the results of mention detection task, results for Product and Event classes are poor. We can observe reasonable or even good precision, while recall is very poor for almost all entity types.

3.3 Entity Normalization

For entity normalization we apply Stanza (Qi et al., 2020) language specific lemmatizers. Since Stanza performs lemmatization on word level each word in multi-word named entity is lemmatized separately. Such approach was useful for person lemmatization, however failed for other categories of named entities, in particular long organization names.

Evaluation results for the normalization task are summarized in Table 5. In almost all cases the system trained on data provided by shared task organizers (TLD1) achieved the highest F-score. For most of languages results are between 43 (Czech) and 52 (Ukrainian), except Bulgarian with only 15 F-Score. The reasons for such low results are multiple: first, errors in detection entity mentions automatically translate into missing normalized forms for normalization; second, multi-word entities are normalized by converting each word to its base form and third, stanza models used for have varying performance in different languages.

	TLD1	TLD2	TLD3	TLD4
bg	15.76	14.80	**15.85**	13.71
cs	**43.36**	40.56	42.74	40.03
pl	**48.40**	45.94	47.45	45.96
ru	**44.12**	42.20	43.64	42.28
sl	**32.07**	30.31	31.57	29.92
uk	**52.10**	49.78	50.71	50.25

Table 5: Evaluation results (F-score) for normalization task

4 Conclusion

In this paper we proposed modular architecture that allows to find Named Entities in six Slavic languages and links identified entities to the same entity in other documents in different languages. Each module can be separately updated to improve system performance.

As the next step, constituent modules of this system could be improved, for example with entity normalization rules for multi-word entities or implementing longer context for obtaining entity embeddings for linking.

Acknowledgments

The research has been supported by the European Regional Development Fund within the research project "Multilingual Artificial Intelligence Based Human Computer Interaction" No. 1.1.1.1/18/A/148.

References

Mikhail Arkhipov, Maria Trofimova, Yuri Kuratov, and Alexey Sorokin. 2019. Tuning multilingual transformers for language-specific named entity recognition. In *Proceedings of the 7th Workshop on Balto-Slavic Natural Language Processing*, pages 89–93, Florence, Italy. Association for Computational Linguistics.

Steven Bird, Ewan Klein, and Edward Loper. 2009. *Natural Language Processing with Python: Analyzing Text with the Natural Language Toolkit*. O'Reilly, Beijing.

Sravan Bodapati, Hyokun Yun, and Yaser Al-Onaizan. 2019. Robustness to capitalization errors in named entity recognition. In *Proceedings of the 5th Workshop on Noisy User-generated Text (W-NUT 2019)*, pages 237–242, Hong Kong, China. Association for Computational Linguistics.

Jacob Devlin, Ming-Wei Chang, Kenton Lee, and Kristina Toutanova. 2019. BERT: Pre-training of deep bidirectional transformers for language understanding. In *Proceedings of the 2019 Conference of the North American Chapter of the Association for Computational Linguistics: Human Language Technologies, Volume 1 (Long and Short Papers)*, pages 4171–4186, Minneapolis, Minnesota. Association for Computational Linguistics.

Fangxiaoyu Feng, Yinfei Yang, Daniel Cer, Naveen Arivazhagan, and Wei Wang. 2020. Language-agnostic bert sentence embedding.

Sopan Khosla and Carolyn Rose. 2020. Using type information to improve entity coreference resolution. In *Proceedings of the First Workshop on Computational Approaches to Discourse*, pages 20–31, Online. Association for Computational Linguistics.

Stephen Mayhew, Nitish Gupta, and Dan Roth. 2020. Robust named entity recognition with truecasing pretraining. In *The Thirty-Fourth AAAI Conference on Artificial Intelligence, AAAI 2020, The Thirty-Second Innovative Applications of Artificial Intelligence Conference, IAAI 2020, The Tenth AAAI Symposium on Educational Advances in Artificial Intelligence, EAAI 2020, New York, NY, USA, February 7-12, 2020*, pages 8480–8487. AAAI Press.

Peng Qi, Yuhao Zhang, Yuhui Zhang, Jason Bolton, and Christopher D. Manning. 2020. Stanza: A Python natural language processing toolkit for many human languages. In *Proceedings of the 58th Annual Meeting of the Association for Computational Linguistics: System Demonstrations*.

Altaf Rahman and Vincent Ng. 2009. Supervised models for coreference resolution. In *Proceedings of the 2009 Conference on Empirical Methods in Natural Language Processing*, pages 968–977, Singapore. Association for Computational Linguistics.

W. Shen, J. Wang, and J. Han. 2015. Entity linking with a knowledge base: Issues, techniques, and solutions. *IEEE Transactions on Knowledge and Data Engineering*, 27(2):443–460.

Antti Virtanen, Jenna Kanerva, Rami Ilo, Jouni Luoma, Juhani Luotolahti, Tapio Salakoski, Filip Ginter, and Sampo Pyysalo. 2019. Multilingual is not enough: Bert for finnish.

Ikuya Yamada, Akari Asai, Hiroyuki Shindo, Hideaki Takeda, and Yuji Matsumoto. 2020. LUKE: Deep contextualized entity representations with entity-aware self-attention. In *Proceedings of the 2020 Conference on Empirical Methods in Natural Language Processing (EMNLP)*, pages 6442–6454, Online. Association for Computational Linguistics.

Ikuya Yamada, Hiroyuki Shindo, Hideaki Takeda, and Yoshiyasu Takefuji. 2016. Joint learning of the embedding of words and entities for named entity disambiguation. In *Proceedings of The 20th SIGNLL Conference on Computational Natural Language Learning*, pages 250–259, Berlin, Germany. Association for Computational Linguistics.

Zhicheng Zheng, Fangtao Li, Minlie Huang, and Xiaoyan Zhu. 2010. Learning to link entities with knowledge base. In *Human Language Technologies: The 2010 Annual Conference of the North American Chapter of the Association for Computational Linguistics*, pages 483–491, Los Angeles, California. Association for Computational Linguistics.

Artūrs Znotiņš. 2015. NLP-PIPE: Latvian NLP tool pipeline. CLARIN-LV digital library at MII, Universiy of Latvia.

Artūrs Znotiņš and Guntis Barzdins. 2020. *LVBERT: Transformer-Based Model for Latvian Language Understanding*, pages 111–115. IOS Press Ebooks.

Using a Frustratingly Easy Domain and Tagset Adaptation for Creating Slavic Named Entity Recognition Systems

Luis Adrián Cabrera-Diego
La Rochelle Université, L3i,
La Rochelle, 17031, France
luis.cabrera_diego@univ-lr.fr

Jose G. Moreno
Université Paul Sabatier, IRIT,
Toulouse, 31062, France
jose.moreno@irit.fr

Antoine Doucet
La Rochelle Université, L3i,
La Rochelle, 17031, France
antoine.doucet@univ-lr.fr

Abstract

We present a collection of Named Entity Recognition (NER) systems for six Slavic languages: Bulgarian, Czech, Polish, Slovenian, Russian and Ukrainian. These NER systems have been trained using different BERT models and a Frustratingly Easy Domain Adaptation (FEDA). FEDA allow us creating NER systems using multiple datasets without having to worry about whether the tagset (e.g. Location, Event, Miscellaneous, Time) in the source and target domains match, while increasing the amount of data available for training. Moreover, we boosted the prediction on named entities by marking uppercase words and predicting masked words. Participating in the 3rd Shared Task on SlavNER[1], our NER systems reached a strict micro F-score of up to 0.908. The results demonstrate good generalization, even in named entities with weak regularity, such as book titles, or entities that were never seen during the training.

1 Introduction

Named Entity Recognition (NER) is a fundamental task in domain of Natural Language Processing (NLP) that consists of extracting entities that semantically refer to aspects such as locations, people or organizations (Luoma et al., 2020). Since the creation of BERT (Devlin et al., 2019), multiple NER systems have brought the state of the art to new levels of performance. Nonetheless, there are many challenges that still need to be faced, especially in the case of less-resources languages.

In the *2nd Shared Task on SlavNER* (Piskorski et al., 2019), the top-two systems in the detection Named Entities (NEs), Tsygankova et al. (2019) and Arkhipov et al. (2019), managed to reach a relaxed partial micro F-score of 0.9, followed by two other systems with values slightly better than 0.8 (Moreno et al., 2019). For the *3rd Shared Task on SlavNER*, we consider that in order to improve the scores, in terms of the strict evaluation, and NEs related to products and events, it is necessary to include additional data that could improve the generalization of the models to any kind of topic.

While in the literature there are multiple techniques for training models over additional datasets, such as transfer learning and domain adaptation, using these techniques might pose additional questions. For example, to determine which layers to freeze, fine-tune or substitute. Furthermore, different datasets might use dissimilar tagsets, which might be incompatible (Nozza et al., 2021).

In this paper, we present the participation of laboratory *L3i* in the 3rd Shared Task on SlavNER. Specifically, we participate with multiple NER systems for Slavic languages using different BERT models and training over diverse datasets through a *Frustratingly Easy Domain Adaptation* (FEDA) algorithm (Daumé III, 2007; Kim et al., 2016).[2] The FEDA algorithm has for objective to learn common and domain-specific patterns between multiple datasets, while keeping separately patterns belonging only to the domain-specific data (Daumé III, 2007). Particularly, the use of FEDA allow us sharing the knowledge and patterns found in multiple datasets without having to worry about which different tagsets are used among them.

Apart from the FEDA algorithm, we explore some other techniques that might improve the performance of our NER system based on the ideas of Cabrera-Diego et al. (2021). Specifically, we analyze whether the marking and enrichment of uppercase tokens can improve the detection of NEs. As well, we use the prediction of masked tokens as a way to improve NER systems' generalization.

[1] bsnlp.cs.helsinki.fi/shared-task.html, last visited on 9 March 2021

[2] github.com/EMBEDDIA/NER_FEDA

Proceedings of the 8th BSNLP Workshop on Balto-Slavic Natural Language Processing, pages 98–104
April 20, 2021. ©2021 Association for Computational Linguistics

The rest of the paper is organized as follows. In Section 2, we introduce the background for the proposed work. This is followed by the methodology in Section 3. The data and the experimental settings are described in Section 4 and Section 5, respectively. In Section 6, we present the results obtained. Finally, the conclusions and future work are detailed in Section 7.

2 Background

Uppercase sentences: Although most of the NER corpora found in the literature provide texts following standard case rules, it is not infrequent to find datasets containing some sentences in which all the words are in uppercase, e.g. English CoNLL 2003 (Tjong Kim Sang and De Meulder, 2003) or SSJ500k (Krek et al., 2019). In NLP systems based on BERT or similar, where Byte Pair Encoding (BPE) tokenizers are used, the presence of uppercase sentences might pose a greater challenge than standard case sentences. The reason is that an uppercase word have different BPE tokens with respect to its lower and title-case versions, and in consequence different dense representation (Powalski and Stanislawek, 2020; Sun et al., 2020).

Weak generalization: One of the most challenging aspects of NER systems is to deal with NEs that have a weak or zero regularity, such as names of movies, and NEs that were never seen during training (Lin et al., 2020b). Some methods found in the literature for improving generalization consists of learning manually defined triggers (Lin et al., 2020a), but also permuting NEs and reducing context such as in Lin et al. (2020b).

FEDA: Originally proposed by Daumé III (2007), the FEDA was firstly designed for sparse machine learning algorithms. Later, Kim et al. (2016), proposed a neural network version of this domain adaptation algorithm. While the former resides in duplicating input features, the latter consists of activating specific neural network layers.

3 Methodology

Consider $\mathcal{D} = \{D_1, D_2, \ldots, D_n | n > 1\}$ a collection of datasets from which we want to train a model. Furthermore, consider a classifier C a stack of two linear layers in which in between we set an activation layer ReLU and a dropout. The first linear layer has a size of 512, while the output h produced by C has a size of l, which is the number of different labels found in $\mathcal{D}$. Thus, the proposed model for doing the FEDA consists of adding on top of BERT $n+1$ classifiers such that we have $\mathcal{C} = \{C_0, C_1, C_2, \ldots, C_n\}$. The classifier C_0 represents a general classifier that will receive as input the sentences from all the datasets in $\mathcal{D}$, while $C_k \in \{\mathcal{C} | 0 < k \leq n\}$ represent a specialized classifier that will focus only on the sentences that belong to the dataset $D_k \in \{\mathcal{D} | 0 < k \leq n\}$. For each sentence belonging to a dataset D_k, we do the element-wise sum between h_0 and h_k, i.e. $H_k = h_0 + h_k$. Finally, H_k is introduced it into a CRF layer, which will determine the labels of each word in a sentence. Figure 1 depicts the proposed architecture.

For increasing the generalization of our NER systems, we explore the prediction of masked tokens during the training as proposed by Cabrera-Diego et al. (2021). Firstly, this method converts randomly selected tokens, within a sentence, into BERT's special token *[MASK]*. Then, the NER system has to predict correctly the sentence's NEs, despite the missing information, as well as predicting the masked tokens. The prediction of masked tokens is done by introducing BERT's output into a linear layer, which has the same size of the pretrained vocabulary. During training, the loss produced by the prediction of masked tokens is added to the loss produced by the recognition of NEs; during testing, this layer is inactive.

Although Powalski and Stanislawek (2020) propose *UniCase*, an architecture for training a language model that learns the casing of a word separately to the tokenization, in this work, we use a simpler method that does not require to retrain a language model. Specifically, we use a marking and enrichment approach, where an uppercase word is tagged with two special BERT's tokens, defined by us as *[UP]* and *[up]*, and where we include additional case versions. For instance, the word "ROME" becomes "[UP] [ROM, ##E] [Rome] [r,##ome] [up]". It is important to indicate that the prediction of the NE type is done uniquely over the first token, which correspond to the special token [UP]. In other words, the output produced by BERT for the rest of the tokens is masked. The marking of the uppercase words is based on the ideas proposed by Cabrera-Diego et al. (2021).

4 Datasets

We use the data provided by the organizers for the 3rd Shared Task on SlavNER. However, for the

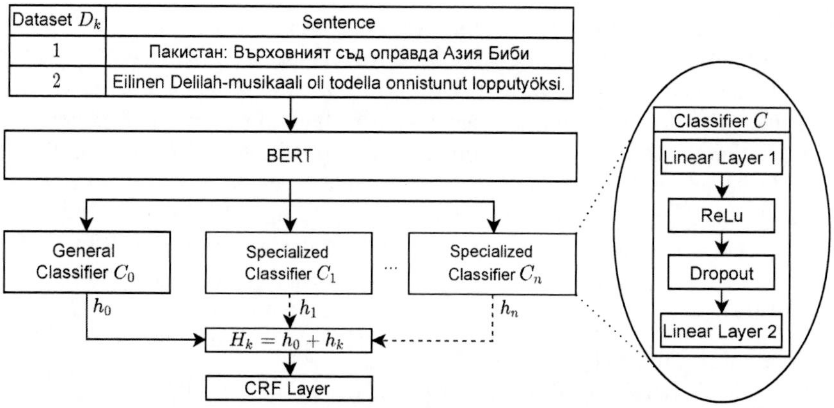

Figure 1: Our FEDA-based architecture for NER with BERT.

development of our internal models, we use the topics of *Nord Stream* and *Ryanair* as testing partition, while the rest as training and development. For the final models, all the data provided is split into training and development sets.

Besides the data provided by SlavNER's organizers, we use the follwing NER corpora:

SlavNER 2017 (Piskorski et al., 2017): Slavic Corpus annotated with 4 NE types: Location, Miscellaneous, Organization and Person.

Collection Named Entities 5 (CNE5) (Mozharova and Loukachevitch, 2016)[3]: Russian NER corpus manually annotated with five NE types: Geopolitical, Location, Media, Person and Organization.

Czech Named Entity Corpus 2.0 (CNEC) (Ševčíková et al., 2007): Czech corpus annotated with fine-grained NE. In this work, we have used 6 types of NE: Location, Organization, Media, Artifact, Person and Time.

FactRuEval[4]: Russian corpus annotated with three NE types: Location, Organization and Person.

Finnish NER (Luoma et al., 2020): Although Finnish is not a language to process in SlavNER, it has similar NE types to those used in the shared task: Date, Event, Location, Organization, Person, Product and Time. We use this dataset to enrich the NEs knowledge, specially on events and products.

National Corpus of Polish (NKJP)[5] (Przepiórkowski et al., 2012): Polish corpus tagged with five NE types: Person, Organization, Geopolitical, Location, Date and Time.

NER-UK[6]: Collection of 264 Ukrainian documents manually annotated with four types of NE: Location, Miscellaneous, Organization and Person.

Polish Corpus of Wrocław University of Technology (KPWr)[7] (Marcińczuk et al., 2016): Polish dataset annotated with nine super NE types, from these six were chosen: Event, Location, Organization, Person, Place and Product. Location and Place were merged as the former.

SSJ500k (Krek et al., 2019): Slovene corpus annotated with four types of NE: Location, Miscellaneous, Organization and Person.

Wikiann (Pan et al., 2017): It is a multilingual NER corpus based on Wikipedia articles; it was annotated automatically using three types of NEs: Location, Organization and Person. We use of the corpus partitions used by Rahimi et al. (2019).

We use for all the additional corpora their training, development and testing partitions; if these are not provided, we create them using a stratified approach to ensure a proportional number of NEs.

5 Experimental Setup

Regarding BERT, we use different pre-trained models: *CroSloEngual* (Ulčar and Robnik-Šikonja, 2020), *Polish BERT*[8], *RuBERT* (Kuratov and Arkhipov, 2019) and *Language-Agnostic BERT Sentence Embedding (LaBSE)* (Feng et al., 2020).

All the files coming from SlavNER are tokenized and, those used for training and development are annotated at token-level. For Bulgarian and Slovene, we tokenize the documents using Reldi-Tokenizer[9], while for the rest of languages, we use the neural parser proposed by Kanerva et al. (2018). Further-

[3] labinform.ru/pub/named_entities

[4] github.com/dialogue-evaluation/factRuEval-2016

[5] nkjp.pl

[6] github.com/lang-uk/ner-uk

[7] clarin-pl.eu/dspace/handle/11321/270

[8] huggingface.co/dkleczek/bert-base-polish-cased-v1

[9] github.com/clarinsi/reldi-tokeniser

more, we over-tokenize all the files, i.e. we separate all the punctuation from tokens within a sentence, to solve some cases where abbreviation periods or dashes were not considered as part of a NE. For example, in Slovene, Roman numerals are followed by a period, such as in *Benedikt XVI.* nevertheless, some NE annotations did not consider the period. Some rules and manual corrections were applied to the tokenization where we determined the fix was critical. For instance, in Polish, *W. Brytania* (Great Britain) was being split into two sentences by the tokenizer. We automatically annotated the files by searching the longest match in the tokenized format and the annotation file. In case of ambiguity, the annotation tool requested a manual intervention. For the final submission, we converted the token-level output to a document-level one.

All the NEs types are encoded using BIOES (Beginning, Inside, Outside/Other, End, Single). As well, to reduce the number of entities types, we normalize those where the theoretical meaning is the same, i.e. PERS into PER or EVENT into EVT.

For the models where masked tokens have to be predicted, we only affect sentences in the training partitions that are longer than 3 actual tokens, i.e. not BPE tokens. At each epoch, we select randomly 25% of each sentence's tokens and substitute them with *[MASK]*. If a token after being processed by BERT's tokenizer produces more than one BPE token, we mask only one of them.[10] Regarding the models that are trained with marked uppercase tokens, at each training epoch, we randomly convert 5% of all the sentences into uppercase. This is done to provide some examples of uppercase sentences to datasets that do not present this phenomenon.

In Table 2, we present the final models created for recognizing NEs. As well, we detail which are the datasets used for training them and which are the additional features that they make use. The combinations of datasets and features used for the final models were selected according to their performance on internal models. To enrich the knowledge in Bulgarian, we added the Macedonian Wikiann dataset, as both languages are considered as mutually intelligible. All the models were trained up to 20 epochs using an early stop approach. In Table 1, we present a summary of the hyperparameters used for training the NER systems.

[10]For Polish BERT, we mask all the tokens as this model was trained using whole word masking.

Hyperparameter	**Value**
Maximum Epochs	20
Early Stop Patience	2
Learning Rate	2×10^{-5}
Scheduler	Linear with warm-up
Warm-up Ratio	0.1
Optimizer	AdamW with bias correction
AdamW ϵ	1×10^{-8}
Random Seed	12
Dropout rate	0.5
Weight decay	0.01
Clipping gradient norm	1.0
BERT's Sequence Size	128
Linear Layer 1 Size	512
Training Mini-Batch:	
Latin 1 & 2	5
Ru	8
Pl	28
Others	16

Table 1: Hyperparameters used for training the models.

6 Results

In Table 3, we present the performance of our systems in terms of strict micro F-score. We can observe, that the marking of uppercase words worked better, in general, for the *Covid-19* topic, specially on the Cyrillic-2 model. As well, single language models worked better on the *Covid-19* topic, while the model Latin-1 worked better on the *U.S. Elections* topic. In most languages, the hardest NEs to predict were related to products and events due to their weak regularity or because they never appeared on the training datasets.

From a manual inspection, we have observed that multiple events were considered as products, such as *Miss USA*, *Pizzagate* and *Covid-19*. Some products were marked as organizations such as *Zoom*, *COVAX*, *Apple TV+*, although fewer organizations were tagged as products, such as *Pfizer/Moderna* and *BBC*. Nonetheless, many of these NEs could be both types depending on the context in which happen. In certain documents, organizations were marked as locations and vice-versa, such as *Ostravské Fakultní Nemocnice* (Ostrava University Hospital) and *Szpitala Wojskowego w Szczecinie* (Military Hospital in Szczecin).

We have found interesting examples regarding products despite their irregularity. For example, the Cyrillic and Latin models managed to detect partially the 2020 book "*Nelojalen: resnična zgodba nekdanjega osebnega odvetnika predsednika Donalda Trumpa*" (Disloyal: A Memoir: The True Story of the Former Personal Attorney to President Donald J. Trump). Specifically, the entity was

Model		Features	BERT Model	*C*	Training datasets
Script-based	Cyrillic-1 Cyrillic-2	None Uppercase	LaBSE	8	SlavNER-17 (Ru, Uk); SlavNER-21 (Bg, Ru, Uk); Wikiann (Bg, Mk, Ru, Uk); FactRuEval; CNE5; NER-UK; Finnish NER
	Latin-1 Latin-2	None Uppercase	LaBSE	8	SlavNER-17 (Cs, Pl, Sl); SlavNER-21 (Cs, Pl, Sl); Wikiann (Cs, Pl, Sl); SSJ500k; KPWr; CNEC; Finnish NER
Single language	Bg	Uppercase	LaBSE	5	SlavNER-21 (Bg); Wikiann (Bg, Mk); Finnish NER
	Cs	Uppercase	LaBSE	5	SlavNER-21 (Cs); Wikiann (Cs); CNEC; Finnish NER
	Pl	Mask.+Upper.	Polish BERT	5	SlavNER-21 (Pl); Wikiann (Pl); KPWr; NKJP
	Ru	Mask.+Upper.	RuBERT	5	SlavNER-21 (Ru); Wikiann (Ru); FactRuEval; CNE5
	Sl	Mask.+Upper.	CroSloEngual	4	SlavNER-21 (Sl); Wikiann (Sl); SSJ500k
	Uk	Uppercase	LaBSE	4	SlavNER-21 (Uk); Wikiann (Uk); NER-UK

Table 2: Datasets used for training each of the model explored in this work. The number of classifiers (C) consider both the general and specialized ones used in the architecture.

	Covid-19							U.S. Elections							
Model	**Bg**	**Cs**	**Pl**	**Ru**	**Sl**	**Uk**	**All**	**Bg**	**Cs**	**Pl**	**Ru**	**Sl**	**Uk**	**All**	**Global**
Cyrillic-1	0.716	0.714	0.760	0.657	0.732	0.722	0.715	0.843	0.837	0.841	0.741	0.837	0.787	0.793	0.764
Cyrillic-2	0.720	0.730	0.783	0.642	0.744	**0.727**	0.721	**0.865**	0.857	0.849	0.746	0.858	**0.813**	0.807	0.775
Latin-1	0.730	0.765	0.791	0.662	0.752	0.706	0.733	0.850	**0.890**	**0.908**	**0.762**	**0.898**	0.789	**0.824**	**0.790**
Latin-2	**0.733**	0.763	0.792	**0.666**	0.758	0.688	**0.734**	0.854	**0.890**	0.891	0.759	0.884	0.782	0.819	0.787
Single lang.	0.725	**0.766**	**0.793**	0.611	**0.775**	0.701	0.729	0.813	0.889	0.887	0.742	0.891	0.781	0.807	0.778

Table 3: Strict micro F-scores obtained by each model for every language and topic. The *Global* column is the strict micro F-score regarding all the test data.

split into two "*Nelojalen: resnična zgodba nekdanjega osebnega odvetnika predsednika*" as a product and *Donalda Trumpa* (Donald Trump) as a person. But there were some exact matches, such as the book "*Cyberwar: How Russian Hackers and Trolls Helped Elect a President*" or the document "*Preveč in nikoli dovolj: kako je moja družina ustvarila najnevarnejšega moža na svetu*" (Treaty on Measures for the Further Reduction and Limitation of Strategic Offensive Arms). Furthermore, some scientific articles were tagged as products, such as "*A Study to Evaluate Efficacy, Safety, and Immunogenicity of mRNA-1273 Vaccine in Adults Aged 18 Years and Older to Prevent COVID-19*", although they did not appear in the gold standard.

Some models considered *BioNTech* as an organization and *Instagram* as a product despite these NEs were never seen during the training. As well, some medication-related products were correctly found such as *AZD1222*, канакинумаб (Canakinumab), *Remdesivir* or *Zithromax*, even if they did not exist on the training corpora.

We observed, specially in Cyrillic-scripted languages, that some named entities were incorrect because they were predicted without punctuation marks. For example: *Moderna Inc* vs *Moderna Inc.*, гам-ковид-вак vs «гам-ковид-вак» and спутником vs "спутником". In Latin-scripted languages, we observed the opposite although less frequently. For instance, *Roberta F. Kennedyho Jr.* vs *Roberta F. Kennedyho Jr.* In some documents the punctuation mark is included in certain NEs but not in others, such as in *Korea Pln.* vs *Korea Pln* but *Korei Pln.*.

7 Conclusions and Future Work

This work presented the participation of Laboratory *L3i* in the 3rd Shared Task on SlavNER. Specifically, we proposed a collection of BERT-based NER systems that were trained using multiple datasets through FEDA.

The results showed us that our NER systems worked better on the *U.S. Elections* topic (strict micro F-score between 0.762 and 0.908) than on the *Covid-19* topic (0.666 - 0.775). Overall, a competitive strength of our NER systems is that they managed to predict named entities occurring with weak regularity or that were never seen before.

In the future, we will apply the proposed architecture on other languages and datasets.

Acknowledgments

This work has been supported by the European Union's Horizon 2020 research and innovation program under grants 770299 (NewsEye) and 825153 (Embeddia).

References

Mikhail Arkhipov, Maria Trofimova, Yuri Kuratov, and Alexey Sorokin. 2019. Tuning Multilingual Transformers for Language-Specific Named Entity Recognition. In *Proceedings of the 7th Workshop on Balto-Slavic Natural Language Processing*, pages 89–93, Florence, Italy. Association for Computational Linguistics.

Luis Adrián Cabrera-Diego, Jose G. Moreno, and Antoine Doucet. 2021. Simple ways to improve NER in every language using markup. In *Proceedings of the 2nd International Workshop on Cross-lingual Event-centric Open Analytics*, Online. CEUR-WS.

Hal Daumé III. 2007. Frustratingly Easy Domain Adaptation. In *Proceedings of the 45th Annual Meeting of the Association of Computational Linguistics*, pages 256–263, Prague, Czech Republic. Association for Computational Linguistics.

Jacob Devlin, Ming-Wei Chang, Kenton Lee, and Kristina Toutanova. 2019. BERT: Pre-training of Deep Bidirectional Transformers for Language Understanding. In *Proceedings of the 2019 Conference of the North American Chapter of the Association for Computational Linguistics: Human Language Technologies, Volume 1 (Long and Short Papers)*, pages 4171–4186, Minneapolis, Minnesota. Association for Computational Linguistics.

Fangxiaoyu Feng, Yinfei Yang, Daniel Cer, Naveen Arivazhagan, and Wei Wang. 2020. *Language-agnostic BERT Sentence Embedding*. ArXiv cs.CL eprint: 2007.01852.

Jenna Kanerva, Filip Ginter, Niko Miekka, Akseli Leino, and Tapio Salakoski. 2018. Turku Neural Parser Pipeline: An End-to-End System for the CoNLL 2018 Shared Task. In *Proceedings of the CoNLL 2018 Shared Task: Multilingual Parsing from Raw Text to Universal Dependencies*. Association for Computational Linguistics.

Young-Bum Kim, Karl Stratos, and Ruhi Sarikaya. 2016. Frustratingly Easy Neural Domain Adaptation. In *Proceedings of COLING 2016, the 26th International Conference on Computational Linguistics: Technical Papers*, pages 387–396, Osaka, Japan. The COLING 2016 Organizing Committee.

Simon Krek, Kaja Dobrovoljc, Tomaž Erjavec, Sara Može, Nina Ledinek, Nanika Holz, Katja Zupan, Polona Gantar, Taja Kuzman, Jaka Čibej, Špela Arhar Holdt, Teja Kavčič, Iza Škrjanec, Dafne Marko, Lucija Jezeršek, and Anja Zajc. 2019. Training corpus ssj500k 2.2. Slovenian language resource repository CLARIN.SI.

Yuri Kuratov and Mikhail Arkhipov. 2019. *Adaptation of Deep Bidirectional Multilingual Transformers for Russian Language*. ArXiv cs.CL eprint: 1905.07213.

Bill Yuchen Lin, Dong-Ho Lee, Ming Shen, Ryan Moreno, Xiao Huang, Prashant Shiralkar, and Xiang Ren. 2020a. TriggerNER: Learning with Entity Triggers as Explanations for Named Entity Recognition. In *Proceedings of the 58th Annual Meeting of the Association for Computational Linguistics*, pages 8503–8511, Online. Association for Computational Linguistics.

Hongyu Lin, Yaojie Lu, Jialong Tang, Xianpei Han, Le Sun, Zhicheng Wei, and Nicholas Jing Yuan. 2020b. A Rigorous Study on Named Entity Recognition: Can Fine-tuning Pretrained Model Lead to the Promised Land? In *Proceedings of the 2020 Conference on Empirical Methods in Natural Language Processing (EMNLP)*, pages 7291–7300, Online. Association for Computational Linguistics.

Jouni Luoma, Miika Oinonen, Maria Pyykönen, Veronika Laippala, and Sampo Pyysalo. 2020. A Broad-coverage Corpus for Finnish Named Entity Recognition. In *Proceedings of the 12th Language Resources and Evaluation Conference*, pages 4615–4624, Marseille, France. European Language Resources Association.

Michał Marcińczuk, Marcin Oleksy, Marek Maziarz, Jan Wieczorek, Dominika Fikus, Agnieszka Turek, Michał Wolski, Tomasz Bernaś, Jan Kocoń, and Paweł Kedzia. 2016. *Polish Corpus of Wrocław University of Technology 1.2*. CLARIN-PL digital repository.

Jose G. Moreno, Elvys Linhares Pontes, Mickaël Coustaty, and Antoine Doucet. 2019. TLR at BSNLP2019: A multilingual named entity recognition system. In *Proceedings of the 7th Workshop on Balto-Slavic Natural Language Processing*, pages 83–88, Florence, Italy. Association for Computational Linguistics.

Valerie Mozharova and Natalia Loukachevitch. 2016. Two-stage approach in Russian named entity recognition. In *2016 Conference on Intelligence, Social Media and Web (ISMW FRUCT)*, pages 1–6, St. Petersburg, Russia.

Debora Nozza, Pikakshi Manchanda, Elisabetta Fersini, Matteo Palmonari, and Enza Messina. 2021. LearningToAdapt with word embeddings: Domain adaptation of Named Entity Recognition systems. *Information Processing & Management*, 58(3):102537.

Xiaoman Pan, Boliang Zhang, Jonathan May, Joel Nothman, Kevin Knight, and Heng Ji. 2017. Cross-lingual Name Tagging and Linking for 282 Languages. In *Proceedings of the 55th Annual Meeting of the Association for Computational Linguistics (Volume 1: Long Papers)*, pages 1946–1958, Vancouver, Canada. Association for Computational Linguistics.

Jakub Piskorski, Laska Laskova, Michał Marcińczuk, Lidia Pivovarova, Pavel Přibáň, Josef Steinberger, and Roman Yangarber. 2019. The Second Cross-Lingual Challenge on Recognition, Normalization, Classification, and Linking of Named Entities across Slavic Languages. In *Proceedings of the 7th Workshop on Balto-Slavic Natural Language Processing*, pages 63–74, Florence, Italy. Association for Computational Linguistics.

Jakub Piskorski, Lidia Pivovarova, Jan Šnajder, Josef Steinberger, and Roman Yangarber. 2017. The First Cross-Lingual Challenge on Recognition, Normalization, and Matching of Named Entities in Slavic Languages. In *Proceedings of the 6th Workshop on Balto-Slavic Natural Language Processing*, pages 76–85, Valencia, Spain. Association for Computational Linguistics.

Rafal Powalski and Tomasz Stanislawek. 2020. *Uni-Case – Rethinking Casing in Language Models.* ArXiv cs.CL eprint: 2010.11936.

Adam Przepiórkowski, Mirosław Bańko, Rafał L. Górski, and Barbara Lewandowska-Tomaszczyk. 2012. *Narodowy korpus jezyka polskiego.* Naukowe PWN, Warsaw, Poland.

Afshin Rahimi, Yuan Li, and Trevor Cohn. 2019. Massively Multilingual Transfer for NER. In *Proceedings of the 57th Annual Meeting of the Association for Computational Linguistics*, pages 151–164, Florence, Italy. Association for Computational Linguistics.

Lichao Sun, Kazuma Hashimoto, Wenpeng Yin, Akari Asai, Jia Li, Philip Yu, and Caiming Xiong. 2020. *Adv-BERT: BERT is not robust on misspellings! Generating nature adversarial samples on BERT.* ArXiv cs.CL eprint: 2003.04985.

Erik F. Tjong Kim Sang and Fien De Meulder. 2003. Introduction to the CoNLL-2003 Shared Task: Language-Independent Named Entity Recognition. In *Proceedings of the Seventh Conference on Natural Language Learning at HLT-NAACL 2003*, pages 142–147.

Tatiana Tsygankova, Stephen Mayhew, and Dan Roth. 2019. BSNLP2019 Shared Task Submission: Multisource Neural NER Transfer. In *Proceedings of the 7th Workshop on Balto-Slavic Natural Language Processing*, pages 75–82, Florence, Italy. Association for Computational Linguistics.

Matej Ulčar and Marko Robnik-Šikonja. 2020. FinEst BERT and CroSloEngual BERT. In *Proceeding of the 23rd International Conference on Text, Speech, and Dialogue (TSD 2020)*, pages 104–111, Brno, Czech Republic. Springer International Publishing.

Magda Ševčíková, Zdeněk Žabokrtský, and Oldřich Krůza. 2007. Named Entities in Czech: Annotating Data and Developing NE Tagger. In *Text, Speech and Dialogue*, pages 188–195, Pilsen, Czech Republic. Springer Berlin Heidelberg.

Benchmarking Pre-trained Language Models for Multilingual NER: TraSpaS at the BSNLP2021 Shared Task

Marek Šuppa*
Comenius University in Bratislava
marek@suppa.sk

Ondrej Jariabka*
Comenius University in Bratislava
o.jariabka@gmail.com

Abstract

In this paper we describe TraSpaS, a submission to the third shared task on named entity recognition hosted as part of the Balto-Slavic Natural Language Processing (BSNLP) Workshop. In it we evaluate various pre-trained language models on the NER task using three open-source NLP toolkits: character level language model with Stanza, language-specific BERT-style models with SpaCy and Adapter-enabled XLM-R with Trankit. Our results show that the Trankit-based models outperformed those based on the other two toolkits, even when trained on smaller amounts of data. Our code is available at https://github.com/NaiveNeuron/slavner-2021.

1 Introduction

This paper describes the TraSpaS submission to the third shared task of the Balto-Slavic Natural Language Processing (BSNLP) Workshop at EACL 2021. The task focuses on recognizing named entities (NER), their normalization and linking across six Slavic languages. The participants are provided training data comprised of news articles crawled from the web, centered around four specific topics and labeled on the document level, while the testing data consists of news articles focused on two topics, which are completely different from those included in the training data. This setup poses a significant research challenge, as it features languages with Latin as well as Cyrillic scripts, substantial class imbalance in the training data, specific set of named entity tags (which makes it difficult to find comparable datasets) as well as document-level annotation, which does not map directly to the more generally used token-level annotation and requires custom preprocessing. Our solution utilizes three open-source NLP toolkits, namely **Tra**nkit (Nguyen et al., 2021), **spa**Cy and **S**tanza (Qi et al., 2020), yielding the name TraSpaS. We chose these particular toolkits for their popularity, ability to exploit large pre-trained language models for the NER task, as well as their potential to be used in production deployments.

The research question we are trying to pose in this work can be paraphrased as follows: can the universal open-source NLP toolkits (such as SpaCy, Stanza or Trankit) be used to achieve competitive performance on Multilingual Named Entity Recognition? This has been tested to some extent in the previous edition of the shared task with NLP-Cube[1], albeit with not very encouraging results: on average it reached F1 scores of around 0.2 whereas the top three best performing systems regularly reported F1 scores of over 0.85. We hypothesize that the situation has changed significantly since then, mostly thanks to large pre-trained Transformer-based language models, which are being made accessible thanks to Huggingface's Transformers (Wolf et al., 2020). Hence, we believe that the customized setup that was previously required in order for models like BERT to be used may no longer be necessary and that competitive performance can be obtained using an off-the-shelf toolkit. Furthermore, this comparison sheds more light on multilingual transfer learning, as Stanza uses LSTM-based pre-trained language models and both spaCy and Trankit generally utilize variants of BERT. Moreover, since spaCy and Stanza defaults to using single-source models (i.e. one model per each language) and Trankit works primarily in the multi-source setup, our experiments allow us to compare these two approaches as well. We further investigate the impact of various tokenizers and additional data on final performance and perform a detailed error analysis.

*These authors contributed equally to the work

[1] https://github.com/adobe/NLP-Cube

Proceedings of the 8th BSNLP Workshop on Balto-Slavic Natural Language Processing, pages 105–114
April 20, 2021.

Our results indicate that the multi-source approach implemented using Trankit yielded the strongest performance, both on the development as well as the test set. The impact of additional data is pronounced in the case of single-source approach but does not lead to significant increase in performance of multi-source systems. The error analysis shows that all of the presented system struggle with the `EVT` (events) tag, which is the least populated in the training set. The highest error rate is between the `PRO` (products) and `ORG` (organizations) tags. We speculate that this might be due to many ambiguities between these two domains, such as "Uber", a product of the Uber company or "Ryanair Choice", a specific product which contains the name of the Ryanair airline. Some of these errors might be caused by the disambiguation rules outlined in the Task Guidelines.

2 Related Work

The Balto-Slavic NLP Workshop has previously organized two shared tasks. In the first one, held in 2017, no training data was provided and as reported in (Piskorski et al., 2017), due to the relatively high complexity of the task, only two teams have submitted the results within the task's deadline. The second one was held in 2019 and featured document-level annotated data in four languages (Bulgarian, Czech, Polish and Russian) on four specific topics, two of which were released as training set, with the remained serving as the test set. As (Piskorski et al., 2019) reports, most teams participating in this task used embeddings provided by the BERT model (Devlin et al., 2018), often in its multilingual version, coupled with cross-lingual training (Tsygankova et al., 2019) and CRF (Arkhipov et al., 2019) or NCRF++ (Emelyanov and Artemova, 2019) as the top-most layer. The work presented in (Tsygankova et al., 2019) is of particular note, as the authors show that multi-source training outperforms the single-source approach.

As one of the standard tasks of Natural Language Processing (NLP), Named Entity Recognition (NER) has been extensively studied in the past. In recent years, performance improvements have been obtained by the introduction of the Conditional Random Field (CRF) (Manning et al., 2014), especially when combined with neural representation of the input text, yielding the BiLSTM-CRF model (Lample et al., 2016). Further improvements can be attributed to the widespread use of contextual embeddings (Howard and Ruder, 2018; Peters et al., 2018; Devlin et al., 2018; Akbik et al., 2018) provided by large-scale language models. An example of such a model in the multilingual setup would be multilingual BERT (Devlin et al., 2018), which was trained on the text of top 104 largest Wikipedias. Its performance on the NER task has recently been improved by XLM (Lample and Conneau, 2019) which leverages cross-lingual language model pre-traning, and XLM-R (Conneau et al., 2019) which applies this pre-training approach to CommonCrawl data, which is significantly larger than data obtained from Wikipedia.

The increasing proliferation of open-source NLP toolkits has significantly lowered the barrier for inclusion of sophisticated language processing tools in larger systems. These include CoreNLP (Manning et al., 2014), FLAIR (Akbik et al., 2019), UDPipe (Straka, 2018), NLP Cube (Boroș et al., 2018) and spaCy[2], which is focused on industry usage and hence optimized for efficiency. Historically, the NLP toolkits have primarily supported a few major languages but recently the trend has reversed, with toolkits aiming to support the processing of multilingual text. Stanza (Qi et al., 2020) is one such toolkit, which provides pretrained models for 66 languages. These models are generally based on BiLSTM architecture, which is then amended for the target downstream task. Trankit (Nguyen et al., 2021) is a recently introduced toolkit based on the XLM-R language model, which also makes use of Adapters architecture (Pfeiffer et al., 2020). This allows the XLM-R model to be reused across languages and only a small number of parameters to be finetuned for a specific language and/or component of the toolkit.

3 The BSNLP2021 Shared Task

The BSNLP2021 Shared Task is the third installment of the Multilingual Named Entity Challenge in Slavic languages, organized as part of the 8th Workshop on Balto-Slavic Natural Language Processing. Similarly to its previous editions, it focuses on recognizing named entities in text of Web news articles, their normalization and linking across languages.

3.1 Dataset

In contrast to its previous editions, the dataset for this edition has been comprised of six languages:

[2] `https://spacy.io`

	ASIA BIBI						BREXIT					
	BG	CS	PL	RU	SL	UK	BG	CS	PL	RU	SL	UK
Documents	101	86	86	118	4	6	600	284	499	153	52	50
PER	976	712	863	933	41	43	3 539	1 159	3 120	1 523	651	319
LOC	543	400	504	664	27	60	4 690	1 541	4 912	853	552	607
ORG	231	247	336	455	9	36	4 366	1 460	5 141	1 035	533	193
PRO	70	46	57	48	3	1	499	265	845	140	35	18
EVT	17	3	13	1	0	0	1 813	546	1 426	445	375	208
Total Tags	1 837	1 408	1 773	2 101	80	140	14 907	4 971	15 444	3 996	2 146	1 345
Unique Tags	305	254	416	311	43	80	903	897	2 115	516	513	198
Ratio	6.02	5.54	4.26	6.76	1.86	1.75	16.51	5.54	7.3	7.74	4.18	6.79
Tokens	30 632	20 708	26 042	27 909	1 678	1 818	187 009	59 325	203 066	36 757	31 129	14 354
Unique Tokens	4 323	3 481	4 826	4 283	637	712	13 340	9 649	23 102	5 519	6 683	2 856

	NORD STREAM						OTHER	RYANAIR					
	BG	CS	PL	RU	SL	UK	SL	BG	CS	PL	RU	SL	UK
Documents	130	160	151	150	74	40	97	86	161	144	147	52	63
PER	350	567	540	375	742	64	934	168	136	148	67	138	35
LOC	1 425	1 981	1 952	1 730	2 018	608	765	431	976	946	995	527	586
ORG	649	590	1 009	941	804	613	753	283	1 035	817	842	618	462
PRO	396	451	955	536	343	8	176	74	74	122	74	148	20
EVT	7	19	14	5	54	15	64	6	12	6	0	11	0
Total Tags	2 827	3 608	4 470	3 587	3 961	1 308	2 692	962	2 233	2 039	1 978	1 442	1 103
Unique Tags	375	637	674	547	818	289	1 341	272	390	437	354	587	166
Ratio	7.54	5.66	6.63	6.56	4.84	4.53	2.01	3.54	5.73	4.67	5.59	2.46	6.64
Tokens	31 313	33 768	42 905	39 124	44 624	15 020	57 611	18 407	35 634	30 258	25 703	28 898	13 790
Unique Tokens	4 475	6 170	7 131	6 327	7 363	3 435	13 150	3 608	5 190	5 503	3 930	6 757	2 375

Table 1: Summary statistics of the BSNLP2021 Shared Task dataset.

Bulgarian, Czech, Polish, Russian, Slovene and Ukrainian. Three of these languages use Latin script (Czech, Polish and Slovene), with the remaining three being written in Cyrillic script. The dataset contains both the training and the test data from the previous edition of the Shared Task. These relate to news stories about a varied set of topics: ASIA BIBI (a Pakistani woman involved in a blasphemy case), BREXIT, RYANAIR and NORD STREAM. These were selected such that their coverage could be expected across multiple languages. In the interest of completeness we also mention that the dataset also contains a topic denoted OTHER, which features news labelled text articles only in Slovene.

The training data is annotated with five Named Entity classes: person names (PER), locations (LOC), organizations (ORG), products (PRO) and events (EVT). The annotations are provided on the document level, in the form of a surface form along with the corresponding tag, the normalized form an the link to the cross-lingual concept. Note that this form of annotation does not provide token-level information and may lead to ambiguities during conversion to more common BIO tagging formats.

The summary statistics of the dataset can be found in Table 1. The distribution of documents shows that BREXIT is by far the largest topic, having as much as 4.5x (in case of Bulgarian) documents as the second largest one. With regards to the document distribution across languages, we can conclude that it is on a similar level, except for Slovene (SL) and Ukrainian (UK), which tend to feature less documents across all topics as compared to the other four languages. This is especially pronounced in the case of ASIA BIBI with only four and six documents written in Slovene and Ukrainian, respectively. This is particularly interesting, as the ASIA BIBI topic has been used as the development set in previous work (Tsygankova et al., 2019; Emelyanov and Artemova, 2019). Despite losing the ability to compare directly with prior work, the presented statistics suggest that using a different topic as the development set may better approximate the test data (two sets of documents, each related to a specific topic, different from the topics in the existing training data sets).

The distribution of tags also highlights an imbalance in the provided training data. While the PER, LOC and ORG tags are distributed relatively evenly, the PRO and EVT tags have less examples in the training data. For instance, the ASIA BIBI topic does not contain EVT-tagged tokens in Slovene and Ukrainian, whereas the RYANAIR topic is missing them for Russian and Ukrainian. We therefore expect the recognition accuracy (as measured by the F-measure) to be lower for these two tags. This is in line with the results of the second edition of the BSNLP2021 Shared Task (Piskorski et al., 2019), where even the best model's performance on a specific language was markedly worse for these two tags.

3.2 Evaluation Metrics

When it comes to evaluation of NER systems, the most commonly used metric is the token-level F1 score, which further expects token-level annotations. Since data provided in this shared task are annotated on the document level a different type of metric needs to be used. The task definition[3] specifies two evaluation types that are to be used to evaluate this task: relaxed and strict evaluation.

Relaxed evaluation An entity is thought to be extracted correctly if the system response includes at least one annotation of a named mention of this entity. Whether the extracted entity is base form or not, does not play a role. Depending on whether partial matches count or the exact string must match, this type of evaluation can be executed with **partial match** or **exact match** criteria.

Strict evaluation The system response needs to capture and list all variant of an entity in order for it to be considered extracted correctly. Unless

[3] http://bsnlp.cs.helsinki.fi/shared-task.html

otherwise stated, all NER metrics in this document were computed via strict evaluation.

3.3 Subtasks

The shared task features three separate subtasks: Recognition, Lemmatization and Linking. We primarily focus on the Recognition part of the task by using the provided data to train custom models, as described in Section 4. For Lemmatization we use the pre-trained models that are provided by the toolkits in question. Since spaCy provides pre-trained Lemmatization models only for Russian and Polish, we use the surface form as the default lemma in all the other languages. As the Linking subtask is out of our focus, we return the same entity ID (`ORG-RAND`) for each detected entity.

4 Experimental Setup

4.1 Preprocessing

Since the training data provided, as part of the shared task, is annotated on the document level, a conversion step into a more commonly used format is necessary. To do so, we first need to split the raw text of each document into sentences and tokens. We therefore use NLTK (Bird, 2006) as well as pre-trained tokenizers from Stanza and Trankit. As NLTK does not provide a tokenizer for Bulgarian, Russian and Ukrainian, we use the English tokenizer for these languages instead. Further discussion on the effect of various tokenizers can be found in Section 6.2.

After tokenization, we proceed to convert the document-level annotations to token-level annotations (BIO format), which can be readily consumed by all three considered NLP toolkits. We do so by iterating over the annotations for each document and assigning token-level tags belonging to the exact matches of the named entity found in the respective raw document. Any token that was not covered by this procedure was deemed to be "other" (`O`). This approach may lead to two types of errors

1. Tagging a token with a specific tag when in reality it was of the "other" (`O`) class.

2. Tagging a token with a wrong tag.

The first type of error is difficult to assess without manual inspection, as it can only take place when depending on context the same surface form is and is not considered to be a named entity. Given the rich morphology of the Slavic languages we are dealing with, we believe this kind of error will be quite rare and can safely be ignored.

The second type of error can happen in cases when the same surface form is assigned multiple distinct named entity tags. In our analysis we found that this happened in only 155 cases in the whole training dataset. As such, we concluded this type of error would have minimal effect on the final performance and in cases we were detected multiple named entity tags to be associated with the same surface form the first occurrence was used in the conversion procedure outlined above.

During preprocessing we also noticed that despite it not being mentioned explicitly, in at least one example[4] the annotated surface form could not be found in the document's raw text but was located in its title. To cope with this, we consider the title to be part of the document text as well and tag it with the procedure outlined above as well.

4.2 Training and Development sets

As discussed in Section 3.1, given the language and tag distribution of the provided dataset, we chose the RYANAIR topic as the development set[5] for our experiments. All the other topics were used for training.

4.3 Additional data

Encouraged by the results reported in (Tsygankova et al., 2019), we investigate the effect of providing additional data for model training. Specifically, we use two datasets: English CoNLL 2003 and the WikiANN dataset (Pan et al., 2017; Rahimi et al., 2019). The former dataset is, as its name suggests, comprised of NER-annotated English documents, whereas the latter consists of NER-annotated Wikipedia documents written in 282 languages.

Apart from the `PER`, `LOC` and `ORG` tags, the English CoNLL 2003 data also contains the `MISC` tag. To make the dataset compatible with our existing datasets, we simply replace all occurrences of the `MISC` tag with the "other" (`O`) tag. Since the WikiANN dataset contains only the `PER`, `LOC` and `ORG` tags, we simply take all the data it has for the six languages that are part of the shared task.

[4]The surface form in question is "Japonci" and can be found in the file named `brexit_cs.txt_file_10.out`.

[5]The terms "development set" and "validation set" are used interchangeably throughout the document.

Possible interpretation	Choose
ORG + PER	PER
ORG + PRO	ORG

Table 2: Named Entity type disambiguation rules applied in postprocessing

4.4 Models

SpaCy With spaCy we trained a single model per language, using its defaults for training custom, accuracy-optimized NER models. For all languages this meant using embeddings from multilingual BERT (bert-base-multilingual-uncased), except for Ukrainian, for which spaCy provides a pre-trained RoBERTa-style model. Since we were not able to fine-tune this model to a performance that would be different from random, we opted for using the efficiency-optimized version of the Ukrainian model, which utilizes word vectors trained on the training dataset.

Stanza A separate model was trained for each language. It uses a forward and backward character-level LSTM model, whose outputs at the end of the word are concatenated with word embeddings and passed to a Bi-LSTM sequence tagger combined with a CRF-based decoder. This yield an architecture similar to that of (Akbik et al., 2018).

We trained the NER tagger with pre-trained word2vec word vectors from CoNLL 2017 Shared Task.

Trankit While Trankit can work in single-source as well as multi-source setup, in preliminary experiments we found that its multi-source performance was consistently significantly better. Therefore, in our experiments, we used Trankit in the multi-source setup, in which XLM-R (xlm-roberta-base) serves as the basis of the model and a custom NER-specific Adapter (Pfeiffer et al., 2020) is trained.

4.5 Postprocessing

When providing the the prediction output, we take the title as well as the text of the document and pass it to the pretrained model. The model's output is generally in the BIO format which is then converted to the output format specified by the shared task's guidelines.

Given the specifics of document-level annotation, the model can predict distinct tags for the surface form within the scope of a single document. If that happens, we choose the tag that was predicted most frequently for this surface form. In case of equal probability (i.e. two tags, each predicted only once) we apply the disambiguation rules[6] outlined in Table 2.

5 Results

The main results can be seen in Table 3, which lists the best performance of all benchmarked toolkits for each language. The (nltk), (st) and (tt) tags highlight that a particular model's training data has been tokenized with the NLTK, Stanza or Trankit tokenizer, respectively. The + WikiANN and + CoNLL2003 symbols indicate that the training data was extended with the WikiANN or CoNLL2003 datasets, as described in 4.3.

The table is split into four parts. In the first column are the names of the evaluated models, along with the aforementioned tags that alter their training set. The following six columns present the performance of respective models on the per-language subsets of the development set. The next five columns visualize the performance across the NER tags, while the last column is the F1 score computed on the whole development set. The presented metrics were computed using the official evaluation tool provided by the organizers of the shared task [7]. The test set results can be found in Table 5 in Appendix B.

6 Discussion

In this section we discuss several observations which follow from the results presented in Table 3. We can generally conclude that the multi-source approach implemented in Trankit tends to yield better results than the single-source (one model per each language) approach utilized by spaCy and Stanza, which is in line with the results reported in (Tsygankova et al., 2019). Across all modelsthe PRO and EVT tags report the worst performance, which is in line with our expectation from Section 3.1.

In the following subsections we discuss the impact of various pre-built models, the various evaluated tokenization methods, the inclusion of additional data and conduct an error analysis on the considered system.

[6] Rules adapted from http://bsnlp.cs.helsinki.fi/System_response_guidelines-1.2.pdf

[7] http://bsnlp.cs.helsinki.fi/program/BSNLP-NER-Evaluator-19.0.4.zip

	BG	CS	PL	RU	SL	UK	PER	LOC	ORG	PRO	EVT	All
spaCy												
+ (nltk) ③	75.59	88.69	90.29	84.73	83.01	79.11	78.32	92.29	81.75	57.38	40.68	85.14
Stanza												
+ (nltk)	79.54	82.82	78.21	85.81	71.12	86.78	58.04	90.87	78.71	48.08	18.87	80.83
+ (st) ①	81.14	82.71	78.46	85.60	73.34	90.14	64.33	91.84	77.25	46.98	10.35	81.61
+ (st) + WikiANN ②	86.25	90.58	88.42	89.09	83.90	92.29	76.43	95.17	87.61	56.42	28.07	88.55
Trankit												
+ (nltk) ④	85.82	92.72	**93.84**	92.62	87.41	**93.82**	87.48	**96.62**	90.42	**61.33**	**74.07**	91.60
+ (tt)	83.44	92.88	91.84	92.90	85.93	93.83	86.15	96.07	90.01	59.38	63.16	90.83
+ (st)	**86.43**	**93.31**	92.29	**93.26**	**88.52**	92.83	87.55	96.51	**91.41**	60.95	64.51	**91.81**
+ (st) + CoNLL2003	86.02	92.50	92.85	92.60	88.21	93.91	85.71	**96.62**	90.58	59.88	64.15	91.40
+ (st) + WikiANN ⑤	85.57	89.82	91.83	91.08	87.28	90.91	**88.54**	94.61	88.48	57.07	62.50	89.83

Table 3: F1 score results on the RYANAIR topic (dev set). The F1 scores are multiplied by 100 for convenience. Numbers in circles represent IDs of submitted systems. Their results on the test set can be found in Table 5.

6.1 Impact of Transformer-based pre-trained models

As the results across the whole dataset suggest (column All in Table 3), the Transformer-based pre-training using variants of BERT, which can be found in both spaCy and Trankit, generally yields better results than the pre-trained LSTM-based language model used in Stanza. While a Stanza-based model has eventually reported performance superior to that of spaCy, it only did so in a setup where additional data was used in its training.

A related effect can be observed in the case of Ukrainian (UK), where the spaCy model performed significantly worse than all the other presented models. We hypothesize this may be due to the fact that a BERT-based model was not used for this language/toolkit pair, as described in Section 4.4.

6.2 Impact of tokenizers

We can observe the impact of various tokenizers introduced in Section 4.1 in the results reported for the Stanza and Trankit toolkits in Table 3. They indicate that the Stanza tokenizer (denoted by `+ (st)`) yields the best results but that its impact is relatively minor, with the largest difference on the order of 0.01 F1-score point (90.83 vs 91.81).

6.3 Impact of additional data

The effect of including additional data in training can be see in Stanza, as well as Trankit models. In particular, the results in Table 3 show that the inclusion of the WikiANN dataset (marked with `WikiANN`) helps the Stanza model better performance than that reported by spaCy (88.55 vs 85.14). The largest gains were reported on Polish (PL) and Slovene (SL) part of the development set, where the performance increased by more than 10% in absolute F1 scores, from 78.46 to 88.42 in case of Polish and from 73.34 to 83.90 for Slovene. The same phenomenon was not observed on Trankit-based models where the inclusion of the WikiANN dataset actually hampered the final performance, compared to the model that only used the training data provided with the shared task. Similarly, the inclusion of the CoNLL 2003 dataset (denoted as `CoNLL2003`) also did not help increase the final performance. We hypothesize this may be due to the very specific domain of the development set, which only tangentially overlaps with the data included in the additional datasets.

6.4 Error analysis

Stanza As the Table 3 shows, the worst performance of Stanza systems is recorded for the `EVT` tags and the best score is achieved for the `LOC` tags. Figure 1 indicates that the `EVT`'s error distribution does not prominently feature any other tag. We believe this may be caused by the limited population of `EVT` in the dataset shown in Table 1. Moreover, this is further supported by the fact that the best score is achieved on `LOC` tag, which is also the most populous one.

Furthermore, we see that by far the biggest error rate (69.79%) is between the `PRO` and `ORG` tags (last row of the confusion matrix). The system is incapable of disambiguation between said tags, as the dataset itself can contain such ambiguities as is also mentioned in the Task Guidelines. We speculate that these ambiguities may be resolved using a knowledge base, which would directly as-

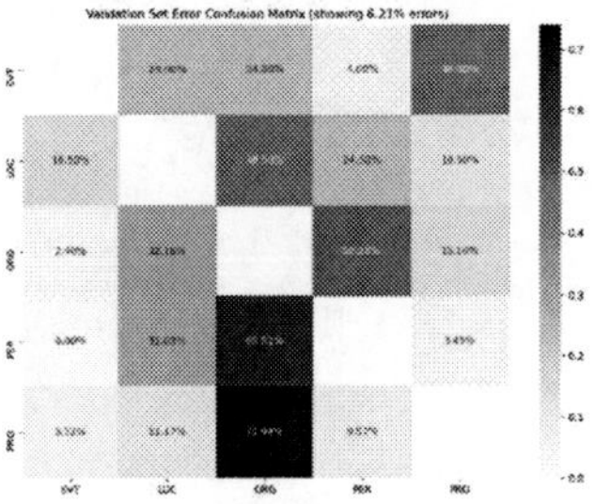

Figure 1: Confusion matrices showing *only* the errors made by the Stanza + (st) + WikiANN system. The error rate was 6.21%.

sociate specific terms with either products (PRO) or organizations (ORG).

Figure 2 shows the distribution of errors by language, where we can see that system achieves the worst performance on Russian language closely followed by Slovene. The models of both languages struggle with the ORG tag, with the highest error between true label PRO. In our experiments both languages benefited from longer training times. This fact might be used to improve the performance of the specific language models with longer training time and higher regularization as both languages are largely populated in the dataset.

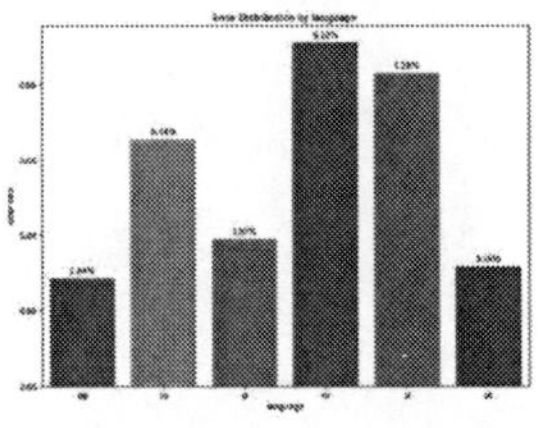

Figure 2: Error distribution across languages by Stanza + (st) + WikiANN system on the full dataset.

Trankit From Table 3, we can see that the best performing model is a Trankit with Stanza tokenizer. In Figure 3 we can see that overall errors made by all three subsystems on the validation set is quite lower compared to the one achieved by the Stanza system (Figure 1). This suggests that the Trankit system is more robust and can generalize better or that the Stanza system might suffer from overfitting, although we didn't see any evidence of such behavior during training.

Similarly to the other systems, we can see that Trankit also performs badly on the EVT tag and confuses it for other tags (LOC, ORG, PRO) with none of them having a prevalent error rate. We speculate that this is again symptom of its uniqueness and low frequency in the event tag domain.

Interestingly, the distribution of the LOC tag's errors changes with the addition of the Stanza tokenizer. This pushes most of the errors to the mismatch between LOC and ORG tags. This highlights the impact of various tokenizers on the overall performance of the model, and might indicate that better performance can be achieved by simply finetuning the tokenizers on a particular dataset.

All Trankit systems show the highest error rates between PRO and predicted ORG tags (last row of the confusion matrix). As we mentioned in the Section 6.4, this inability to disambiguate can be a consequence of the training set containing many such ambiguities, which is also mentioned in the Task Guidelines. For example, *"Ryanair Choice"* from document with id cs-new-36 contains the name of the company within the name of a product. It seems that from the context of the sentence *"Mezi výhody* Ryanair Choice *patří možnost..."* (translated to English as "The advantages of *Ryanair Choice* include"), our models are not able to disambiguate between the two acceptable tags and the rules mentioned in Table 2 then push the prediction to ORG, resulting in an incorrect prediction. For instance, "Boeing 747" is another example of company name included in the product tag, which could be swayed to the ORG prediction by the nature of the disambiguation rules. More examples of such errors in the RYANAIR topic across various languages can be found in Figure 4 in Appendix A.

Another set of problematic examples consist of those the where products have company names and the only disambiguation clue comes from a small part of the context sentence. One such example is *Uber* from file pl-261 and the sentence *"... stolicy regionu tanich platform taksówkarskich, takich jak* Uber *i Cabify."* (translated to English as "... the region's capital of low-cost taxi platforms such as *Uber* or Cabify). The sentence mentions Uber (the platform) which ought to be categorized as product offered by a company named Uber. The only clue for disambiguation between PRO and ORG in the considered sentence is the word "platform", which might be easily missed by the models. Moreover, the sentence would still make sense even without the word "platform" and in that context "Uber" would probably be tagged as ORG.

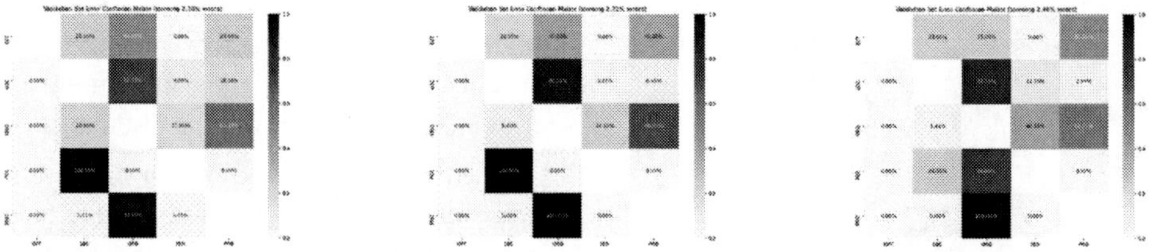

Figure 3: Confusion matrices showing *only* errors made by the Trankit + (st) + WikiANN (left, error rate 2.30%), Trankit + st (center, error rate 2.46%) and Trankit + st + CoNLL2003 (right, error rate 2.46%) system on validation set (RYANAIR topic.). The 100% error rate in the fourth row, for the left and center figure, is caused by a single example and can be ignored.

SpaCy SpaCy placed somewhere in the middle between all tested models which is shown in Table 1 and it also suffers from issues mentioned in the previous sections. Tts errors are visualized in Figure 4, which presents the confusion matrix between the predicted and true tags only for the 3.02% of errors made by the spaCy system on the dev set.

SpaCy system is more similar to Trankit in the types of error it makes, which is visible on the LOC and ORG tags (rows 2 and 3). While Stanza errors for LOC are split between ORG and PER tags, most of spaCy's errors are concentrated on the ORG tag, similarly to Trankit. This is not surprising, as both frameworks use BERT-based models. Errors in location domain often comes from multiword names of locations, such as "Letitě Václava Havla" (Vaclav Havel Airport) in cz-114, "Letališče Franza Liszta" (Francz Liszt Airport) in sl-75 or "Združeni arabski Emirati" (United Arab Emirates) in sl-75.

SpaCy does not improve on the PRO - ORG tag miss-matches (last row of the confusion matrix) and comparably to previously discussed systems, the language with the most errors on the validation set was Bulgarian, with the most miss-classified word "Райънеър", which stands for "Ryanair" and it's variants, such as, "Ryanaira" or "Ryanairze".

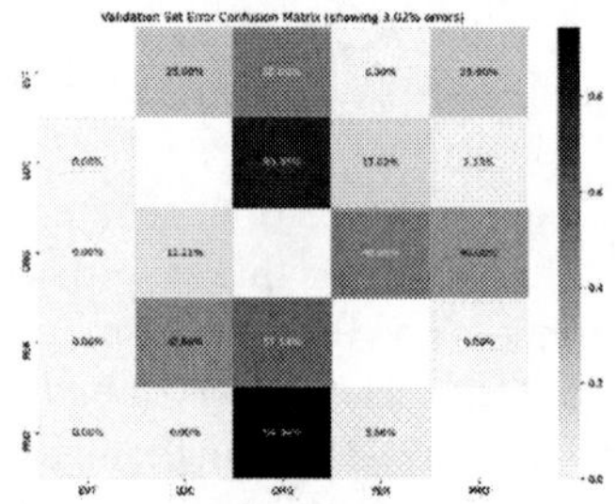

Figure 4: Confusion matrix showing only the errors of the SpaCy system on validation set (RYANAIR topic). The error rate was 3.02%.

7 Conclusions

This paper describes the TraSpaS submission to the BSNLP 2021 shared task on multilingual named entity recognition in which three open-source NLP toolkits were benchmarked. The results show that the approach implemented using the Trankit toolkit, based on the XLM-R pre-trained language, produced a model with the best results on both the development as well as the test set. While additional data did help in the case of the other two frameworks, the effect on the Trankit-based models was mostly negative. Error analysis on the development set indicates that many errors of our models could be attributed due to ambiguities in the training data.

References

Alan Akbik, Tanja Bergmann, Duncan Blythe, Kashif Rasul, Stefan Schweter, and Roland Vollgraf. 2019. Flair: An easy-to-use framework for state-of-the-art nlp. In *Proceedings of the 2019 Conference of the North American Chapter of the Association for Computational Linguistics (Demonstrations)*, pages 54–59.

Alan Akbik, Duncan Blythe, and Roland Vollgraf. 2018. Contextual string embeddings for sequence labeling. In *Proceedings of the 27th international conference on computational linguistics*, pages 1638–1649.

Mikhail Arkhipov, Maria Trofimova, Yurii Kuratov, and Alexey Sorokin. 2019. Tuning multilingual transformers for language-specific named entity recognition. In *Proceedings of the 7th Workshop on Balto-Slavic Natural Language Processing*, pages 89–93.

Steven Bird. 2006. Nltk: the natural language toolkit. In *Proceedings of the COLING/ACL 2006 Interactive Presentation Sessions*, pages 69–72.

Tiberiu Boroș, Stefan Daniel Dumitrescu, and Ruxandra Burtica. 2018. NLP-cube: End-to-end raw text processing with neural networks. In *Proceedings of the CoNLL 2018 Shared Task: Multilingual Parsing from Raw Text to Universal Dependencies*, pages 171–179, Brussels, Belgium. Association for Computational Linguistics.

Alexis Conneau, Kartikay Khandelwal, Naman Goyal, Vishrav Chaudhary, Guillaume Wenzek, Francisco Guzmán, Edouard Grave, Myle Ott, Luke Zettlemoyer, and Veselin Stoyanov. 2019. Unsupervised cross-lingual representation learning at scale. *arXiv preprint arXiv:1911.02116*.

Jacob Devlin, Ming-Wei Chang, Kenton Lee, and Kristina Toutanova. 2018. Bert: Pre-training of deep bidirectional transformers for language understanding. *arXiv preprint arXiv:1810.04805*.

Anton A Emelyanov and Ekaterina Artemova. 2019. Multilingual named entity recognition using pretrained embeddings, attention mechanism and ncrf. *arXiv preprint arXiv:1906.09978*.

Jeremy Howard and Sebastian Ruder. 2018. Universal language model fine-tuning for text classification. *arXiv preprint arXiv:1801.06146*.

Guillaume Lample, Miguel Ballesteros, Sandeep Subramanian, Kazuya Kawakami, and Chris Dyer. 2016. Neural architectures for named entity recognition. *arXiv preprint arXiv:1603.01360*.

Guillaume Lample and Alexis Conneau. 2019. Cross-lingual language model pretraining. *arXiv preprint arXiv:1901.07291*.

Christopher Manning, Mihai Surdeanu, John Bauer, Jenny Finkel, Steven Bethard, and David McClosky. 2014. The Stanford CoreNLP natural language processing toolkit. In *Proceedings of 52nd Annual Meeting of the Association for Computational Linguistics: System Demonstrations*, pages 55–60, Baltimore, Maryland. Association for Computational Linguistics.

Minh Nguyen, Viet Lai, Amir Pouran Ben Veyseh, and Thien Huu Nguyen. 2021. Trankit: A light-weight transformer-based toolkit for multilingual natural language processing. In *Proceedings of the 16th Conference of the European Chapter of the Association for Computational Linguistics: System Demonstrations*.

Xiaoman Pan, Boliang Zhang, Jonathan May, Joel Nothman, Kevin Knight, and Heng Ji. 2017. Cross-lingual name tagging and linking for 282 languages. In *Proceedings of the 55th Annual Meeting of the Association for Computational Linguistics (Volume 1: Long Papers)*, pages 1946–1958.

Matthew E Peters, Mark Neumann, Mohit Iyyer, Matt Gardner, Christopher Clark, Kenton Lee, and Luke Zettlemoyer. 2018. Deep contextualized word representations. *arXiv preprint arXiv:1802.05365*.

Jonas Pfeiffer, Andreas Rücklé, Clifton Poth, Aishwarya Kamath, Ivan Vulić, Sebastian Ruder, Kyunghyun Cho, and Iryna Gurevych. 2020. Adapterhub: A framework for adapting transformers. *arXiv preprint arXiv:2007.07779*.

Jakub Piskorski, Laska Laskova, Michał Marcińczuk, Lidia Pivovarova, Pavel Přibáň, Josef Steinberger, and Roman Yangarber. 2019. The second cross-lingual challenge on recognition, normalization, classification, and linking of named entities across slavic languages. In *Proceedings of the 7th Workshop on Balto-Slavic Natural Language Processing*, pages 63–74.

Jakub Piskorski, Lidia Pivovarova, Jan Šnajder, Josef Steinberger, and Roman Yangarber. 2017. The first cross-lingual challenge on recognition, normalization, and matching of named entities in slavic languages. In *Proceedings of the 6th Workshop on Balto-Slavic Natural Language Processing*, pages 76–85.

Peng Qi, Yuhao Zhang, Yuhui Zhang, Jason Bolton, and Christopher D. Manning. 2020. Stanza: A Python natural language processing toolkit for many human languages. In *Proceedings of the 58th Annual Meeting of the Association for Computational Linguistics: System Demonstrations*.

Afshin Rahimi, Yuan Li, and Trevor Cohn. 2019. Massively multilingual transfer for NER. In *Proceedings of the 57th Annual Meeting of the Association for Computational Linguistics*, pages 151–164, Florence, Italy. Association for Computational Linguistics.

Milan Straka. 2018. Udpipe 2.0 prototype at conll 2018 ud shared task. In *Proceedings of the CoNLL 2018 Shared Task: Multilingual Parsing from Raw Text to Universal Dependencies*, pages 197–207.

Tatiana Tsygankova, Stephen Mayhew, and Dan Roth. 2019. Bsnlp2019 shared task submission: Multisource neural ner transfer. In *Proceedings of the 7th Workshop on Balto-Slavic Natural Language Processing*, pages 75–82.

Thomas Wolf, Julien Chaumond, Lysandre Debut, Victor Sanh, Clement Delangue, Anthony Moi, Pierric Cistac, Morgan Funtowicz, Joe Davison, Sam Shleifer, et al. 2020. Transformers: State-of-the-art natural language processing. In *Proceedings of the 2020 Conference on Empirical Methods in Natural Language Processing: System Demonstrations*, pages 38–45.

A Sample of miss-categorized terms (PRO vs ORG)

words	language
Pixabay	cs
Skyscanner	cs
Ryanair Choice	cs
Cabify	pl
Wizz Tours	pl
Uber	pl
CNN	sl
737	sl
БНТ	bg
БНР	bg
Марица	bg
Дарик	bg
DW	ru
Ryanair	ru
Corriere della Sera	ru
DW	ru
ЄП	uk
Boeing 737	uk

Table 4: Examples of miss-categorised words between PRO and ORG tags on validation set (RYANAIR topic).

B Test set results

ID	BG	CS	PL	RU	SL	UK	All
①	72.93	70.66	73.79	60.18	72.03	65.39	67.74
②	72.12	69.37	76.43	60.19	72.03	63.79	67.63
③	65.29	71.06	79.61	57.14	72.65	48.28	64.61
④	**79.00**	**78.33**	**82.08**	**64.12**	**81.48**	**75.36**	**77.41**
⑤	77.19	74.69	81.07	60.03	79.53	69.88	74.56

Table 5: Results of the submitted systems on the test set. The numbers represent the F1 scores, multiplied by 100 for convenience. The definition of the systems can be found in Table 3.

Named Entity Recognition and Linking Augmented with Large-Scale Structured Data

Paweł Rychlikowski
University of Wrocław
prych@cs.uni.wroc.pl

Bartłomiej Najdecki
University of Wrocław
bnajdecki@gmail.com

Adrian Łańcucki
NVIDIA Corporation
alancucki@nvidia.com

Adam Kaczmarek
VoiceLab AI
adam.kaczmarek@voicelab.ai

Abstract

In this paper we describe our submissions to the 2nd and 3rd SlavNER Shared Tasks held at BSNLP 2019 and BSNLP 2021, respectively. The tasks focused on the analysis of Named Entities in multilingual Web documents in Slavic languages with rich inflection. Our solution takes advantage of large collections of both unstructured and structured documents. The former serve as data for unsupervised training of language models and embeddings of lexical units. The latter refers to Wikipedia and its structured counterpart - Wikidata, our source of lemmatization rules, and real-world entities. With the aid of those resources, our system could recognize, normalize and link entities, while being trained with only small amounts of labeled data.

1 Introduction

Intelligent analysis of texts written in natural languages, despite the advancements made with deep neural networks, is still regarded as challenging. The *lingua franca* of science is English, and new methods are typically evaluated firstly on English data, and often on other Germanic or Romance languages. This puts a certain bias on the development and design of modern NLP methods, which are not always transferable, and the metrics comparable, across languages and language families.

Due to the complexity and inherent vagueness of intelligent language processing, is has been naturally split into simple tasks, one of which is named entity recognition (NER), concerned in this paper. The output of a NER system is traditionally a set labelled phrases recognized in a given text. In order to process a document, one has to not only find and label the entities, but also link appropriately subsequent occurrences of the same entity. The task becomes harder, if the linking can be made across languages, when the entities are globally present.

We describe our submission to the *3rd Multilingual Named Entity Challenge in Slavic languages*, held at the 8th Workshop on Balto-Slavic Natural Language Processing (BSNLP) in conjunction with the EACL 2021 conference. The system was similar to the one submitted to the *2nd Multilingual Named Entity Challenges in Slavic languages* (Piskorski et al., 2019) held at 7th BSNLP Workshop in conjunction with ACL 2019 conference, and we discuss the differences between both systems.

The aim of those shared tasks was to recognize, normalize, and ultimately link - on a document, language and cross-language level - all named entities in collections of documents concerning the same topic, e.g., the 2020 US presidential election. Named entities have been split into five categories: PER (person), LOC (location), ORG (organization), PRO (product), and EVT (event). The 2019 edition featured four Slavic languages (Czech, Russian, Bulgarian, Polish), and the 2021 edition featured six languages (the previous four plus Ukrainian and Sloven).

In our solution we have combined models trained unsupervised on large datasets, and fine-tuned on small ones in a supervised way, with simple, white-box algorithms that perform later stages of processing in a stable and predictable manner. In addition, we have taken advantage of similarities between certain languages in order to augment the data and further improve the results.

2 Our Approach

Our system chains three modules for named entity recognition, lemmatization, and linking, which correspond to the objectives of the BSNLP Shared Task. We describe them in detail in the following sections. Our submissions for the 2019 and the 2021 shared tasks were similar, and differed

Proceedings of the 8th BSNLP Workshop on Balto-Slavic Natural Language Processing, pages 115–121
April 20, 2021.

Table 1: Class label mapping to the shared task label set in additional training datasets: KPWr (Marcińczuk et al., 2016), CNEC (Ševčíková et al., 2014), and FactRuEval (Starostin et al., 2016)

KPWr	PER	nam_adj_person, nam_liv_*
	LOC	nam_adj_city, nam_oth_address_-street, nam_fac_*, nam_loc_*
	EVT	nam_eve_*
	PRO	nam_oth_tech, nam_pro_*, nam_-oth_license, nam_oth_stock_in-dex
	ORG	nam_org_*
CNEC	PER	p (personal names)
	LOC	g (geographical names)
	EVT	ia (conferences), tc (centuries), tf (feasts), tp (epochs)
	PRO	cs (article titless), mn (periodicals), oa (cultural artifacts), op (products), or (directives)
	ORG	ic (cultural/edu/science institutions), if (companies), io (govt. inst.), mt (tv stations)
FactRu	PER	name, surname, nickname, patronymic
	LOC	geo_adj, loc_descr, loc_name
	PRO	job, prj_name, prj_desc
	ORG	facility_descr, org_descr

only in the first element of the chain - the entity recognition method.

2.1 Recognition

2.1.1 Additional Training Data

Because the training datasets were small, we looked for other labeled datasets. There is no common standard of labelling NER datasets, and those extra datasets had to be remapped into the label set of the shared task. However, their addition did improve the recognition scores, and we describe them in the following paragraphs.

PL We used 1343 documents from KPWr with Named Entity annotations pre-processed with `liner2-convert` (Marcińczuk et al., 2017) tool, flattening and mapping original categories as shown in Table 1.

RU, BG, UK For languages with Cyrillic script we used FactRuEval2016 (Starostin et al., 2016) corpus consisting of 255 documents with 11754 annotated spans. Interestingly, the addition of this dataset improved scores for BG and UK despite the language mismatch.

CS, SL For Czech and Slovene we used Czech Named Entity Corpus (Ševčíková et al., 2014) containing 8993 sentences with manually annotated 35220 named entities, classified according to a two-level hierarchy.

2.1.2 Flair-based Recognition System

Recognition in our 2019 submission was realized with Flair (Akbik et al., 2018), a model made of the embedding layer and a bi-directional LSTM with a Conditional Random Field output (BiLSTM-CRF). The embedding layer aggregated pre-trained word representations of varying granularity and origin (word embeddings, subword embeddings (Heinzerling and Strube, 2018), contextual *forward* and *backward* character embeddings inherent to Flair).

Because of the data scarcity, we adopted the philosophy of making our systems „neural gazetteers". To this end, we tried to collect as much various embeddings as possible. This line of reasoning applied especially to word-level embeddings. Ideally we wanted our systems to have, for every language, embeddings trained on Wikipedia, Common Crawl[1], and a collection of news articles.

We found it beneficial to mix word pieces and character embeddings between languages. For instance, our model for Russian used Bulgarian embeddings.This is especially useful when the model of specific granularity in the target language is unavailable. Lastly, we also found it beneficial to mix training data for seemingly related languages, and improved the scores by adding our additional FactRuEval data to the Bulgarian training dataset.

Our recurrent recognition model underperformed in comparison to the top 2019 contestants, notably those based on BERT (Arkhipov et al., 2019; Devlin et al., 2019). We present an excerpt from the 2019 recognition results in Section 3.1.

2.1.3 FLERT-based Recognition System

For our submission to the 2021 BSNLP Shared Task we have used FLERT (Schweter and Akbik, 2020), a state-of-the-art architecture for named entity recognition. It is a BERT-style transformer approach, in which a XLM-RoBERTa model (Conneau et al., 2019), initially trained on a 100-language Common Crawl corpus (Wenzek et al., 2020), is fine-tuned on a small, language-specific corpus. This model departs from training an output CRF. We found that FLERT models train fast, and outperform our previously used Flair models by a significant margin.

[1] `http://commoncrawl.org`

2.2 Lemmatization

In the process of lemmatization of compound phrases, some words are converted into their lemmas, and some words remain unchanged. Occasionally some words are changed into other forms, e.g., adjectives might be transformed to nominatives with an appropriate gender. In the low-data regime of the shared task, we have opted for a simple rule-based system and data augmentation.

We pose the lemmatization task as splitting a word w into two concatenated parts $w = w_1w_2$, and computing the lemma as w_1v_2, where $(w_2, v_2) \in R_{lem}$, and R_{lem} is a small set of single-word lemmatization rules.

We use two main additional sources of information:

Wikipedia We take advantage of numerous links between articles, from which we extract pairs `[[text anchor|document title]]`. The anchors often are the inflected forms, and document titles the lemmatized forms of the same entity. In order to filter out spurious we consider a pair *(anchor, title)* a correct lemmatization if both the anchor and the text have the same number of words, and every i-th word in a title is either equal to the i-th word in an anchor, or is its possible lemma.

Finally, we heuristically recognize a small set of of words for later use, which we call **stopper words**. We define them as words shared between the anchor and the title, such that all words that follow them are identical in the anchor and the title, e.g., in the *(anchor, title)* pair

(Bazylikę św. Pawła za Murami,
Bazylika św. Pawła za Murami),

a stoper word is *"św."*.

Universal Dependencies (UD) (Universal Dependencies Consortium, 2021) is a large collection of treebanks in multiple languages. We extract morphosyntactic information (word, lemma, POS-tags and additional parameters[2]) from the words present in UD subsets for our target languages. Using that information, we construct single-word lemmatization rules. We say that the word w is a possible lemma of v if there is a one word lemmatization rule transforming v into w.

[2] We take the 'international version' of these parameters

PoliMorfologik For the Polish language, we additionally use PoliMorfologik (Woliński et al., 2012), a comprehensive morphosyntactic dictionary, which allows us to extract a large collection of lemmatization rules.

2.2.1 Lemmatization Schemas

Lemmatization of every phrase gives rise to a lemmatization schema. It works as follows: for every word we take its suffix (the longest suffix which occurs in the list of 2000 most popular suffices), in that way we obtain the left-hand side of the rule. The right-hand side describes, how this suffices should be transformed. For instance for the pair

(Václavem Havlem, Václav Havel)

we obtain a rule

(-vem, -vlem) $\longrightarrow$ *(-v, -vel)*.

Our lemmatization algorithm takes a phrase (named entity found in the first stage) and returns its lemma. It follows that we do not consider every information from the words surrounding the phrase/context. Afterwards, we try to apply the following heuristics in a given order:

1. Try to find the (rightmost) stopper word. If there is one, then leave unchanged suffix of the phrase after the stopper (including the stopper itself), find the lemma for the prefix.
2. Try to apply rule based agreement phrase lemmatization (only for Polish)
3. Try to find the lemmatization schema suitable for the phrase. If there are more than one such rule, use the one which gives ‚more natural lemmatization' (which prefers common words and words occurring in lemmas)
4. Replace every word with its most popular lemma (in the training data, and in Wikipedia), if the word doesn't occur leave it unchanged

2.3 Entity Linking

A recognized entity, associated with a category and a normalized lemma, has to be linked with other occurrences of this entity (in this document, in other documents, and ultimately across the documents in all languages). The task is difficult due to the subtle differences between seemingly identical

Table 2: Relations between Wikidata categories and named entity categories

Label	Top-level Wikidata Entities
PER	human (Q5), nationality (Q231002), ethnic group (Q41710)
LOC	locality (Q3257686), location (Q2221906), spatial entity (Q58416391), geologic province (Q214045)
EVT	event (Q1656682), social phenomenon (Q602884), occurrence (Q1190554)
PRO	type of manufactured good (Q22811462), tangible good (Q1485500), broadcasting program (Q11578774), intellectual work (Q15621286), television station (Q1616075)
ORG	organization (Q43229), trade agreement (Q252550), company (Q783794)

entities. Consider *Donald Trump* entity: its one occurrence could be linked with *the 45th president of the United States*, or *Donald Trump Jr*, depending on the role in the text, but not with both at the same time.

We divide the task into two phases: 1) initial assignment of identifiers, and 2) refinement of identifiers. Our linking algorithm relies on three kinds of matches: exact matches of entity names, partial matches, and fuzzy matches with word embeddings. In order to ground the recognized entities regardless of the language, as well as extend our inventory of entities and their possible names, we use Wikidata[3] as a catalogue of entities.

2.3.1 Wikidata

Wikidata is a structured database of entities extracted from Wikipedia. Every entity has a unique identifier, e.g. `Q123456`, a list of labels and languages for each label, a description and subclasses/instances of properties, and relationships to other Wikidata entities (*instance of*, *part of*, etc.), which form a graph.

Thanks to the hierarchy of the relations, we have selected a handful of top-level Wikidata entities (Table 2), and collected all their descendants into sets of *wikidata_entities*. These are further weighted by their Term Frequency in Wikidata, so we could resolve collisions in favor of the most popular entities.

2.3.2 Initial Assignment of Identifiers

In a typical, coherent paragraph, the narrative develops with every new sentence. Upon introduction, the entities are named carefully (e.g., with a full name, expanded acronym), to be shortened later, when it is clear from the context what they refer to. For this reason we designed a stateful algorithm, that processes and refines a local list of *doc_entities* caught in the document.

Algorithm 1 outlines the linking procedure. Assignment of identifiers is performed separately for every document with the ADD_AND_LINK function. It processes a lemmatized set of entities recognized earlier modules of our system. Two kinds of entity dictionaries: *doc_entities*, which is local to a function, and a global *wikidata_entities*, which we prepare earlier using Wikidata. Those dictionaries map the textual mentions to identifiers from Wikidata and the target language, e.g., *Donald Trump* maps to `[(Q22686, en), (Q22686, pl), (Q22686, cs), (Q3713655, cs)]` (the last identifier refers to *Donald Trump Jr*).

We process document entities starting from the longest ones, and for each select the best entity id with the BEST_ID function. It firstly prefers the matching entries from the *doc_entities* dictionary, and secondly the most popular Wikidata entries (by Term Frequency) from *wikidata_entities*. For instance, with the local *doc_entities* dictionary, after processing *Donald Trump*, a subsequent shorter mention *Trump* should be linked with it.

The function ALIASES handles only PRO and ORG labels, and returns a list of all short forms and acronyms specific to those labels, present in Wikidata, e.g., *Sony Ericsson* is aliased as *SE*.

2.3.3 Refinement of Identifiers

The refinement stage uses dense embeddings of phrases in order to uncover high similarities between them, that might have been otherwise missed. We use FastText (Bojanowski et al., 2017), which is suited for morphologically rich Slavic languages, since the representations are built from generic subword units.

The refinement is carried out in two phases. In the first one, all phrases with the same identifier are grouped together. In the second one, two groups are merged into one if there exist two mentions (one per each group) with sufficiently similar embeddings measured by their dot product. Phrases are embedded as sums of embeddings of their words. When we merge two groups, we assign to them the identifier with a higher Wikidata term frequency. We refine identifiers only on the single language level.

[3] `http://www.wikidata.org`

Algorithm 1 Basic routines of the linking algorithm

```
function ADD_AND_LINK(ners)
    doc_entities, linked ← {}, {}
    for (phrase, lemma, type) in SORTED(ners) do        ▷ Descending by the # of words in a phrase
        P_1 ← GET_IDENTIFIERS(phrase, doc_entities)
        P_2 ← GET_IDENTIFIERS(lemma, doc_entities)
        id ← BEST_ID(lemma, P_1 + P_2 + [lemma + type])
        linked[(phrase, lemma, type)] ← id
        doc_entities ← doc_entities ∪ ALIASES(lemma, id)
    return linked

function GET_IDENTIFIERS(phrase, doc_entities)
    res ← []
    for (doc_phrase, id) in doc_entities do              ▷ IDs matching in the document
        if SAME_ENTITY(doc_phrase, phrase) then
            APPEND(res, id)
    if phrase ∈ wikidata_entities then                    ▷ The most common ID for a phrase
        APPEND(res, wikidata_entities[lemma])
    return res
```

3 Evaluation

We present experiments carried out on different levels of the entity recognition pipeline. The data used in those experiments comes from the BSNLP 2019 Shared Task test set (*Nord Stream* and *Ryanair* subsets). Our algorithms are tested in the submitted form and have not been further adapted to those datasets.

3.1 The 2019 Shared Task

Recognition Table 3 summarizes *strict* recognition results on the test data.

Lemmatization We analyzed the influence of various part of lemmatization on the performance of our method. The results are shown in Table 4. Our baseline is the identity function, in which we assume a phrase being its own lemma.

One should be aware that due to the small amount of test data, the results should be treated as approximate. Some differences can be caused by bad lemmatization of one phrase (especially if the phrase occurs many times in test data). It seems that all implemented heuristic are reasonable and improve over the baseline. Moreover, it is easy to see that links from Wikipedia are useful source of information in this task.

Entity Linking Table 5 shows the result of linking. Even though our recognizer did not hold up to the competition, the linking algorithm was able to close the gap in F1 score. In order to test the algorithm in ablation, we include linking results on ground truth lemmatized data (Lemma Oracle).

Table 3: 2019 BSNLP Shared Task selected results (*strict* recognition evaluation, test set, F1 metric). For every submitter, the best solution is shown with respect to the average performance on all languages.

Model	Testset	BG	CS	PL	RU	All
RIS-slav_lemma	NordS	0.84	0.89	0.89	0.78	0.85
CogComp-7	NordS	0.84	0.89	0.86	0.72	0.83
IIUWR.PL-5	NordS	0.71	0.83	0.86	0.65	0.78
TLR	NordS	0.73	0.74	0.72	0.60	0.70
Cog_Tech_Cent-4	NordS	-	-	-	0.69	0.69
Sberiboba	NordS	0.63	0.71	0.68	0.60	0.66
JRC-TMA-CC-4	NordS	0.67	0.50	0.42	0.52	0.52
NLP_Cube	NordS	0.14	0.16	0.09	0.11	0.12
CogComp-6	Ryanair	0.88	0.94	0.91	0.94	0.92
RIS-slav_lemma	Ryanair	0.86	0.94	0.92	0.91	0.91
Cog_Tech_Cent-4	Ryanair	-	-	-	0.91	0.91
IIUWR.PL-4	Ryanair	0.76	0.87	0.84	0.79	0.82
TLR	Ryanair	0.76	0.83	0.82	0.83	0.82
Sberiboba	Ryanair	0.65	0.84	0.81	0.72	0.77
JRC-TMA-CC-1	Ryanair	0.64	0.55	0.52	0.79	0.64
NLP_Cube	Ryanair	0.15	0.13	0.19	0.18	0.16

3.2 The 2021 Shared Task

We present the results of our FLERT-based submission, which are partial results of the entire shared task available at the time of writing.

One of the sets of articles in the training data is devoted to COVID-19. This situation is unusual: the phrase very often used in test data, does not

Table 4: Accuracy of our rule-based lemmatization algorithm on the 2019 BSNLP Shared Task training data. Abbreviations: **p** – phrase lemmatization rules, **w** – separate lemmatization of words, **W** – additional Wikipedia data, **a** – handwritten agreement rules (Polish only), **s** – uses *stoper words*.

Method	BG	CS	PL	RU	Avg
Baseline	89.02	59.23	54.51	54.79	63.00
+a	89.02	59.23	58.53	54.79	64.12
+w	89.91	64.39	74.17	57.23	70.41
+p	89.18	67.47	79.12	57.53	72.34
+wW	92.73	71.29	81.27	86.71	82.62
+pW	88.53	81.78	80.77	89.16	84.97
+paswW	91.60	81.69	82.42	89.28	86.14
+pasW	92.33	81.86	83.57	89.99	**86.83**

appear at all in the training data (also in the data used to pre-train language model).

We have verified that our NER models struggle with assigning consistent labels to the phrase *COVID-19*, which is common in the test data. An additional difficulty is the ambiguity of this phrase, which may refer to a disease and possibly remain unclassified as a named entity, or a pandemic and be classified as EVT. We decided to do a simple post-processing which assigns EVT to all COVID-19 phrases recognized by the NER module.

We think that this situation is so unusual that in a real system, used in the industry, it would be handled using a special ad-hoc rule. Moreover, we wanted to know, what are the result of this fixed assignment, and submitted two versions of our solutions.

Table 5: 2019 BSNLP Shared Task results (cross-language linking, test data). For every team we present their highest scoring submission wrt. the F1 metric. (*) The oracle model (first row for every dataset) is our entity linking algorithm run on the ground truth lemmatized data after the competition.

Model	Testset	F1	Prec.	Rec.
Ours + Lemma Oracle	Ryanair	0.76*	0.83*	0.70*
Ours (IIUWR.PL-5)	Ryanair	0.49	0.80	0.35
JRC-TMA-CC-2	Ryanair	0.27	0.67	0.17
CogComp-3	Ryanair	0.13	0.07	0.73
RIS-merge	Ryanair	0.10	0.06	0.70
Sberiboba	Ryanair	0.10	0.06	0.30
NLP_Cube	Ryanair	0.00	0.67	0.00
Ours + Lemma Oracle	NordS	0.59*	0.74*	0.50*
Ours (IIUWR.PL-5)	NordS	0.42	0.73	0.29
JRC-TMA-CC-2	NordS	0.31	0.69	0.20
RIS-merge_lemma	NordS	0.11	0.06	0.72
CogComp-3	NordS	0.11	0.06	0.68
Sberiboba	NordS	0.06	0.03	0.36
NLP_Cube	NordS	0.00	0.46	0.00

Table 6: 2021 BSNLP Shared Task selected results (test set, F1 metric): *strict* recognition, normalization, language-level linking (coreference). NC refers to the submission without fixed labelling of COVID-19 occurrences as EVT.

Task	Testset	CS	RU	BG	UK	SL	PL	All
Recon.	US Elect.	0.87	0.70	0.82	0.79	0.88	0.86	0.79
	COVID-19	0.80	0.57	0.72	0.75	0.77	0.81	0.73
(NC)	US Elect.	0.87	0.70	0.82	0.79	0.88	0.85	0.78
	COVID-19	0.80	0.55	0.68	0.72	0.75	0.78	0.71
Norm.	US Elect.	0.52	0.26	0.51	0.26	0.62	0.62	0.43
	COVID-19	0.45	0.27	0.33	0.51	0.53	0.57	0.45
Link.	US Elect.	0.66	0.39	0.69	0.52	0.66	0.70	0.56
	COVID-19	0.66	0.39	0.68	0.61	0.66	0.73	0.62
(NC)	US Elect.	0.66	0.39	0.68	0.52	0.66	0.70	0.55
	COVID-19	0.66	0.39	0.67	0.61	0.66	0.72	0.62

4 Conclusion

This paper describes our submissions to the 2019 and 2021 BSNLP Shared Tasks on named entity recognition on Slavic languages. Even though the training data was scarce, we have used large-scale datasets: corpora of unstructured text in the unsupervised training phase of training of the recognition model, and structured Wikipedia and Wikidata knowledge bases in order to extract rules and entities for lemmatization and linking phases. The linking algorithm is a strong point of our submission. In the 2019 task it allowed to close the performance gap between our solution and competitors, introduced by a weak initial recognition model. The results suggest that, perhaps, there is still a white spot in between supervised and unsupervised neural learning, where the structure of the data matters more than volume, and simple rule-based system excel.

Acknowledgment

The authors thank Polish National Science Center for funding under the OPUS-18 2019/35/B/ST6/04379 grant. We also would like to thank Adam Wawrzyński and Wojciech Janowski from VoiceLab AI for their support during conducting experiments and model training.

References

Alan Akbik, Duncan Blythe, and Roland Vollgraf. 2018. Contextual string embeddings for sequence labeling. In *Proceedings of the 27th International Conference on Computational Linguistics*, pages 1638–1649, Santa Fe, New Mexico, USA. Association for Computational Linguistics.

Mikhail Arkhipov, Maria Trofimova, Yuri Kuratov, and Alexey Sorokin. 2019. Tuning multilingual transformers for language-specific named entity recognition. In *Proceedings of the 7th Workshop on Balto-Slavic Natural Language Processing*, pages 89–93, Florence, Italy. Association for Computational Linguistics.

Piotr Bojanowski, Edouard Grave, Armand Joulin, and Tomas Mikolov. 2017. Enriching word vectors with subword information. *Transactions of the Association for Computational Linguistics*, 5:135–146.

Alexis Conneau, Kartikay Khandelwal, Naman Goyal, Vishrav Chaudhary, Guillaume Wenzek, Francisco Guzmán, Edouard Grave, Myle Ott, Luke Zettlemoyer, and Veselin Stoyanov. 2019. Unsupervised cross-lingual representation learning at scale. *arXiv preprint arXiv:1911.02116*.

Jacob Devlin, Ming-Wei Chang, Kenton Lee, and Kristina Toutanova. 2019. BERT: Pre-training of deep bidirectional transformers for language understanding. In *Proceedings of the 2019 Conference of the North American Chapter of the Association for Computational Linguistics: Human Language Technologies, Volume 1 (Long and Short Papers)*, pages 4171–4186, Minneapolis, Minnesota. Association for Computational Linguistics.

Benjamin Heinzerling and Michael Strube. 2018. BPEmb: Tokenization-free pre-trained subword embeddings in 275 languages. In *Proceedings of the Eleventh International Conference on Language Resources and Evaluation (LREC 2018)*, Miyazaki, Japan. European Language Resources Association (ELRA).

Michał Marcińczuk, Jan Kocoń, and Marcin Oleksy. 2017. Liner2 — a generic framework for named entity recognition. In *Proceedings of the 6th Workshop on Balto-Slavic Natural Language Processing*, pages 86–91. Association for Computational Linguistics.

Michał Marcińczuk, Marcin Oleksy, Marek Maziarz, Jan Wieczorek, Dominika Fikus, Agnieszka Turek, Michał Wolski, Tomasz Bernaś, Jan Kocoń, and Paweł Kędzia. 2016. Polish corpus of wrocław university of technology 1.2. CLARIN-PL digital repository.

Jakub Piskorski, Laska Laskova, Michał Marcińczuk, Lidia Pivovarova, Pavel Přibáň, Josef Steinberger, and Roman Yangarber. 2019. The second cross-lingual challenge on recognition, normalization, classification, and linking of named entities across Slavic languages. In *Proceedings of the 7th Workshop on Balto-Slavic Natural Language Processing*, pages 63–74, Florence, Italy. Association for Computational Linguistics.

Stefan Schweter and Alan Akbik. 2020. Flert: Document-level features for named entity recognition.

Magda Ševčíková, Zdeněk Žabokrtský, Jana Straková, and Milan Straka. 2014. Czech named entity corpus 2.0. LINDAT/CLARIAH-CZ digital library at the Institute of Formal and Applied Linguistics (ÚFAL), Faculty of Mathematics and Physics, Charles University.

A. S. Starostin, V. V. Bocharov, S. V. Alexeeva, A. A. Bodrova, A. S. Chuchunkov, S. S. Dzhumaev, I. V. Efimenko, D. V. Granovsky, V. F. Khoroshevsky, I. V. Krylova, M. A. Nikolaeva, I. M. Smurov, and S. Y. Toldova. 2016. Factrueval 2016: Evaluation of named entity recognition and fact extraction systems for russian. In *FactRuEval 2016: Evaluation of Named Entity Recognition and Fact Extraction Systems for Russian*, pages 688–705.

Universal Dependencies Consortium. 2021. Universal dependencies.

Guillaume Wenzek, Marie-Anne Lachaux, Alexis Conneau, Vishrav Chaudhary, Francisco Guzmán, Armand Joulin, and Edouard Grave. 2020. CCNet: Extracting high quality monolingual datasets from web crawl data. In *Proceedings of The 12th Language Resources and Evaluation Conference*, pages 4003–4012, Marseille, France. European Language Resources Association.

Marcin Woliński, Marcin Miłkowski, Maciej Ogrodniczuk, Adam Przepiórkowski, and Łukasz Szałkiewicz. 2012. PoliMorf: a (not so) new open morphological dictionary for Polish. In *Proceedings of the Eighth International Conference on Language Resources and Evaluation, LREC 2012*, pages 860–864, Istanbul, Turkey. European Language Resources Association (ELRA).

Slav-NER: the 3rd Cross-lingual Challenge on Recognition, Normalization, Classification, and Linking of Named Entities across Slavic languages

Jakub Piskorski,[1] Bogdan Babych,[2] Zara Kancheva,[3] Olga Kanishcheva,[4] Maria Lebedeva,[5] Michał Marcińczuk,[6] Preslav Nakov,[7] Petya Osenova,[3] Lidia Pivovarova,[8] Senja Pollak,[9] Pavel Přibáň,[10] Ivaylo Radev,[3] Marko Robnik-Šikonja,[11] Vasyl Starko,[12] Josef Steinberger,[10] Roman Yangarber[8]

[1]Polish Academy of Sciences, Warsaw, Poland jpiskorski@gmail.com
[2]Heidelberg University, Germany bogdan.babych@iued.uni-heidelberg.de
[3]IICT-BAS, Bulgarian Academy of Sciences, Bulgaria {petya,zara,radev}@bultreebank.org
[4]Kharkiv Polytechnic Institute, Ukraine kanichshevaolga@gmail.com
[5]Pushkin State Russian Language Institute, Moscow, Russia mylebedeva@pushkin.institute
[6]Wrocław University of Science and Technology, Poland michal.marcinczuk@pwr.edu.pl
[7]Qatar Computing Research Institute, HBKU pnakov@hbku.edu.qa
[8]University of Helsinki, Finland first.last@helsinki.fi
[9]Jozef Stefan Institute, Slovenia senja.pollak@ijs.si
[10]University of West Bohemia, Czech Republic {pribanp,jstein}@kiv.zcu.cz
[11]University of Ljubljana, Slovenia Marko.RobnikSikonja@fri.uni-lj.si
[12]Ukrainian Catholic University, Lviv, Ukraine vstarko@gmail.com

Abstract

This paper describes Slav-NER: the 3rd Multilingual Named Entity Challenge in Slavic languages. The tasks involve recognizing mentions of named entities in Web documents, normalization of the names, and cross-lingual linking. The Challenge covers six languages and five entity types, and is organized as part of the 8th Balto-Slavic Natural Language Processing Workshop, co-located with the EACL 2021 Conference. Ten teams participated in the competition. Performance for the named entity recognition task reached 90% F-measure, much higher than reported in the first edition of the Challenge. Seven teams covered all six languages. Detailed evaluation information is available on the shared task web page.

1 Introduction

Analyzing named entities (NEs) in Slavic languages poses a challenging problem, due to the rich inflection and derivation, free word order, and other morphological and syntactic phenomena exhibited in these languages (Przepiórkowski, 2007; Piskorski et al., 2009). Encouraging research on detection and normalization of NEs—and on the closely related problem of cross-lingual, cross-document *entity linking*—is of paramount importance for improving multilingual and cross-lingual information access in these languages.

This paper describes the 3rd Shared Task on multilingual NE recognition (NER), which aims at addressing these problems in a systematic way. The shared task was organized in the context of the 8th BSNLP: Balto-Slavic Natural Language Processing Workshop, co-located with the EACL 2021 conference. The task covers six languages—Bulgarian, Czech, Polish, Russian, Slovene and Ukrainian—and five types of NE: person, location, organization, product, and event. The input text collection consists of documents collected from the Web, each collection centered on a certain "focal" event. The rationale of such a setup is to foster the development of "end-to-end" NER and cross-lingual entity linking solutions, which are not tailored to specific, narrow domains. This paper also serves as an introduction and a guide for researchers wishing to explore these problems using the training and test data, which are released to the public.[1]

The paper is organized as follows. Section 2 reviews prior work. Section 3 describes the task; Section 4 describes the annotation of the dataset. The evaluation methodology is introduced in Section 5. Participant systems are described in Section 6, and the results obtained by these systems are presented in Section 7. We present the conclusions and lessons learned in Section 8.

2 Prior Work

The work described here builds on the 1st and 2nd Shared Task on Multilingual Named Entity Recognition, Normalization and cross-lingual Match-

[1]bsnlp.cs.helsinki.fi/shared_task.html

Proceedings of the 8th BSNLP Workshop on Balto-Slavic Natural Language Processing, pages 122–133
April 20, 2021.

ing for Slavic Languages, (Piskorski et al., 2017, 2019), which, to the best of our knowledge, are the first attempts at such shared tasks covering multiple Slavic languages.

High-quality recognition and analysis of NEs is an essential step not only for information access, such as document retrieval and clustering, but it also constitutes a fundamental processing step in a wide range of NLP pipelines built for higher-level analysis of text, such as Information Extraction, see, e.g. (Huttunen et al., 2002). Other NER-related shared tasks have been organized previously. The first *non-English* monolingual NER evaluations—covering Chinese, Japanese, Spanish, and Arabic—were held in the context of the Message Understanding Conferences (MUCs) (Chinchor, 1998) and the ACE Programme (Doddington et al., 2004). The first *multilingual* NER shared task, which covered several European languages, including Spanish, German, and Dutch, was organized in the context of the CoNLL conferences (Tjong Kim Sang, 2002; Tjong Kim Sang and De Meulder, 2003). The NE types covered in these campaigns were similar to the NE types covered in our Challenge. Worth mentioning in this context is Entity Discovery and Linking (EDL) (Ji et al., 2014, 2015), a track of the NIST Text Analysis Conferences (TAC). EDL aimed to extract entity mentions from a collection of documents in multiple languages (English, Chinese, and Spanish), and to partition the entities into cross-document equivalence classes, by either linking mentions to a knowledge base or directly clustering them. An important difference between EDL and our task is that EDL required linking entities to a pre-existing knowledge base.

Related to cross-lingual NE recognition is NE transliteration, i.e., linking NEs across languages that use different scripts. A series of NE Transliteration Shared Tasks were organized as a part of NEWS—Named Entity Workshops—(Duan et al., 2016), focusing mostly on Indian and Asian languages. In 2010, the NEWS Workshop included a shared task on Transliteration Mining (Kumaran et al., 2010), i.e., mining of names from parallel corpora. This task included corpora in English, Chinese, Tamil, Russian, and Arabic.

Research on NE focusing on Slavic languages includes tools for NE recognition for Croatian (Karan et al., 2013; Ljubešić et al., 2013), NE recognition in Croatian tweets (Baksa et al., 2017), a manually annotated NE corpus for Croatian (Agić and Ljubešić, 2014), tools for NE recognition in Slovene (Štajner et al., 2013; Ljubešić et al., 2013), a Czech corpus of 11K annotated NEs (Ševčíková et al., 2007), NER tools for Czech (Konkol and Konopík, 2013), tools and resources for fine-grained annotation of NEs in the National Corpus of Polish (Waszczuk et al., 2010; Savary and Piskorski, 2011), NER shared tasks for Polish organized under the umbrella of POLEVAL[2] evaluation campaigns (Ogrodniczuk and Łukasz Kobyliński, 2018, 2020). and a recent shared task on NE Recognition in Russian (Starostin et al., 2016).

3 Task Description

The data for this edition of the shared task consists of sets of documents in six Slavic languages: Bulgarian, Czech, Polish, Russian, Slovene and Ukrainian. To accommodate entity linking, each set of documents is chosen to revolve around one certain entity—e.g., a person, an organization or an event. The documents were obtained from the Web, by posing a keyword query to a search engine or publicly available crawled data repositories, and extracting the textual content from the respective sources.

The task is to recognize, classify, and "normalize" all named-entity mentions in each of the documents, and to link across languages all named mentions referring to the same real-world entity. Formally, the Multilingual Named Entity Recognition task is subdivided into three sub-tasks:

- **Named Entity Mention Detection and Classification:** Recognizing all named mentions of entities of five types: persons (PER), organizations (ORG), locations (LOC), products (PRO), and events (EVT).
- **Name Normalization:** Mapping each named mention of an entity to its corresponding *base form*. By "base form" we generally mean the lemma ("dictionary form") of the inflected word-form. In some cases normalization should go beyond inflection and transform a derived word into a base word's lemma, e.g., in case of personal possessives (see below). Multi-word names should be normalized to the *canonical multi-word expression*—rather than a sequence

[2] `http:\\poleval.pl`

of lemmas of the words making up the multi-word expression.

- **Entity Linking.** Assigning a unique identifier (ID) to each detected named mention of an entity, in such a way that mentions referring to the same real-world entity should be assigned the same ID—referred to as the cross-lingual ID.

The task does not require positional information of the name entity mentions. Thus, for all occurrences of the same form of a NE mention (e.g., an inflected variant, an acronym or abbreviation) within a given document, no more than one annotation should be produced.[3] Furthermore, distinguishing typographical case is not necessary since the evaluation is case-insensitive. If the text includes lowercase, uppercase or mixed-case variants of the same entity, the system should produce only one annotation for all of these mentions. For instance, for "*ISIS*" and "*isis*" (provided that they refer to the same NE type), only one annotation should be produced. The recognition of common-noun or pronominal references to named entities does not constitute part of the task.

3.1 Named Entity Classes

The task defines the following five NE classes.

Person names (PER): Names of real (or fictional) persons). Person names should not include titles, honorifics, and functions/positions. For example, in the text fragment "...*President Vladimir Putin...*", only "*Vladimir Putin*" is recognized as a person name. Both initials and pseudonyms are also considered named mentions of persons. Similarly, toponym-based named references to groups of people (that do not have a formal organization unifying them) should also be recognized, e.g., "*Germans*." In this context, mentions of a single member belonging to such groups, e.g., "*German*," should be assigned the same cross-lingual ID as plural mentions, i.e., "*Germans*" and "*German*" when referring to the nation receive the same cross-lingual ID.

Named mentions of other groups of people that do have a formal organization unifying them should be tagged as PER, e.g., in the phrase "*Spart'ané vyhráli*" (Spartans won), "*Spart'ané* are to be tagged as PER.

[3]Unless the different occurrences have different entity types (different *readings*) assigned to them, which is rare.

Personal possessives derived from a person's name should be classified as a Person, and the base form of the corresponding name should be extracted. For instance, in "*Trumpov tweet*" (Croatian) one is expected to classify "*Trumpov*" as PER, with the base form "*Trump*."

Locations (LOC): All toponyms and geopolitical entities—cities, counties, provinces, countries, regions, bodies of water, land formations, etc.—including named mentions of *facilities*—e.g., stadiums, parks, museums, theaters, hotels, hospitals, transportation hubs, churches, streets, railroads, bridges, and similar facilities.

In case named mentions of facilities *also* refer to an organization, the LOC tag should be used. For example, from the text "*San Rafaelle Hospital hired new staff due to Covid-19 pandemic*" the mention "*San Rafaelle Hospital*" should be classified as LOC.

Organizations (ORG): All organizations, including companies, public institutions, political parties, international organizations, religious organizations, sport organizations, educational and research institutions, etc.

Organization designators and potential mentions of the seat of the organization are considered to be part of the organization name. For instance, from the text "*...Zakład Ubezpieczeń Społecznych w Bydgoszczy...*" (The Social Insurance Institution in Bydgoszcz), the full phrase "*Zakład Ubezpieczeń Społecznych w Bydgoszczy*" should be extracted.

Products (PRO): All names of *products and services*, such as electronics ("*Samsung Galaxy A41*"), cars ("*Honda Pilot*"), newspapers ("*Der Spiegel*"), web-services ("*Pintertest*"), medicines ("*Oxycodone*"), awards ("*Pulitzer Prize*"), books ("*Animal Farm*"), TV programmes ("*Wiadomości TVP*"), etc.

When a company name is used to refer to a *service*, e.g., "*na Instagramie*" (Polish for "on Instagram"), the mention of "*Instagramie*" is considered to refer to a service/product and should be tagged as PRO. However, when a company name refers to a service, expressing an opinion of the company, it should be tagged as ORG.

This category also includes legal documents and treaties, e.g., "*Układ z Schengen*" (Pol-

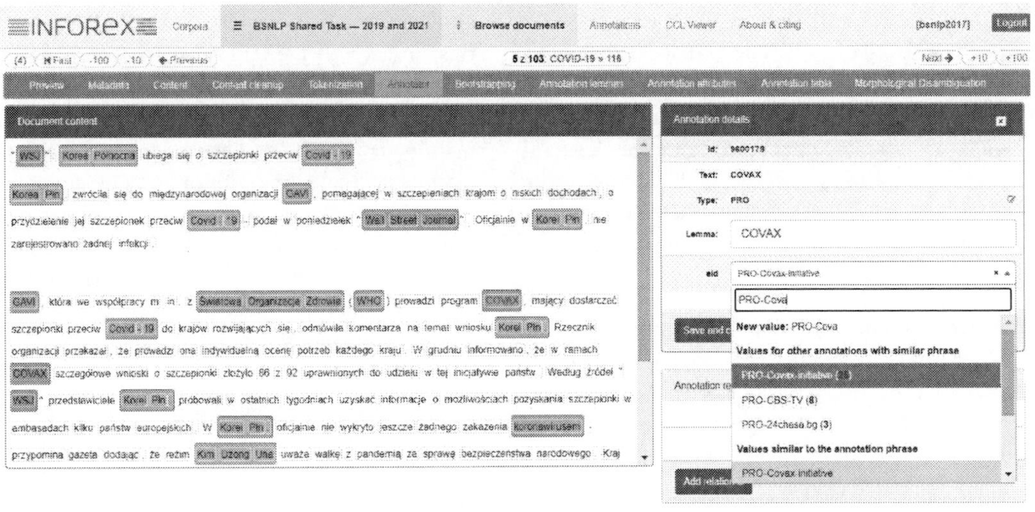

Figure 1: Screenshot of the Inforex Web interface, the tool used for data annotation.

Jacob Serrano (23) z americké Floridy se stal vůbec prvním Američanem, který byl očkován experimentální vakcínou proti koronaviru, ta vznikla za spolupráce vědců z Oxfordské univerzity a farmaceutické společnosti AstraZeneca. Podle WHO jde zatím o nejslibnější očkovací látku. Serrano se neváhal zapojit se do boje s koronavirem, který způsobuje nemoc covid-19, nákaza ho totiž připravila o 7 příbuzných, uvedl list Daily Mail.

114

Američanem	Američan	PER	GPE-USA
AstraZeneca	AstraZeneca	ORG	ORG-AstraZeneca
Daily Mail	Daily Mail	PRO	PRO-Daily-Mail
Floridy	Florida	LOC	GPE-Florida
Jacob Serrano	Jacob Serrano	PER	PER-Jacob-Serrano
Oxfordské univerzity	Oxfordská univerzita	ORG	ORG-University-of-Oxford
Serrano	Serrano	PER	PER-Jacob-Serrano
WHO	WHO	ORG	ORG-World-Health-Org
covid-19	covid-19	EVT	EVT-Covid-19
koronavirem	koronavirus	EVT	EVT-Covid-19
koronaviru	koronavirus	EVT	EVT-Covid-19

Figure 2: Example input and output formats.

ish: "Schengen Agreement") and initiatives, e.g., "*Horizon 2020*".

Events (EVT): This category covers named mentions of events, including conferences, e.g. "24. Konference Žárovného Zinkování" (Czech: "Hot Galvanizing Conference"), concerts, festivals, holidays, e.g., "*Święta Bożego Narodzenia*" (Polish: "Christmas"), wars, battles, disasters, e.g., "*Katastrofa Smoleńska*" (Polish: "the Smoleńsk air disaster"), outbreaks of infectious diseases ("*Spanish Flu*"). Future, speculative, and fictive events—e.g., "'Polexit"—are considered event mentions too.

3.2 Complex and Ambiguous Entities

In case of complex named entities, consisting of nested named entities, only the *top-most* entity should be recognized. For example, from the text "*Università Commerciale Luigi Bocconi*" one should not extract "*Luigi Bocconi*", but only the top-level entity.

In case one word-form (e.g., "*Georgia*") is used to refer to more than one different real-world entities in different contexts in the same document (e.g., a person and a location), two annotations should be returned, associated with different cross-lingual IDs.

In case of coordinated phrases, like "*European and German Parliament*," two names should be extracted (as ORG). The lemmas would be "*European*" and "*German Parliament*", and the IDs should refer to "*European Parliament*" and "*German Parliament*" respectively.

In rare cases, plural forms might have two annotations—e.g., in the phrase "*a border between Irelands*"—"*Irelands*" should be extracted twice with identical lemmas but different IDs.

3.3 System Input and Response

Input Document Format: Documents in the collection are represented in the following format. The first five lines contain the following metadata (in the respective order): `<DOCUMENT-ID>`,

<LANGUAGE>, <CREATION-DATE>, <URL>, <TITLE>, <TEXT>. The text to be processed begins from the sixth line and runs till the end of file. The <URL> field stores the origin from which the text document was retrieved. The values of <CREATION-DATE> and <TITLE> were not provided for all documents, due to unavailability of such data or due to errors in parsing during data collection.

System Response. For each input file, the system should return one output file as follows. The first line should contain only the <DOCUMENT-ID>, which corresponds to the input. Each subsequent line contains one annotation, as tab-separated fields:

```
<MENTION> TAB <BASE> TAB <CAT> TAB <ID>
```

The <MENTION> field should be the NE as it appears in text. The <BASE> field should be the base form of the entity. The <CAT> field stores the category of the entity (ORG, PER, LOC, PRO, or EVT) and <ID> is the cross-lingual identifier. The cross-lingual identifiers may consist of an arbitrary sequence of alphanumeric characters. An example document in Czech and the corresponding response is shown in Figure 2.

The detailed descriptions of the tasks are available on the web page of the Shared Task.[4]

4 Data

For Russian, Polish, Czech and Bulgarian, the training and test data sets from the 2019 Shared Task were used as training data for 2021. For the new languages—Ukrainian and Slovene—new training sets were annotated. The test data in all six languages covered two major current topics: the COVID-19 pandemic and the 2020 USA Presidential elections (USA 2020 ELECTIONS).

The 2019 training data consist of four sets of documents extracted from the Web, each related to a given *focus* entity. We tried to choose entities related to events in 2018 and 2019 covered in mainstream news in many languages. ASIA BIBI, which relates to a Pakistani woman involved in a blasphemy case, BREXIT, RYANAIR, which faced a massive strike, and NORD STREAM, a controversial Russian-European project.

Each dataset was created as follows. For the focus entity, we posed a search query to Google and/or publicly available crawled data repositories, in each of the target languages. The query returned documents in the target language. We removed duplicates, downloaded the HTML—mainly news articles—and converted them into plain text. Since the result of HTML parsing may include not only the main text of a Web page, but also spurious text, some additional manual cleaning was applied whenever necessary. The resulting set of "cleaned" documents were used to manually select documents for each language and topic, for the final datasets.

Documents were annotated using the Inforex[5] web-based system for annotation of text corpora (Marcińczuk et al., 2017). Inforex allows parallel access and resource sharing by multiple annotators. It let us share a common list of entities, and perform entity-linking semi-automatically: for a given entity, an annotator sees a list of entities of the same type inserted by all annotators and can select an entity ID from the list. A snapshot of the Inforex interface is in Figure 1.

In addition, Inforex keeps track of all lemmas and IDs inserted for each surface form, and inserts them automatically, so in many cases the annotator only confirms the proposed values, which speeds up the annotation process a great deal. All annotations were made by native speakers. After annotation, we performed automatic and manual consistency checks, to reduce annotation errors, especially in entity linking.

Training and test data statistics are presented in Table 1 and 2 respectively.

The testing datasets—COVID-19 and USA 2020 ELECTIONS—were released to the participants who were given circa 2 days to return up to 5 system responses. The participants did not know the topics in advance, and did not receive the annotations. The main drive behind this decision was to push participants to build a general solution for Slavic NER, rather than to optimize their models toward a particular set of names.

5 Evaluation Methodology

The NER task (exact case-insensitive matching) and Name Normalization (or "lemmatization") were evaluated in terms of precision, recall, and F1-measure. For NER, two types of evaluations were carried out:

[4] http://bsnlp.cs.helsinki.fi/System_response_guidelines-1.2.pdf

[5] github.com/CLARIN-PL/Inforex

	Brexit						Asia Bibi					
	PL	CS	RU	BG	SL	UK	PL	CS	RU	BG	SL	UK
Documents	500	284	153	600	52	50	88	89	118	101	4	6
PER	2 650	1 108	1 308	2 515	532	242	683	570	643	583	36	39
LOC	3 524	1 279	666	2 407	403	336	403	366	567	388	24	57
ORG	3 080	1 039	828	2 455	301	166	286	214	419	245	10	30
EVT	1 072	471	261	776	165	62	14	3	1	8	0	0
PRO	668	232	137	490	31	17	55	42	49	63	2	1
Total	10 994	4 129	3 200	8 643	1 445	823	1 441	1 195	1 679	1 287	72	127
Distinct												
Surface forms	2 820	1 111	783	1 200	596	234	508	303	406	412	51	87
Lemmas	2 133	840	568	1 091	411	177	412	248	317	360	41	77
Entity IDs	1 506	583	268	772	288	127	273	160	178	230	31	64

	Nord Stream						Ryanair					
	PL	CS	RU	BG	SL	UK	PL	CS	RU	BG	SL	UK
Documents	151	161	150	130	74	40	146	163	150	87	52	63
PER	538	570	392	335	548	78	136	161	72	147	107	33
LOC	1 430	1 689	1 320	910	1 362	339	821	871	902	344	384	455
ORG	837	477	792	540	460	449	529	707	500	238	408	193
EVT	15	9	5	6	50	14	7	12	0	4	8	0
PRO	405	364	510	331	243	8	114	66	82	79	101	20
Total	3 225	3 116	3 020	2 122	2 664	948	1 607	1 817	1 556	812	1008	701
Distinct												
Surface forms	845	770	892	504	902	336	514	475	400	323	673	187
Lemmas	634	550	583	448	600	244	419	400	332	315	520	137
Entity IDs	441	392	321	305	465	177	322	306	251	245	428	108

Table 1: Overview of the training datasets.

	Covid-19						USA 2020 Elections					
	PL	CS	RU	BG	SL	UK	PL	CS	RU	BG	SL	UK
Documents	103	155	83	151	178	85	66	85	163	151	143	83
PER	419	478	559	351	834	215	566	447	3203	1539	2589	672
LOC	369	474	701	759	1228	364	827	277	3457	1093	1268	541
ORG	402	318	628	589	965	455	243	99	2486	557	578	384
EVT	240	393	435	465	612	269	86	63	396	170	118	257
PRO	137	155	400	168	274	143	87	56	846	240	254	124
Total	1567	1818	2723	2332	3913	1446	1810	942	10398	3599	4807	1978
Distinct												
Surface forms	688	941	1436	1092	2190	622	484	377	3440	1117	1605	537
Lemmas	557	745	1133	1016	1774	509	356	279	2593	1019	1129	390
Entity IDs	404	562	796	764	1400	369	278	200	1669	668	833	270

Table 2: Overview of the test datasets.

- **Relaxed:** An entity mentioned in a given document is considered to be extracted correctly if the system response includes *at least one* annotation of a named mention of this entity (regardless of whether the extracted mention is in base form);

- **Strict:** The system response should include exactly one annotation *for each* unique form of a named mention of an entity in a given document, i.e., identifying all variants of an entity is required.

In relaxed evaluation we additionally distinguish between *exact* and *partial matching*: in the latter case, an entity mentioned in a given document is considered to be extracted correctly if the system response includes at least one partial match of a named mention of this entity.

We evaluate systems at several levels of granularity: we measure performance for (a) all NE types and all languages, (b) each given NE type and all languages, (c) all NE types for each language, and (d) each given NE type per language.

In the name normalization task, we take into account only correctly recognized entity mentions and only those that were normalized (on both the annotation and system's sides). Formally, let $N_{correct}$ denote the number of all correctly recognized entity mentions for which the system returned a correct base form. Let N_{key} denote the number of all normalized entity mentions in the gold-standard answer key and $N_{response}$ denote the number of all normalized entity mentions in the system's response. We define precision and recall for the name normalization task as:

$$Recall = \frac{N_{corrrect}}{N_{key}} \qquad Precision = \frac{N_{corrrect}}{N_{response}}$$

In evaluating document-level, single-language and cross-lingual entity linking we adopted the Link-Based Entity-Aware metric (LEA) (Moosavi and Strube, 2016), which considers how important the entity is and how well it is resolved. LEA is defined as follows. Let $K = \{k_1, k_2, \ldots, k_{|K|}\}$ denote the set of key entities and $R = \{r_1, r_2, \ldots, r_{|R|}\}$ the set of response entities, i.e., $k_i \in K$ ($r_i \in R$) stand for set of mentions of the same entity in the key entity set (response entity set). LEA recall and precision are then defined as follows:

$$Recall_{LEA} = \frac{\sum_{k_i \in K} \left(imp(k_i) \cdot res(k_i)\right)}{\sum_{k_z \in K} imp(k_z)}$$

$$Precision_{LEA} = \frac{\sum_{r_i \in R} \left(imp(r_i) \cdot res(r_i)\right)}{\sum_{r_z \in R} imp(r_z)}$$

where imp and res denote the measure of importance and the resolution score for an entity, respectively. In our setting, we define $imp(e) = \log_2 |e|$ for an entity e (in K or R), $|e|$ is the number of mentions of e—i.e., the more mentions an entity has the more important it is. To avoid biasing the importance of the more frequent entities log is used. The resolution score of key entity k_i is computed as the fraction of correctly resolved co-reference links of k_i:

$$res(k_i) = \sum_{r_j \in R} \frac{link(k_i \cap r_j)}{link(k_i)}$$

where $link(e) = (|e| \times (|e| - 1))/2$ is the number of unique co-reference links in e. For each k_i, LEA checks all response entities to check whether they are partial matches for k_i. Analogously, the resolution score of response entity r_i is computed as the fraction of co-reference links in r_i that are extracted correctly:

$$res(r_i) = \sum_{k_j \in K} \frac{link(r_i \cap k_j)}{link(r_i)}$$

LEA brings several benefits. For example, LEA considers resolved co-reference relations instead of resolved mentions and has more discriminative power than other metrics for co-reference resolution (Moosavi and Strube, 2016).

The evaluation was carried out in "case-insensitive" mode: all named mentions in system response and test corpora were lower-cased.

6 Participant Systems

Six teams submitted descriptions of their systems as BSNLP Workshop papers. We briefly review these systems here; for complete descriptions, please see the corresponding papers. Two additional teams submitted their results with short descriptions of their systems, which appear in this section.

The **UL FRI** system, (Prelevikj and Zitnik, 2021), generated results for several settings, models and languages, although the team's main motivation is to develop effective NER tools for Slovenian. The system uses contemporary BERT and RoBERTa multilingual pre-trained models, which include Slovene among other languages. The system was further trained on the SlavNER dataset for the NER task and used the Dedupe method for the Entity Matching task. The best performing models were pre-trained on Slovene. The results also indicate that two-step prediction of NE could be beneficial. The team made their code publicly available.

The **Priberam Labs** system, (Ferreira et al., 2021), focuses on the NER task. It uses three components: a multilingual contextual embedding model, a character-level embedding model, and a bi-affine classifier model. The paper reports results for different multilingual contextual embedding models, which included Multilingual BERT, XLM-RoBERTa, or the Slavic BERT. For different languages the best-performing models where different, but having the same language within the large pre-trained model usually improved the results—e.g., Slavic BERT, which used additional resources for Bulgarian, Russian and Polish, also performed best for these languages. The system uses heuristics to predict and resolve spans of NEs, and in this way it is able to tag overlapping entities. The code for the system is made available.

The **TLD** system, (Vīksna and Skadina, 2021), uses a staged approach. The first stage is identification of NEs in context, which is treated as a sequence labeling problem and is performed by a multilingual BERT model from Google, modified by the team. Entity linking is the second stage, which uses a list of LaBSE embeddings; matched entries need to pass a pre-defined threshold of cosine similarity with existing entries; otherwise they are added as new values to the list. The third stage is normalisation of identified entities, which is performed using models provided with Stanza.

The **L3i** system, (Cabrera-Diego et al., 2021), combines BERT models with the "Frustratingly Easy" domain adaptation algorithm. It also uses other techniques to improve system's NER performance, such as marking and enrichment of uppercase tokens, prediction of NE boundaries with a multitask approach, prediction of masked tokens, fine-tuning the language model to the domain of the document.

The **TraSpaS** system, (Suppa and Jariabka, 2021), tests the assumption that the universal open-source NLP toolkits (such as SpaCy, Stanza or Trankit) could achieve competitive performance on the Multilingual NER task, using large pre-trained Transformer-based language models available from HuggingfaceTransformers, which have not been available in previous editions of the Shared Task. The team tests the generalizability of the models to new low-resourced domains, and to languages such as Slovene and Ukrainian.

The **UWr-VL** system, (Rychlikowski et al., 2021), utilizes large collections of unstructured and structured documents for unsupervised training of embedding of lexical units and for recognizing and linking multiple real-world NEs. In particular, the team makes use of CommonCrawl news articles, Wikipedia, and its structured counterpart Wikidata as knowledge sources, to address the problem of data scarcity, building neural gazetteer via collecting different embeddings from these knowledge sources. The system further uses standard neural approaches to the NER task, with a RNN classifier, in order to determine for every input word the probability of labelling it with various beginning and end NE tags.

Two more systems generated the results for the shared task—**CTC-NER** from the Cognitive Technologies Center team, and **PAISC_wxd**:

CTC-NER is a baseline prototype of a NER component of an entity recognition system currently under development at the Cognitive Technologies Center. The system has a hybrid architecture combining rule-based and ML techniques; the ML-component is loosely related to (Antonova and Soloviev, 2013). The languages currently processed include Russian, English and Ukrainian.

PAISC_wxd uses the XLM-Roberta model, followed by BiLSTM-CRF on top. In addition, the system uses data enhancement based on machine translation.

7 Evaluation Results

Figure 3 shows the performance of the systems averaged across all languages and both test corpora. For each team that provided a solution for all six languages (7 teams except **CTC-NER**), we present the best scores ($F1$, $Precision$, and $Recall$) obtained by the team in three evaluation modes.[6]

As the plots show, the best performing model, Priberam, yields F-measure 85.7% according to the *relaxed partial* evaluation, and 79.3% according to the strict evaluation. The Priberam submission scores highest in precision — 89,4% relaxed partial, and 85.1% strict — but much lower in recall — 82.2% relaxed partial, and 74.3% strict.

Among the teams that submitted results for *cross-lingual entity linking*, only two achieved results comparable with the benchmarks achieved on the Second Challenge, and this year's results surpass those benchmarks by a substantial margin. The best results for each team, averaged across two corpora, are shown in Table 3. These results

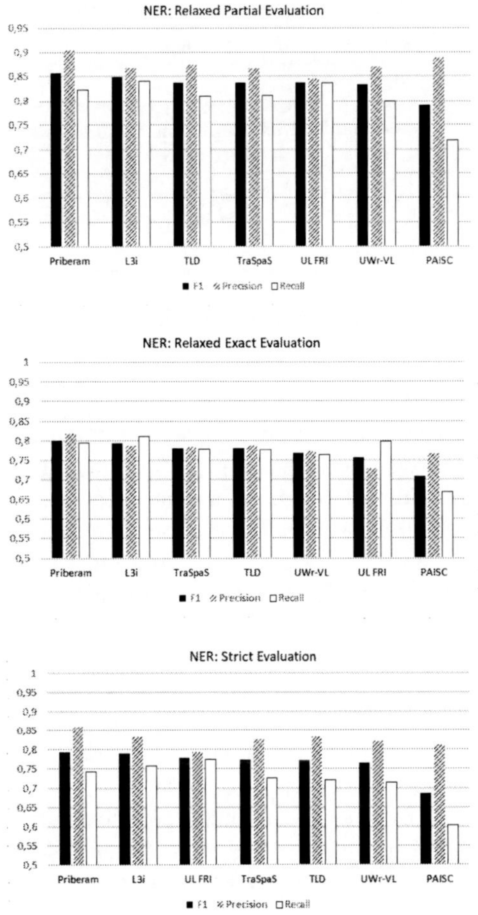

Figure 3: Best average performance scores obtained by the teams on the two test data

show that this task is much more difficult than entity extraction. The best performing model, TLD, achieves F-measure 50.4%.

Note that in our setting the performance on entity linking depends on the performance on name recognition and normalization: each system had to link entities that it had extracted from documents upstream, rather than link a set of correct entities.

Tables 4 and 5 present the F1-measures separated by language, for all tasks for the COVID-19 and USA 2020 ELECTIONS data sets These tables show only the top-performing model for each team. For recognition, we show only the *relaxed* evaluation, since the results obtained on the three evaluation schemes are correlated, as can be seen from Figure 3.

The tables indicate some variation in scores obtained on the test corpora This variation could be

[6]Complete results available on the Workshop's Web page: `bsnlp.cs.helsinki.fi/final-rank-2021.pdf`

COVID-19		USA 2020 ELECTIONS	
System	F1	System	F1
TLD	47.5	TLD	52.0
UWr-VL	32.8	UWr-VL	27.9
Priberam	5.8	Priberam	8.0
L3i	4.4	TraSpaS	7.9
PAISC	2.8	L3i	7.3
TraSpaS	2.7	PAISC	6.2
UL FRI	1.9	CTC-NER	2.9
CTC-NER	1.2	UL FRI	0.4

Table 3: Cross-lingual entity linking.

due to a number of factors, including actual differences in the test data, as well as differences in annotation across languages. This variation should and will be investigated in greater depth.

In Table 6 we present the results of the evaluation by entity type. As seen in the table, performance was higher overall for LOC and PER, and substantially lower for ORG and PRO, which corresponds with our findings from the previous editions of the shared task, where ORG and MISC were the most problematic categories (Piskorski et al., 2017). The PRO category also exhibits higher variance across languages and corpora than other categories, which might point to possible annotation artefacts. The results for the EVT category are less informative, since the task heavily depends on detecting the repeated central events of the corpora.

8 Conclusion

This paper reports on the 3rd Multilingual Named Entity Challenge focusing on recognizing mentions of NEs in Web documents in six Slavic languages, normalization of the NEs, and cross-lingual entity linking. The Challenge has attracted substantial interest, following the prior Challenges in 2017 and 2019, with 10 teams registering for the competition and eight teams submitting results from working systems, with multiple variants. Most systems use state-of-the-art neural network models. Overall, the results of the best-performing systems are quite strong for extraction and normalization, while cross-lingual linking is the most challenging of the tasks.

We show summary results for the main aspects of the challenge and the best-performing model for each team. For detailed, in-depth evaluations of all participating systems and their performance please consult the Shared Task's Web page and the papers by the respective teams.

To stimulate further research into NLP for Slavic languages, including cross-lingual entity linking, our training and test datasets, the detailed annotations, and scripts used for evaluations are made available to the public on the Shared Task's Web page.[7] The annotation interface is released by the Inforex team, to support further annotation of additional data for future tests.

This challenge covered six Slavic languages. For future editions of the Challenge, we plan to expand the data sets, covering a wider range of entity types, and supporting cross-lingual entity linking. We plan to expand the training and test data to include *non-Slavic* languages. We will also undertake further refinement of the underlying annotation guidelines—a highly complex task in a real-world setting. More complex phenomena also need to be addressed, e.g., coordinated NEs, contracted versions of multiple NEs, etc.

We believe that the reported results and the annotated datasets will help stimulate further research on robust, end-to-end analysis of real-world texts in Slavic languages.

Acknowledgments

Work on Bulgarian was in part supported by the Bulgarian National Interdisciplinary Research e-Infrastructure for Resources and Technologies for the Bulgarian Language and Cultural Heritage, part of the EU infrastructures CLARIN and DARIAH – CLaDA-BG, Grant number DO1-377/18.12.2020.

Work on Czech was in part supported by ERDF "Research and Development of Intelligent Components of Advanced Technologies for the Pilsen Metropolitan Area (InteCom)" (no. CZ.02.1.01/0.0/0.0/17 048/0007267), and by Grant No. SGS-2019-018 "Processing of heterogeneous data and its specialized applications."

Work on Inforex and on Polish was supported in part by investment in the CLARIN-PL research infrastructure funded by the Polish Ministry of Science and Higher Education.

We thank the students of Pushkin State Russian Language Institute for their assistance with annotation of Russian data.

This work has been partially supported by the European Union Horizon 2020 research and in-

[7] bsnlp.cs.helsinki.fi/shared_task.html

COVID-19		Language											
Phase	*Metric*	bg		cs		pl		ru		sl		uk	
Recognition	Relaxed Partial	Priberam	83.2	UWr-VL	86.7	Priberam	87.8	L3i	76.0	UWr-VL	87.6	UWr-VL	84.8
		L3i	82.8	Priberam	86.3	UWr-VL	86.9	Priberam	75.1	Priberam	87.5	L3i	80.6
		TLD	82.2	TLD	84.1	TLD	86.4	PAISC	74.4	L3i	85.6	TLD	80.1
		UL FRI	81.6	L3i	83.9	L3i	85.0	TLD	72.9	TLD	84.2	Priberam	79.9
		UWr-VL	81.2	TraSpaS	82.0	UL FRI	83.4	UL FRI	71.9	TraSpaS	83.9	PAISC	78.3
		TraSpaS	80.9	UL FRI	80.4	TraSpaS	82.5	TraSpaS	70.2	PAISC	80.1	UL FRI	78.3
		PAISC	79.7	PAISC	77.6	PAISC	81.0	CTC-NER	69.3	UL FRI	79.1	TraSpaS	78.1
								UWr-VL	67.1			CTC-NER	65.0
Normalization		UWr-VL	33.3	TraSpaS	47.0	UWr-VL	57.4	CTC-NER	40.4	UWr-VL	53.0	TraSpaS	53.7
		UL FRI	21.4	TLD	45.2	UL FRI	47.2	UL FRI	39.9	UL FRI	40.5	UWr-VL	51.5
		TLD	13.8	UWr-VL	44.8	TraSpaS	46.2	TraSpaS	38.6	TraSpaS	34.3	UL FRI	50.7
		TraSpaS	10.0	UL FRI	44.4	TLD	45.3	TLD	36.2	TLD	32.3	TLD	46.3
		Priberam	0.0	Priberam	0.0	Priberam	0.0	UWr-VL	27.2	Priberam	0.0	CTC-NER	39.2
		L3i	0.0	L3i	0.0	L3i	0.0	Priberam	0.0	L3i	0.0	Priberam	0.0
		PAISC	0.0	PAISC	0.0	PAISC	0.0	L3i	0.0	PAISC	0.0	L3i	0.0
								PAISC	0.0			PAISC	0.0
Entity linking	Document level	UWr-VL	37.6	TLD	47.0	UWr-VL	61.2	TLD	42.5	UWr-VL	52.0	TLD	48.9
		TLD	24.6	UWr-VL	46.0	TLD	44.7	UWr-VL	30.5	TLD	45.2	UWr-VL	45.3
		L3i	13.3	UL FRI	29.8	UL FRI	26.4	UL FRI	20.4	UL FRI	29.6	UL FRI	24.7
		Priberam	12.4	Priberam	23.9	PAISC	20.4	Priberam	15.5	Priberam	16.8	Priberam	23.7
		TraSpaS	11.5	L3i	22.5	L3i	20.3	PAISC	13.8	L3i	15.6	L3i	22.3
		PAISC	11.4	TraSpaS	22.1	Priberam	20.0	L3i	13.3	TraSpaS	14.9	TraSpaS	22.0
		UL FRI	6.1	PAISC	21.2	TraSpaS	18.4	TraSpaS	12.2	PAISC	13.8	PAISC	17.8
								CTC-NER	3.5			CTC-NER	2.3
	Single language	UWr-VL	67.9	TLD	66.5	UWr-VL	73.0	TLD	47.4	UWr-VL	66.4	TLD	61.7
		TLD	57.1	UWr-VL	66.1	TLD	67.8	UWr-VL	38.9	TLD	59.2	UWr-VL	61.5
		PAISC	16.4	UL FRI	40.2	UL FRI	38.8	UL FRI	20.1	UL FRI	32.7	UL FRI	36.8
		L3i	10.9	PAISC	15.9	PAISC	13.7	Priberam	6.2	TraSpaS	10.0	Priberam	15.9
		Priberam	8.7	L3i	11.2	Priberam	9.3	L3i	4.2	Priberam	7.2	L3i	7.7
		UL FRI	7.6	TraSpaS	11.2	TraSpaS	8.2	PAISC	3.5	L3i	4.2	PAISC	7.5
		TraSpaS	3.6	Priberam	8.0	L3i	7.9	TraSpaS	2.0	PAISC	1.8	TraSpaS	6.3
								CTC-NER	1.8			CTC-NER	2.6

Table 4: F1-measure results for the COVID-19 corpus.

novation programme under grants 770299 (NewsEye).

Work on Slovene was financed through the European Union's Horizon 2020 Research and Innovation Programme under grant agreement No 825153, Project EMBEDDIA: Cross-Lingual Embeddings for Less-Represented Languages in European News Media, as well as Slovenian Research Agency's project: Computer-assisted multilingual news discourse analysis with contextual embeddings (CANDAS, J6-2581).

References

Željko Agić and Nikola Ljubešić. 2014. The SETimes.HR linguistically annotated corpus of Croatian. In *Ninth International Conference on Language Resources and Evaluation (LREC 2014)*, pages 1724–1727, Reykjavík, Iceland.

AY Antonova and AN Soloviev. 2013. Conditional random field models for the processing of Russian. In *Computational Linguistics and Intellectual Technologies: Papers From the Annual Conference "Dialogue"(Bekasovo, 29 May–2 June 2013)*, volume 1, pages 27–44.

Krešimir Baksa, Dino Golović, Goran Glavaš, and Jan Šnajder. 2017. Tagging named entities in Croatian tweets. *Slovenščina 2.0: empirical, applied and interdisciplinary research*, 4(1):20–41.

Luis Adrián Cabrera-Diego, Jose G. Moreno, and Antoine Doucet. 2021. Using a frustratingly easy domain and tagset adaptation for creating slavic named entity recognition systems. In *Proceedings of the 8th Workshop on Balto-Slavic Natural Language Processing*. European Association for Computational Linguistics.

Nancy Chinchor. 1998. Overview of MUC-7/MET-2. In *Proceedings of Seventh Message Understanding Conference (MUC-7)*.

George R. Doddington, Alexis Mitchell, Mark A. Przybocki, Lance A. Ramshaw, Stephanie Strassel, and Ralph M. Weischedel. 2004. The Automatic Content Extraction (ACE) program—tasks, data, and evaluation. In *Fourth International Conference on Language Resources and Evaluation (LREC 2004)*, pages 837–840, Lisbon, Portugal.

Xiangyu Duan, Rafael E. Banchs, Min Zhang, Haizhou Li, and A. Kumaran. 2016. Report of NEWS 2016 machine transliteration shared task. In *Proceedings of The Sixth Named Entities Workshop*, pages 58–72, Berlin, Germany.

Pedro Ferreira, Ruben Cardoso, and Afonso Mendes. 2021. Priberam labs at the 3rd shared task on

USA 2020 ELECTIONS		*Language*											
Phase	*Metric*	bg		cs		pl		ru		sl		uk	
Recognition	Relaxed Partial	L3i	89.8	UWr-VL	91.3	Priberam	92.3	L3i	83.7	Priberam	91.5	TLD	84.6
		Priberam	88.7	Priberam	90.7	L3i	92.0	Priberam	83.4	L3i	91.5	Priberam	84.6
		TraSpaS	88.1	L3i	90.2	TLD	90.8	TraSpaS	81.5	UWr-VL	90.4	L3i	84.5
		UWr-VL	87.3	TLD	88.5	UWr-VL	89.8	TLD	80.9	TLD	89.8	TraSpaS	83.3
		TLD	87.3	UL FRI	88.4	TraSpaS	89.2	UL FRI	80.5	TraSpaS	89.4	UWr-VL	83.3
		UL FRI	86.9	TraSpaS	87.8	UL FRI	89.1	UWr-VL	77.2	UL FRI	88.6	UL FRI	83.2
		PAISC	83.6	PAISC	82.6	PAISC	66.4	PAISC	77.1	PAISC	86.0	PAISC	77.0
								CTC-NER	75.4			CTC-NER	71.1
Normalization		UWr-VL	51.3	UWr-VL	51.9	UWr-VL	62.1	TraSpaS	50.7	UWr-VL	62.4	UL FRI	56.9
		UL FRI	21.9	TraSpaS	42.0	TLD	51.0	UL FRI	48.8	UL FRI	43.9	TraSpaS	56.8
		TLD	19.1	TLD	40.1	UL FRI	50.1	TLD	46.5	TraSpaS	34.2	TLD	55.3
		TraSpaS	17.9	UL FRI	39.7	TraSpaS	42.4	CTC-NER	44.8	TLD	31.9	CTC-NER	36.9
		Priberam	0.0	Priberam	0.0	Priberam	0.0	UWr-VL	25.6	Priberam	0.0	UWr-VL	26.5
		L3i	0.0	L3i	0.0	L3i	0.0	Priberam	0.0	L3i	0.0	Priberam	0.0
		PAISC	0.0	PAISC	0.0	PAISC	0.0	L3i	0.0	PAISC	0.0	L3i	0.0
								PAISC	0.0			PAISC	0.0
Entity linking	Document level	UWr-VL	63.7	UWr-VL	64.3	UWr-VL	67.1	TLD	44.8	UWr-VL	67.3	UWr-VL	58.9
		TLD	58.7	TLD	55.3	TLD	62.3	UWr-VL	35.8	TLD	59.3	TLD	52.2
		Priberam	12.5	UL FRI	37.5	UL FRI	44.9	UL FRI	32.2	UL FRI	43.3	UL FRI	28.8
		L3i	12.1	L3i	30.5	Priberam	18.2	Priberam	12.3	L3i	18.3	Priberam	25.4
		TraSpaS	11.7	Priberam	29.5	L3i	18.0	L3i	12.3	Priberam	17.9	L3i	23.9
		PAISC	11.4	TraSpaS	28.6	TraSpaS	17.4	PAISC	9.9	TraSpaS	17.1	TraSpaS	23.5
		UL FRI	4.5	PAISC	21.6	PAISC	13.4	TraSpaS	9.8	PAISC	15.8	PAISC	16.8
								CTC-NER	2.8			CTC-NER	1.5
	Single language	UWr-VL	68.5	TLD	69.0	TLD	74.9	TLD	50.1	TLD	68.7	TLD	62.2
		TLD	67.1	UWr-VL	66.0	UWr-VL	69.9	UWr-VL	39.3	UWr-VL	66.5	UWr-VL	52.9
		PAISC	12.8	UL FRI	50.0	UL FRI	37.7	UL FRI	13.6	UL FRI	21.3	UL FRI	23.0
		Priberam	10.1	L3i	18.1	Priberam	14.8	Priberam	5.6	Priberam	8.4	TraSpaS	21.4
		TraSpaS	8.6	Priberam	17.7	L3i	14.5	L3i	5.5	L3i	8.3	L3i	20.5
		L3i	8.6	TraSpaS	17.7	TraSpaS	13.4	TraSpaS	5.1	TraSpaS	8.2	Priberam	20.2
		UL FRI	8.3	PAISC	14.1	PAISC	10.7	PAISC	4.4	PAISC	7.2	PAISC	12.9
								CTC-NER	3.6			CTC-NER	9.4

Table 5: Evaluation results (F1-measure) for the USA 2020 ELECTION corpus.

	COVID-19						USA 2020 ELECTIONS					
	bg	cs	pl	ru	sl	uk	bg	cs	pl	ru	sl	uk
Per	98.0	98.1	98.3	83.1	98.2	96.6	93.6	97.4	94.2	93.1	96.3	98.7
Loc	95.8	96.4	96.7	95.1	95.7	97.3	97.5	96.9	97.6	93.1	98.2	93.8
Org	86.5	89.4	91.3	82.9	88.8	87.6	86.6	89.6	86.3	76.6	76.7	81.7
Pro	55.1	76.2	75.6	47.6	63.4	49.4	80.7	87.4	90.2	66.9	77.7	69.9
Evt	52.6	40.1	57.8	52.6	63.5	75.9	29.6	26.1	40.5	55.7	38.0	16.1

Table 6: Recognition F1-measure (relaxed partial) by entity type—best-performing systems for each language.

slavner. In *Proceedings of the 8th Workshop on Balto-Slavic Natural Language Processing*. European Association for Computational Linguistics.

Silja Huttunen, Roman Yangarber, and Ralph Grishman. 2002. Diversity of scenarios in information extraction. In *Proceedings of the Third International Conference on Language Resources and Evaluation (LREC 2002)*, Las Palmas, Spain.

Heng Ji, Joel Nothman, and Ben Hachey. 2014. Overview of TAC-KBP2014 entity discovery and linking tasks. In *Proceedings of Text Analysis Conference (TAC2014)*, pages 1333–1339.

Heng Ji, Joel Nothman, and Ben Hachey. 2015. Overview of TAC-KBP2015 tri-lingual entity discovery and linking. In *Proceedings of Text Analysis Conference (TAC2015)*.

Mladen Karan, Goran Glavaš, Frane Šarić, Jan Šnajder, Jure Mijić, Artur Šilić, and Bojana Dalbelo Bašić. 2013. CroNER: Recognizing named entities in Croatian using conditional random fields. *Informatica*, 37(2):165.

Michal Konkol and Miloslav Konopík. 2013. CRF-based Czech named entity recognizer and consolidation of Czech NER research. In *Text, Speech and Dialogue*, volume 8082 of *Lecture Notes in Computer Science*, pages 153–160. Springer Berlin Heidelberg.

A Kumaran, Mitesh M. Khapra, and Haizhou Li. 2010. Report of NEWS 2010 transliteration mining shared task. In *Proceedings of the 2010 Named Entities Workshop*, pages 21–28, Uppsala, Sweden.

Nikola Ljubešić, Marija Stupar, Tereza Jurić, and Željko Agić. 2013. Combining available datasets for building named entity recognition models of Croatian and Slovene. *Slovenščina 2.0: empirical, applied and interdisciplinary research*, 1(2):35–57.

Michał Marcińczuk, Marcin Oleksy, and Jan Kocoń. 2017. Inforex - a collaborative system for text corpora annotation and analysis. In *Proceedings of the International Conference Recent Advances in Natural Language Processing, RANLP 2017, Varna, Bulgaria, September 2-8, 2017*, pages 473–482. INCOMA Ltd.

Nafise Sadat Moosavi and Michael Strube. 2016. Which coreference evaluation metric do you trust? A proposal for a link-based entity aware metric. In *Proceedings of the 54th Annual Meeting of the Association for Computational Linguistics (ACL 2016)*, pages 632–642, Berlin, Germany.

Maciej Ogrodniczuk and Łukasz Kobyliński, editors. 2018. *Proceedings of the PolEval 2018 Workshop*. Institute of Computer Science, Polish Academy of Sciences, Warsaw, Poland.

Maciej Ogrodniczuk and Łukasz Kobyliński, editors. 2020. *Proceedings of the PolEval 2020 Workshop*. Institute of Computer Science, Polish Academy of Sciences, Warsaw, Poland.

Jakub Piskorski, Laska Laskova, Michał Marcińczuk, Lidia Pivovarova, Pavel Přibáň, Josef Steinberger, and Roman Yangarber. 2019. The second cross-lingual challenge on recognition, normalization, classification, and linking of named entities across Slavic languages. In *Proceedings of the 7th Workshop on Balto-Slavic Natural Language Processing*, pages 63–74, Florence, Italy. Association for Computational Linguistics.

Jakub Piskorski, Lidia Pivovarova, Jan Šnajder, Josef Steinberger, and Roman Yangarber. 2017. The first cross-lingual challenge on recognition, normalization and matching of named entities in Slavic languages. In *Proceedings of the 6th Workshop on Balto-Slavic Natural Language Processing*. Association for Computational Linguistics.

Jakub Piskorski, Karol Wieloch, and Marcin Sydow. 2009. On knowledge-poor methods for person name matching and lemmatization for highly inflectional languages. *Information retrieval*, 12(3):275–299.

Marko Prelevikj and Slavko Zitnik. 2021. Bsnlp 2021 shared task: Multilingual named entity recognition and matching using bert and dedupe for slavic languages. In *Proceedings of the 8th Workshop on Balto-Slavic Natural Language Processing*. European Association for Computational Linguistics.

Adam Przepiórkowski. 2007. Slavonic information extraction and partial parsing. In *Proceedings of the Workshop on Balto-Slavonic Natural Language Processing: Information Extraction and Enabling Technologies*, ACL '07, pages 1–10, Stroudsburg, PA, USA. Association for Computational Linguistics.

Paweł Rychlikowski, Adrian Lancucki, Adam Kaczmarek, Bartłomiej Najdecki, Adam Wawrzyński, and Wojciech Janowski. 2021. Named entity recognition and linking augmented with large-scale structured data. In *Proceedings of the 8th Workshop on Balto-Slavic Natural Language Processing*. European Association for Computational Linguistics.

Agata Savary and Jakub Piskorski. 2011. Language Resources for Named Entity Annotation in the National Corpus of Polish. *Control and Cybernetics*, 40(2):361–391.

Magda Ševčíková, Zdeněk Žabokrtský, and Oldřich Kruza. 2007. Named entities in Czech: annotating data and developing NE tagger. In *International Conference on Text, Speech and Dialogue*, pages 188–195. Springer.

Tadej Štajner, Tomaž Erjavec, and Simon Krek. 2013. Razpoznavanje imenskih entitet v slovenskem besedilu. *Slovenščina 2.0: empirical, applied and interdisciplinary research*, 1(2):58–81.

A. S. Starostin, V. V. Bocharov, S. V. Alexeeva, A. A. Bodrova, A. S. Chuchunkov, S. S. Dzhumaev, I. V. Efimenko, D. V. Granovsky, V. F. Khoroshevsky, I. V. Krylova, M. A. Nikolaeva, I. M. Smurov, and S. Y. Toldova. 2016. FactRuEval 2016: Evaluation of named entity recognition and fact extraction systems for Russian. In *Computational Linguistics and Intellectual Technologies. Proceedings of the Annual International Conference "Dialogue"*, pages 688–705.

Marek Suppa and Ondrej Jariabka. 2021. Benchmarking pre-trained language models for multilingual ner: Traspas at the bsnlp2021 shared task. In *Proceedings of the 8th Workshop on Balto-Slavic Natural Language Processing*. European Association for Computational Linguistics.

Erik Tjong Kim Sang. 2002. Introduction to the CoNLL-2002 shared task: Language-independent named entity recognition. In *Proceedings of the 6th Conference on Natural Language Learning - Volume 20*, COLING-02, pages 1–4, Stroudsburg, PA, USA. Association for Computational Linguistics.

Erik Tjong Kim Sang and Fien De Meulder. 2003. Introduction to the CoNLL-2003 shared task: Language-independent named entity recognition. In *Proceedings of the Seventh Conference on Natural Language Learning at HLT-NAACL 2003 - Volume 4*, CONLL '03, pages 142–147, Stroudsburg, PA, USA. Association for Computational Linguistics.

Rinalds Vīksna and Inguna Skadina. 2021. Multilingual slavic named entity recognition. In *Proceedings of the 8th Workshop on Balto-Slavic Natural Language Processing*. European Association for Computational Linguistics.

Jakub Waszczuk, Katarzyna Głowińska, Agata Savary, and Adam Przepiórkowski. 2010. Tools and methodologies for annotating syntax and named entities in the National Corpus of Polish. In *Proceedings of the International Multiconference on Computer Science and Information Technology (IMCSIT 2010): Computational Linguistics – Applications (CLA'10)*, pages 531–539, Wisła, Poland. PTI.

Association for Computational Linguistics
209 N. Eighth Street
Stroudsburg, Pennsylvania 18360

ISBN 978-1-7138-2958-4

CURRAN ASSOCIATES INC.
proceedings.com